WORLD ON THE BRINK

WORLD ON THE BRINK

G7 Vs. BRICS In The Quest For Dominance

GEW INTELLIGENCE UNIT
Hichem Karoui (Ed.)

Global East-West (London)

Copyright © 2024 by GEW Intelligence Unit

Hichem Karoui (Editor)

All rights reserved. No part of this book may be reproduced in any manner whatsoever without written permission except in the case of brief quotations embodied in critical articles and reviews.

First Printing, 2024

CONTENTS

1. Introduction: The New World Order and the Rise of Coalition-Based Strategies — 1
2. Historical Context and Formation of the G7 — 14
3. BRICS: Genesis and Growth of a Power Bloc — 27
4. The Economics of Competition: Analyzing G7 and BRICS Economies — 40
5. Geostrategic Interests and Political Dynamics in G7 Nations — 52
6. The Pivot to Asia: BRICS' Struggle for Influence — 66
7. Technological Advancements and Their Impact on Global Dominance — 79
8. Energy Resources and Environmental Policies in BRICS vs. G7 — 93
9. Cultural Diplomacy and Soft Power: Contrasting Approaches — 107
10. Military Alliances and Defense Postures: A Comparative Study — 121
11. New Alliances: Shifting Powers in the 21st Century — 134
12. Trade Wars and Economic Sanctions: The Weapons of Choice — 138

13	Public Opinion and Media Influence in Shaping International Policy	150
14	Emerging Markets and Future Economic Leaders: Projections for 2050	163
15	Cybersecurity Challenges in a Digitally Connected World	177
16	Migration and Human Capital: Critical Factors in Global Success	191
17	Healthcare, Pandemics, and International Cooperation	204
18	Global Terrorism and Security Measures by G7 and BRICS	218
19	Legal and Regulatory Frameworks: Ensuring Compliance across Borders	231
20	Gender Equality and Inclusivity in Global Governance	246
21	The Future of Education and Research Collaboration	259
22	Global Leadership: Who Will Guide Tomorrow's World?	273
23	Conclusion: Building a More Cooperative Peaceful World	285
Bibliography		299

CHAPTER 1

Introduction: The New World Order and the Rise of Coalition-Based Strategies

DEFINING THE NEW WORLD ORDER

The 'New World Order' concept has been a subject of intense debate and speculation in global politics. It signifies a shift in the power dynamics and alliances at an international level, redefining the traditional structures that have governed geopolitical interactions for decades. The idea of a 'New World Order' encompasses the evolving relationships between nation-states, non-state actors, and international organizations and the impact of technological advancements, economic interdependence, and ideological shifts on the global landscape. This paradigm shift is driven by many factors, including the rise of emerging economies, changing demographics, the proliferation of information technology, and the increasing interconnectedness of societies. The implications of this new order are far-reaching, influencing areas such as trade, security, human rights, and environmental stewardship. Moreover, the transition to a 'New World Order' challenges established norms and conventions, requiring innovative approaches to address complex transnational issues. Understanding and navigating this evolving global architecture is essential for policymakers, businesses, and civil society to engage in a rapidly changing world effectively. The 'New World Order' demands a holistic analysis of power dynamics, strategic partnerships, and institutional frameworks to adapt to the contemporary complexities of international relations. As we delve deeper into the intricate layers of this new paradigm, it becomes imperative to comprehend the intricacies of coalition-based strategies, geopolitical realignments, and the pursuit of common goals in an increasingly interconnected world. By embracing this paradigm shift with intellectual rigor and foresight, stakeholders can harness the opportunities presented by the 'New World Order' while mitigating potential risks and challenges.

COALITIONS IN GLOBAL POLITICS: AN OVERVIEW

Global politics has witnessed a complex web of interactions where nation-states have increasingly relied on coalition-based strategies to pursue their geopolitical interests. The formation of coalitions has become a defining feature of the contemporary international system, shaping regional diplomatic, economic, and security dynamics. Coalitions, also known as alliances or partnerships, are instrumental in advancing shared objectives, mitigating risks, and amplifying influence in an interconnected world. In this section, we will delve into the nuances of global coalitions, examining their historical developments, current manifestations, and future implications. The nature of coalitions in global politics is multifaceted, encompassing diverse forms such as military alliances, economic blocs, and diplomatic collaborations. These coalitions operate on multiple levels, reflecting converging or diverging interests of participating states. It is essential to comprehend the intricacies of coalition-building, including the factors that drive nations to seek collaborative arrangements, the mechanisms through which these coalitions function, and the potential ramifications they yield. Moreover, understanding the evolving dynamics of global coalitions requires exploring power distribution, aligning values and ideologies, and pursuing collective security and prosperity. While some coalitions emerge out of necessity to address common threats or challenges, others are forged to enhance economic partnerships, trade relations, or technological innovation. As we scrutinize the landscape of global politics, it becomes evident that coalitions serve as instruments of strength and solidarity and embody contested narratives, conflicting ambitions, and power asymmetries. The composition of coalitions often reflects the interplay of historical legacies, regional rivalries, and shifting balances of power. Furthermore, the emergence of new actors and non-state entities has augmented the complexity of coalition dynamics, requiring a reevaluation of traditional paradigms and strategic calculations. In this era of rapid globalization and interdependence, the interconnectivity of issues ranging from climate change and pandemics to cybersecurity and terrorism necessitates comprehensive and inclusive coalition-building. The effectiveness of coalitions in addressing transnational challenges hinges on the consensus-building capacity, institutional frameworks, and normative standards upheld by participating members. In the subsequent sections, we will analyze specific case studies, examine the efficacy of existing coalitions, and envision the trajectory of coalition-based strategies in navigating the shifting contours of global politics.

STRATEGIC IMPERATIVES FOR COALITION FORMATIONS

Coalition formations in the contemporary global landscape are driven by myriad strategic imperatives, reflecting the complex interplay of political, economic, and security objectives. As geopolitical power dynamics evolve, nations identify various imperatives that lead them to forge coalitions with other like-minded entities. One of the primary strategic imperatives for coalition formations is the pursuit of shared interests and goals. In an era characterized by interconnected economies, addressing climate change, trade agreements, and global security threats necessitates collaborative efforts among nations with converging agendas. Moreover, coalition formations can serve as a means to enhance influence and exert leverage on the international stage. By aligning with other powerful or strategically significant actors, states seek to amplify their voices and bolster their positions in shaping the direction of global policies and regulations. Another critical imperative lies in the management of regional or transnational challenges. Whether addressing regional security concerns, mitigating economic disparities, or combating cross-border crime and terrorism, coalitions offer a platform for concerted action and resource pooling. Additionally, coalition formations often become essential in navigating power shifts and balancing hegemonic tendencies. As emerging powers continue to assert themselves and traditional powerhouses realign strategic imperatives, they prompt nations to form alliances that can counterbalance perceived threats or establish new centers of gravity within the international system. Furthermore, coalition formations present opportunities for enhancing collective capabilities and sharing the burden of everyday challenges. Collaborative ventures in defense, technological research, and infrastructure development enable the pooling of resources, knowledge, and expertise, ultimately fostering mutual growth and resilience. It is crucial to recognize that strategic imperatives for coalition formations are not static; they continually adapt to changing circumstances and emergent issues. As such, the evolution of these imperatives influences the configuration and sustainability of coalitions, thereby shaping the course of global governance and geopolitical strategies.

MAJOR GLOBAL PLAYERS AND THEIR ALIGNMENTS

In the complex and interconnected landscape of global politics, the alignments of major global players play a pivotal role in shaping the course of international relations and power dynamics. These alignments are often rooted in historical alliances, geopolitical interests, economic dependencies, and strategic imperatives. Understanding the relationships between these critical actors provides crucial insights into the world order's current state and future trajectory. The United States, as the world's largest economy and a traditional champion of liberal democratic values, has historically led or been a part of various coalition formations such as NATO, the G7, and other security partnerships. Its alliances across different regions, including Europe, Asia, and the Middle East, significantly influence the global balance of power. The European Union, comprising multiple influential member states, is an economic and political force with unique alliances and cooperative arrangements with global partners. Its unified approach to trade, diplomacy, and security significantly influences the world stage. Meanwhile, Russia's historic and strategic ties with countries in Eastern Europe, Central Asia, and the Middle East have given rise to alliances and partnerships that both challenge and complement existing global power structures. As the world's second-largest economy, China has established multilateral partnerships through organizations like the Shanghai Cooperation Organization and the BRICS bloc while asserting its influence through initiatives such as the Belt and Road Initiative. With its growing economic prowess and regional influence, India similarly seeks alignment in various cooperative arrangements, especially within the framework of BRICS and regional groupings in South Asia. Other major players, such as Japan, Brazil, and South Africa, actively seek and engage in alignments that serve their national interests within the context of the evolving world order. The dynamics of these alignments impact not only the political and economic landscapes but also shape crucial issues such as security, trade, technology, and global governance. As these major global players continue to navigate the complexities of international relations, their alignments will inevitably determine the direction and nature of coalition-based strategies and hold implications for the broader global community.

ECONOMIC IMPLICATIONS OF COALITION-BASED STRATEGIES

Coalition-based strategies have significant economic implications that must be carefully considered in the rapidly evolving global landscape. As significant players realign their alliances to secure economic advantages, the repercussions on trade, investment, and market dynamics become increasingly pronounced. The formation of coalitions often leads to the establishment of preferential trading blocs or economic partnerships, influencing the flow of goods, services, and capital across borders. This impacts not only the member nations but also has ripple effects on global supply chains and market competitiveness. Furthermore, coalition-based strategies can introduce complexities in international trade agreements and monetary policies as member countries coordinate their economic agendas. These coalitions may negotiate joint strategies for industrial development, technology transfer, and intellectual property rights protection, altering the traditional power structures within key industries. The economic implications extend beyond trade and production, encompassing macroeconomic stability, currency exchange rates, and fiscal policies. Moreover, they drive discussions on resource allocation, infrastructure investments, and sustainable development initiatives, shaping the trajectory of global economic growth. By leveraging collective resources and expertise, coalition-based strategies offer opportunities to address economic disparities and promote inclusive growth. However, they also pose challenges related to regulatory harmonization, taxation systems, and financial transparency, requiring careful navigation to mitigate potential drawbacks. Understanding the economic implications of coalition-based strategies is essential for policymakers, businesses, and stakeholders to make informed decisions and adapt to the changing global economic order.

POLITICAL OUTCOMES FROM NEW ALLIANCES

The formation of new alliances on the global stage has brought about significant political outcomes that reverberate across nations and regions, reshaping the geopolitical landscape in profound ways. As countries join coalitions, they can exercise collective influence and leverage their combined power to advance shared political objectives. These new alliances have reconfigured traditional power dynamics, challenging the established order and creating a platform for diverse voices to be heard.

One prominent political outcome stemming from new alliances is the shift in decision-making processes within international institutions and fora. As coalitions emerge as influential blocs, their ability to shape the formulation and implementation of global policies becomes more pronounced. This has resulted in a departure from unilateral decision-making by individual nations, giving rise to a more consensus-driven approach in addressing critical issues such as climate change, security, trade, and human rights.

Moreover, the political outcomes from new alliances extend to regional stability and conflict resolution. By forging strategic partnerships, nations within these coalitions are better equipped to address regional conflicts and promote stability through coordinated diplomatic efforts and peace-building initiatives. The collective weight of allied nations often serves as a deterrent to potential aggressors, fostering an environment conducive to dialogue and peaceful resolutions.

Another notable repercussion of new alliances is the amplification of soft power and cultural diplomacy on the global stage. As allied nations collaborate more closely, they engage in concerted efforts to project their values, ideologies, and cultural influences, thereby shaping global narratives and perceptions. This can foster greater understanding and cooperation among nations, transcending traditional divides and fostering a more interconnected world.

Furthermore, these new alliances have had a discernible impact on the traditional spheres of influence and the balance of power. New coalitions have prompted a reevaluation of geopolitical allegiances, compelling long-established powers to recalibrate their relationships and adapt to this evolving landscape. This, in turn, has triggered a realignment of global power structures, with significant implications for international relations and strategic maneuvering across all domains.

In conclusion, the political outcomes arising from new alliances underscore the transformative influence of coalition-based strategies on the contemporary geopolitical environment. As these alliances continue to evolve and assert themselves on the world stage, their enduring impact on political dynamics, global governance, and the pursuit of shared aspirations will undoubtedly continue to unfold.

TECHNOLOGICAL INFLUENCE ON GLOBAL CONFIGURATIONS

The technological landscape is undergoing rapid and profound changes, exerting a meaningful impact on the configuration of global dynamics. Technological advancements have revolutionized how nations interact and have become instrumental in shaping international relations and power structures. The pervasiveness of digital technologies has enabled real-time communication, data sharing, and collaboration on an unparalleled scale. Consequently, it has blurred traditional geographic boundaries, fostering interconnectedness that transcends physical barriers.

Furthermore, the rise of artificial intelligence, machine learning, and big data analytics has empowered states to enhance their strategic decision-making processes, optimize resource allocation, and bolster national security measures. This has ushered in an era where technology plays a pivotal role in safeguarding national interests, projecting influence, and countering potential threats in the cyber realm.

The proliferation of cyber capabilities has transformed warfare and espionage, necessitating a reevaluation of conventional notions of security. Information warfare and cyber-attacks pose formidable challenges in this digital age, compelling nations to fortify their cyber defenses and engage in defensive and offensive cyber operations. The strategic significance of technological prowess has thus emerged as a critical determinant of a nation's global standing, influencing its ability to assert dominance and protect its core interests.

Moreover, emerging technologies such as blockchain and quantum computing have the potential to disrupt existing economic and financial systems, redefining the nature of global commerce and trade. As these technologies mature, they could fundamentally alter the dynamics of international finance, offering new avenues for cross-border transactions, supply chain management, and regulatory oversight.

Beyond security and economic dimensions, technology has also catalyzed societal and cultural transformations, fostering the exchange of ideas, values, and norms across diverse populations. Social media platforms, mobile connectivity, and digital content dissemination have facilitated the amplification of voices, fueling social movements, and contributing to the global exchange of cultural perspectives.

In conclusion, technology's pervasive influence on global configurations is incontrovertible. It permeates all facets of human civilization and underscores the modern world's interconnectedness. Technology's continual evolution will undoubtedly shape the future landscape of international relations, exerting far-reaching implications on diplomacy, governance, trade, security, and human interaction.

SOCIO-CULTURAL IMPACTS AND PUBLIC PERCEPTION

The socio-cultural landscape shapes public perception and attitudes towards global coalitions. Understanding the impact of culture, traditions, and societal norms is crucial in assessing the effectiveness and acceptance of multinational partnerships. Societies are interconnected through shared values, beliefs, and historical experiences, all influencing how individuals perceive international collaborations. Cultural differences can either be a stumbling block or a bridge builder in forming and sustaining coalition-based strategies.

Public perception, shaped by socio-cultural factors, influences a nation's willingness to engage in multilateral engagements. It determines the extent to which citizens are receptive to their country's participation in international alliances. Furthermore, as a powerful influencer of public opinion, the media can significantly sway socio-cultural perceptions through its portrayal of global partnerships.

As societies evolve and cultures intermingle, new paradigms emerge, presenting opportunities and challenges for coalition-based strategies. The convergence of diverse civilizations within global governance frameworks necessitates a deep understanding of cross-cultural communication and sensitivity, cultivating a more inclusive and cohesive approach to navigating international relations.

Moreover, historical narratives, national pride, and collective memory can influence public sentiment toward coalition-based strategies. Perceptions of past victories, defeats, or diplomatic achievements may shape contemporary attitudes toward forming alliances and participating in cooperative endeavors.

Acknowledging the socio-cultural impacts on public perception provides insights into the potential success or resistance towards coalition-based strategies. Effective public diplomacy initiatives must consider cultural nuances and sensitivities, tailoring messaging and engagement approaches to resonate with diverse audiences across geographies.

In conclusion, acknowledging the socio-cultural impacts and understanding public perceptions are essential to strategizing and sustaining cooperation among nations. By fostering an awareness of cultural intricacies and actively engaging with diverse societies, coalition formations can navigate socio-cultural influences adeptly, fostering mutual understanding and strengthening global partnerships.

CHALLENGES TO MULTILATERALISM

Multilateralism confronts numerous challenges in contemporary times as a concept and practice in global governance. One of the foremost challenges lies in the shifting dynamics of power and influence among nation-states as emerging economies assert themselves internationally. This presents a challenge to established multilateral institutions that were designed to reflect the power structures of the post-World War II era. The rise of unilateralism and protectionist policies by certain influential countries further undermines the efficacy of multilateral approaches to addressing global issues. Additionally, the inability of existing multilateral frameworks to keep pace with the rapid evolution of technology and its impact on global affairs presents another significant challenge. As cyberspace and digital economies increasingly shape geopolitics, there is a pressing need to reevaluate how multilateralism can effectively govern these domains. Moreover, the erosion of trust and confidence among member states within multilateral organizations poses a critical challenge. Diverging interests, conflicting priorities, and geopolitical rivalries often hinder consensus-building and collective action, impeding multilateral initiatives' effectiveness. Furthermore, the increasing skepticism and criticism of multilateralism by certain political factions and populist movements within several nations poses an internal challenge. These voices advocate for a retreat from international cooperation and prioritizing national interests over collective responsibilities. Such sentiments can undermine the cohesion necessary for successful multilateral action. Another significant challenge to multilateralism stems from structural constraints and bureaucratic inefficiencies within established international organizations. Adaptability and responsiveness to emerging global issues have been constrained by complex decision-making processes and bureaucratic hurdles, necessitating a reexamination of institutional frameworks. Finally, the lack of universal commitment to multilateralism and effective enforcement mechanisms for international agreements pose fundamental challenges. States with divergent ideologies and priorities may defy or circumvent multilateral decisions, undermining the foundations of collaborative governance. In navigating these multifaceted challenges, it becomes imperative to recalibrate multilateral approaches and institutions to better align with contemporary realities and engender sustainable solutions to complex global issues.

OUTLOOK AND PREDICTIVE SCENARIOS FOR FUTURE COALITIONS

The landscape of global politics is rapidly evolving, and as we confront the challenges of the 21st century, the formation of future coalitions will be pivotal in shaping international relations. One of the key predictive scenarios for future coalitions revolves around the emergence of new regional powerhouses challenging the traditional dominance of existing global players. As economic and technological advancements progress at an unprecedented pace, historically overshadowed countries are now positioning themselves to form strategic alliances to enhance their influence on the world stage.

Moreover, globalization's increasing interconnectedness means that non-state actors, such as multinational corporations, influential NGOs, and even online communities, have the potential to form coalitions that transcend national boundaries. These diverse coalitions could profoundly impact the socio-political landscape, adding new dimensions to traditional power structures and diplomatic relations.

Furthermore, climate change and environmental sustainability are expected to play pivotal roles in the formation of future coalitions. As the global community grapples with the urgency of addressing environmental crises, countries will likely form coalitions focused on promoting sustainable development, mitigating the impacts of climate change, and ensuring environmental stewardship. This alignment of interests in preserving the planet could lead to unprecedented collaborations between nations that were previously at odds, potentially reshaping the geopolitical dynamics.

Another plausible scenario for future coalitions lies in security and defense. With the growing prevalence of cyber threats, hybrid warfare, and unconventional security challenges, countries may seek to forge alliances dedicated to enhancing cybersecurity, sharing intelligence, and coordinating defense strategies. Additionally, the rise of non-traditional security threats, such as pandemics and mass migration, could prompt the establishment of novel coalitions to address these complex issues collectively.

Regarding economic partnerships, the transformative potential of technologies like blockchain, artificial intelligence, and decentralized finance presents new opportunities for cross-border collaborations and trade alliances. Countries could leverage these innovations for mutual economic benefit, paving the way for innovative financial frameworks and intercontinental economic unions.

As we look towards the future, coalition-based strategies will continue to define the course of international relations. The fluidity of global challenges necessitates agile and adaptive alliances capable of responding to multifaceted issues. The dynamic nature of these predictive scenarios underscores the imperative for policymakers, diplomats, and global leaders to anticipate, engage with, and navigate the evolving landscape of coalition formations.

CHAPTER 2

Historical Context and Formation of the G7

ORIGINS OF THE G7: POST-WORLD WAR II ECONOMIC STABILITY

The origins of the G7 can be traced back to the aftermath of World War II when global economies were grappling with the immense challenges of post-war reconstruction and economic stability. The devastating impact of the war had left Europe in ruins, with infrastructure destroyed and economies in disarray. At the same time, the United States emerged as a major economic powerhouse, fostering rapid industrialization and technological advancement. Recognizing the need for coordinated efforts to rebuild and stabilize the global economy, leaders from industrialized nations formed the Group of Six.

This coalition, initially comprising the United States, United Kingdom, France, Italy, Canada, and Japan, sought to promote economic cooperation and foster stability through collective initiatives. The overarching objective was to prevent the recurrence of the economic strife that had paved the way for global conflicts. By promoting open trade, currency stability, and collaboration on economic policies, the member nations aimed to create a framework for sustained growth and prosperity.

The 1944 Bretton Woods Conference played a pivotal role in shaping the economic landscape. It established key institutions such as the International Monetary Fund (IMF) and the World Bank, which provided the necessary financial mechanisms to regulate international monetary systems and facilitate economic recovery. This underscored the growing recognition of the interdependence of global economies and the need for a coordinated approach to ensure stability and growth.

As the group evolved into the Group of Seven with the inclusion of Canada, the focus on creating a forum for advanced industrialized democracies to address economic challenges became more pronounced. Through regular summits and discussions, the G7 aimed to coordinate economic policies, address trade imbalances, and promote initiatives to bolster economic stability. It also served as a platform for addressing critical issues such as energy crises, inflation, and exchange rate volatility.

Overall, establishing the G7 marked a significant milestone in post-World War II history, reflecting a commitment to collaborative economic governance and the pursuit of shared prosperity. By understanding the historical context and the foundational principles that underpin the G7's formation, we gain valuable insights into the broader goals of international economic cooperation and the enduring legacy of this influential coalition.

CHRONOLOGICAL EVOLUTION FROM GROUP OF SIX TO GROUP OF SEVEN

The transformation from the Group of Six to the Group of Seven represents a significant chronological and geopolitical evolution in international economic governance. Emerging from the ashes of World War II, the initial collaboration among six major industrial powers—France, Germany, Italy, Japan, the United Kingdom, and the United

States—laid the foundation for what would become the G7. The pivotal moment came in 1976 when Canada joined, marking the group's transition into the G7. This expansion was aimed at broadening representation within the group and strengthening its global economic influence. Over the years, the G7 underwent notable shifts, adapting to changes in the global economic landscape and expanding its agenda beyond purely economic matters. Each annual summit allowed leaders to address pressing global challenges and coordinate policy responses. The evolution of the G7 also reflected changing power dynamics as emerging economies increasingly sought a seat at the table. The G7's transition to the G8, including Russia in 1998, further exemplified the changing geopolitical climate. However, the suspension of Russia from the group in 2014 highlighted the political tensions that could impact the group's continued evolution. This chronological evolution underscores the dynamic nature of the G7 and the ongoing quest for consensus and cooperation among the world's leading economies.

FOUNDING PURPOSES: ADDRESSING GLOBAL ECONOMIC CHALLENGES

The founding of the Group of Seven (G7) was rooted in the aftermath of World War II and the pressing need for global economic stability. As the war-torn nations sought to rebuild their economies and foster cooperation, the G7 emerged as a platform for addressing critical economic challenges on a global scale. At its core, the G7 was established to promote monetary and fiscal policies that could foster sustainable economic growth while ensuring financial stability across member countries. The founding fathers envisioned a forum where leading industrialized nations could unite to navigate and tackle the complex landscape of international trade, finance, and development. With an emphasis on upholding free market principles, the G7 was positioned as a key player in shaping the post-war economic order, setting norms of conduct, and fostering cooperation among its member states. In addition to economic rehabilitation and reconstruction efforts, the G7 aimed to provide a unified front against emerging economic threats and challenges, amplifying the voice and influence of its member nations on the global stage. Moreover, the G7 founders recognized the necessity of addressing international debt, exchange rate fluctuations, and trade imbalances to bolster global economic resilience and prosperity. Through collaborative discussions and policy initiatives, the G7 sought to promote responsible macroeconomic policies and build consensus on fiscal discipline, inflation control, and sustainable development. The commitment to fostering economic stability and addressing global challenges has remained a fundamental pillar of the G7's mission, reflecting a steadfast dedication to fortifying the global financial architecture and providing strategic guidance during economic uncertainty and turmoil.

KEY SUMMITS AND HISTORIC DECLARATIONS

The G7 has historically been characterized by pivotal summits and groundbreaking declarations that have shaped the global economic landscape. Beginning with the initial gatherings in the 1970s, these summits have provided a platform for member countries to engage in crucial discussions about international economic cooperation, monetary policies, and trade relations. One of the most notable early summits was the 1975 Rambouillet Summit in France, which laid the groundwork for ongoing dialogue and collaboration among advanced economies. This was followed by the 1976 Puerto Rico Summit, where leaders addressed pressing issues such as inflation, unemployment, and energy security, setting the stage for collective policy responses.

Subsequent summits, including the 1981 Ottawa Summit and the 1985 Plaza Accord, were instrumental in shaping global financial reforms and fostering coordination on exchange rate policies. The 1994 Naples Summit marked a significant milestone with discussions on structural reforms and the need for sustained economic growth. Notably, the G7's role expanded beyond economic matters, encompassing foreign policy and global security concerns following events such as the Gulf War and the dissolution of the Soviet Union.

The turn of the century witnessed the 2008 Heiligendamm Summit intensively addressing climate change, development aid, and sustainable growth issues. Furthermore, declarations from the G7 summits have fostered engagement on critical topics such as debt relief for developing nations, pharmaceutical access in low-income countries, and counter-terrorism efforts. The 2015 Schloss Elmau Summit highlighted the significance of collaborative action against global challenges, including cybersecurity threats and geopolitical tensions.

In addition to these foundational summits, the G7 has continually reaffirmed its commitment to fundamental principles through historic declarations. These statements have collectively shaped the agenda for international economic governance, emphasizing shared values, democracy, human rights, and social responsibility. The Tokyo Declaration, issued in 1979, underlined the group's dedication to promoting global prosperity and stability, while subsequent declarations emphasized the importance of free trade, innovation, and inclusive growth.

The entwining of diplomatic protocol and substantive discourse at these summits and through historic declarations has evidenced the G7's enduring impact on the interconnected world economy. These moments of convergence serve as testaments to the spirit of multilateralism, solidarity, and the pursuit of common goals amidst complex geopolitical realities.

ECONOMIC POLICIES AND AGREEMENTS AMONG MEMBER COUNTRIES

The economic policies and agreements among the G7 member countries play a pivotal role in shaping the global economic landscape. These policies reflect the shared goals and priorities of the member states, emphasizing cooperation and coordination to address common challenges while promoting sustainable economic growth. One of the fundamental objectives of the G7 economic policies is to enhance international trade relations by fostering an open, fair, and rules-based trading system. This commitment is underscored by efforts to remove trade barriers, reduce tariffs, and promote investment, thus creating a conducive environment for economic prosperity. Moreover, the G7 economies have focused on formulating and implementing sound macroeconomic policies to ensure stability, curb inflation, and promote employment opportunities. This concerted approach has been instrumental in navigating through volatile economic conditions and bolstering global resilience. The member nations also engage in dialogues and negotiations to forge agreements on key economic issues, such as taxation, financial regulations, and multilateral development assistance. These agreements serve as frameworks for addressing global economic challenges and promote harmonization of policies across borders. Additionally, the G7 member countries demonstrate a commitment to innovation and technological advancement as drivers of economic growth. Collaborative initiatives in research and development, along with investments in digital infrastructure and emerging technologies, underscore their collective vision for harnessing innovation to drive competitiveness and productivity. Furthermore, the G7 economies prioritize sustainable development and environmental stewardship, recognizing the interconnectedness of economic progress and environmental conservation. This is evident through initiatives to promote clean energy technologies, mitigate climate change, and foster sustainable resource management. By aligning their economic policies and agreements, the G7 member countries strive to set standards that benefit their economies and contribute to the prosperity and stability of the global economy. These shared commitments underscore the significance of multilateral cooperation and underline the G7's role as a key architect of international economic governance.

EXPANSION OF SCOPE: SECURITY AND POLITICAL COOPERATION

Expanding the G7 scope from primarily economic concerns to encompass security and political cooperation has been a defining feature of its evolution. Initially conceived as an economic forum to promote dialogue among the world's leading industrialized nations, the G7 gradually recognized the inseparable link between economic stability and broader geopolitical issues. This shift in focus was particularly evident during the latter half of the 20th century, characterized by heightened global tensions and conflicts. Recognizing the intertwined nature of economic prosperity and security laid the groundwork for the G7's expanded role in addressing security challenges.

One of the pivotal moments that underscored the G7's pivot towards security matters was the end of the Cold War. As the geopolitical landscape underwent seismic shifts, the G7 members realized the imperative of collaborative efforts to mitigate threats to global security. From regional conflicts to terrorism and nuclear proliferation, the G7 assumed a proactive stance in addressing these multifaceted challenges through coordinated diplomatic initiatives and strategic interventions. The G7 platform provided a forum for sustained dialogue and consensus-building on pressing security issues, showcasing a collective commitment to upholding stability and peace on a global scale.

Furthermore, the G7's engagement in fostering political cooperation has underpinned its significance as a driving force in shaping international relations. With new political dynamics and power struggles, the G7 has leveraged its influence to advocate for democratic values, human rights, and good governance practices. By prioritizing political cooperation, the G7 has sought to fortify the foundations of global stability and contribute to resolving political crises. This multidimensional approach reflects the G7's recognition that sustainable economic progress is contingent upon a secure and stable geopolitical environment.

Additionally, the G7's expanding involvement in security and political domains has necessitated the development of institutional frameworks and mechanisms for collaboration. Initiatives such as joint security strategies, intelligence sharing, and crisis management protocols exemplify the concerted efforts of G7 members to bolster global security architecture and enhance their collective capacity to respond to complex security challenges. These endeavors have not only reinforced the G7's cohesiveness but also broadened the scope of its impact in addressing a spectrum of contemporary security and political issues.

In conclusion, the G7's evolution from an exclusive economic forum to a multifaceted security and political cooperation platform signifies its adaptability in response to the evolving global landscape. Expanding its scope reflects the G7's recognition of the interconnected nature of economic, security, and political realms, solidifying its role as a pivotal actor in steering international affairs toward peace, stability, and prosperity.

INFLUENCE ON GLOBAL TRADE AND MONETARY SYSTEMS

The G7, comprising the world's most industrially advanced economies, wields significant influence over global trade and monetary systems. The G7 member nations have played a pivotal role in shaping the international trade landscape and developing monetary policies through their combined economic prowess and political clout. The group's impact extends beyond their economies, translating into far-reaching implications for the global economic order. The G7's decisions and agreements hold substantial weight in determining trade regulations, fiscal policies, and exchange rate mechanisms reverberating across international markets. One of the key aspects of the G7's influence on global trade is its ability to foster cooperation and consensus among member nations, often leading to the establishment of multilateral trade agreements and frameworks. These agreements set benchmarks for trade practices and exert considerable influence on the policies of non-member countries. Moreover, the G7's policy coordination and alignment stabilizes global financial markets, fostering greater predictability and confidence among investors and market participants. The group's discussions addressing currency exchange rates, trade tariffs, and regulatory standards serve as an instrumental driving force in formulating globally recognized standards and norms. Additionally, the G7's concerted efforts toward implementing fair and transparent trading practices have demonstrated their commitment to upholding ethical and equitable principles in international commerce. Furthermore, the G7's influence extends into the realm of international financial institutions, where their backing and support for reforms and initiatives significantly impact the functioning and governance of these organizations. By leveraging their collective economic power, the G7 consistently shapes major financial institutions' operations and lending policies, influencing global financial flows and investments. This stewardship has far-reaching implications, affecting the availability of capital, credit access, and investment opportunities in developing and emerging market economies, thereby contributing to the balance of global economic growth. The G7's influence on global trade and monetary systems underscores the group's pivotal role in setting the tone for international commerce and finance. Their actions and policies resonate across borders, shaping the economic landscape and guiding the trajectory of global trade and monetary policies.

CRITICISMS AND CONTROVERSIES SURROUNDING THE G7

The G7, as a leading forum for economic cooperation, has not been immune to criticism and controversies. One of the main criticisms revolves around the representativeness of the group. Critics argue that in today's multipolar world, the G7, dominated by Western powers, does not adequately reflect the global economic landscape. Emerging economies such as China, India, Brazil, and others have voiced concerns about being excluded from crucial economic decisions made within the G7 framework. This lack of inclusivity has raised questions about the legitimacy and relevance of the G7 in addressing global economic challenges. Additionally, there have been allegations of elitism, with detractors noting the disproportionate influence a handful of wealthy nations wielded in shaping international economic policies. Another point of contention is the efficacy of G7 initiatives in addressing pressing issues such as income inequality, environmental sustainability, and reducing poverty on a global scale. Critics argue that despite lofty declarations and commitments, the G7 has struggled to deliver meaningful and equitable solutions to these complex issues. Furthermore, the handling of financial crises and monetary policies by the G7 has drawn criticism. Detractors argue that the economic dominance of the G7 has led to policies that benefit their economies at the expense of developing nations, exacerbating economic disparities and perpetuating a global power imbalance. The G7's role in setting global economic agendas has also faced pushback from other international forums and organizations, with some asserting that the G7 undermines the efforts of more inclusive entities like the G20 or the United Nations in addressing economic challenges. Finally, controversies have arisen over the decision-making process within the G7, with concerns about transparency, accountability, and the influence of corporate interests. These criticisms and controversies surrounding the G7 underscore the imperative for ongoing evaluations and recalibrations to ensure that the group remains relevant and effective in a rapidly evolving global economy.

COMPARATIVE ANALYSIS: G7'S ROLE VERSUS EMERGING ECONOMIES

The comparison between the G7 and emerging economies is integral to understanding the evolving dynamics of the global economic landscape. The G7, composed of advanced industrialized nations, has historically influenced international economic policies. However, the rise of emerging economies, such as the BRICS nations (Brazil, Russia, India, China, and South Africa), has challenged the dominance of the G7 consortium. The comparative analysis of their roles encompasses various dimensions, from economic growth and trade relations to geopolitical influence and development initiatives.

Economic Growth and Trade Relations: As established industrial powers, G7 countries have historically been at the forefront of driving global economic growth through trade and investments. On the other hand, emerging economies have demonstrated remarkable growth rates, reshaping the global economic landscape. The competitive tension arising from this contrast often leads to complex trade negotiations and the reevaluating of traditional economic power structures.

Geopolitical Influence and Development Initiatives: The G7 has historically wielded substantial geopolitical influence, impacting global security and political affairs. Meanwhile, emerging economies have increasingly sought to assert their influence on regional and international platforms. Moreover, emerging economies have pursued ambitious development initiatives, challenging the traditional aid and investment models led by G7 nations.

Access to Resources and Market Integration: G7 nations have historically enjoyed privileged access to critical resources and global market integration. Conversely, emerging economies harbor vast resources and represent burgeoning consumer markets, attracting substantial attention from global investors. The interplay between resource access and market integration reflects shifting patterns of economic influence and underscores the evolving nature of global economic power.

Multilateral Engagement and Global Governance: Recognizing the significance of multilateral engagement, the G7 has played a pivotal role in shaping global governance structures. Emerging economies increasingly assert themselves within international institutions and forums, seeking to redress historical imbalances in global governance. The resultant power shifts require continued recalibration of global governance mechanisms to accommodate diverse perspectives and interests.

Conclusion: The comparative analysis of the G7's role vis-à-vis emerging economies reveals a dynamic and interconnected global economy. While the G7 retains substantial influence, the collective rise of emerging economies signifies a transformative shift in the global economic order. Understanding and navigating the interactions between these entities are crucial for fostering inclusive and sustainable global economic development.

THE G7 IN CONTEMPORARY GLOBAL POLITICS

The G7, comprising some of the world's most industrialized and economically influential nations, significantly shapes contemporary global politics. As the geopolitical landscape evolves, the G7's policies, decisions, and engagements have far-reaching implications for international relations, trade, and security. At the core of the G7's relevance in contemporary global politics is its ability to address emerging challenges while maintaining its historical leadership position.

In recent years, the G7 has demonstrated a keen interest in addressing global issues such as climate change, sustainable development, and economic stability. Its members have consistently engaged in dialogues to foster cooperation and implement policies that promote inclusive growth and uphold democratic values. Beyond economic considerations, the G7 actively addresses security challenges, including terrorism, non-proliferation of weapons of mass destruction, and global conflicts. This proactive approach amplifies the G7's impact on contemporary global politics.

Furthermore, the group's outreach and diplomacy efforts extend beyond its membership, engaging with developing economies, international organizations, and multilateral forums to advocate for coordinated responses to global crises. The G7 significantly influences the global political agenda through its actions and directives, often setting precedents for other regional and intergovernmental bodies.

In light of emerging economies' increasing influence, the G7 faces the challenge of adapting to a rapidly changing global scenario. It seeks to balance established leadership roles with inclusivity, recognizing the growing impact of disparate voices in international decision-making processes. This forward-looking approach is evident in the G7's initiatives to collaborate with emerging economies like those within the BRICS bloc, promote dialogue, and seek common ground on key global issues.

Amid geopolitical uncertainties and shifting power dynamics, the G7's stance on trade, intellectual property rights, and technological advancements has profound implications for contemporary global politics. By navigating complex trade relations, advocating for fair competition, and establishing norms governing emerging technologies, the G7 showcases its significance as a stabilizing force in global economic and political spheres.

In conclusion, the G7 remains a pivotal player in contemporary global politics, wielding substantial influence in fostering global dialogue, shaping policies, and addressing multifaceted challenges. The group's sustained relevance underscores its commitment to steering global affairs toward shared prosperity, peace, and sustainable development.

CHAPTER 3

BRICS: Genesis and Growth of a Power Bloc

BRICS: ORIGIN AND OVERVIEW

The formation of BRICS, comprising Brazil, Russia, India, China, and later South Africa, marks a significant shift in the global economic and political landscape. This collective emerged in the early 21st century as a platform for leveraging shared interests and addressing everyday challenges. The coming together of these diverse nations, each with its unique historical, cultural, and geopolitical background, highlights the convergence of strategic objectives and mutual ambitions. BRICS has provided a forum for these countries to collectively assert their influence on the international stage, aiming to shape a more multipolar world order. The genesis of BRICS can be traced to the increasing recognition of these emerging powers' economic potential and geopolitical significance. As individual nations sought to secure their positions in the global arena, the idea of forming a coalition gained momentum. The ascendancy of BRICS reflects the desire to counterbalance traditional Western powers and institutions' dominance and carve out a more equitable representation of the global community. Moreover, the collaborative ethos of BRICS aligns with the shared goals of fostering inclusive development, promoting sustainable growth, and ensuring a greater say for emerging economies in global governance structures. By exploring the formative years and foundational principles of BRICS, we gain valuable insights into the driving forces behind this dynamic alliance and the opportunities it presents for shaping the geopolitical future.

KEY FOUNDING MEMBERS AND THEIR ROLES

The formation of BRICS as a power bloc was initiated by the participation of five major emerging economies, namely Brazil, Russia, India, China, and later South Africa. Each founding member brought unique economic, political, and strategic significance to the alliance, contributing to the collective strength and influence of BRICS on the global stage. With its vast agricultural resources and growing industrial base, Brazil played a vital role in leveraging the group's position in international trade negotiations and multilateral forums. Russia, rich in natural resources and possessing advanced technological capabilities, has shaped the geopolitical agenda and fostered strategic partnerships within BRICS. India, known for its dynamic and rapidly growing economy, has been pivotal in promoting inclusive development and advocating for the representation of emerging economies in global governance institutions. As the world's second-largest economy, China has been a driving force behind BRICS' efforts to reform international financial architecture and promote a more equitable and balanced global economic order. Lastly, South Africa, the newest addition to the bloc, introduced a unique African perspective and extended BRICS' reach into the African continent, contributing valuable insights into regional dynamics and socioeconomic challenges. The founding members have strategically utilized their strengths and resources to fortify the collective influence of BRICS, showcasing a commitment to mutual cooperation, shared prosperity, and sustainable development. As the alliance continues to evolve, the roles and contributions of these key members are essential in shaping the future trajectory of BRICS and reinforcing its position as a formidable geopolitical and economic force in the international arena.

POLITICAL IDEOLOGIES AND GOVERNANCE STRUCTURES

The political ideologies and governance structures within the BRICS bloc are diverse, reflecting its member nations' varying historical backgrounds, cultural foundations, and socio-economic dynamics. This chapter delves into the complex tapestry of ideologies and structures underpinning these influential countries' functioning. As a coalition of emerging powers, BRICS encompasses a wide spectrum of political systems, from Russia's semi-presidential republic to China's one-party socialist state and India's federal parliamentary democratic system to Brazil's federal presidential representative democratic republic. Understanding these divergent political ideologies is crucial in comprehending how the members of BRICS navigate their collective identity while respecting individual national sovereignty. The governance structures within BRICS nations also contribute to the rich fabric of the coalition. While each nation upholds its distinct approach to governance, the common aspiration for cooperation and shared development acts as the cohesive force underpinning this diverse alliance. The decentralization and delegation of power, the role of political parties, and the influence of civil society are pivotal considerations in this exploration. Additionally, examining the regulatory frameworks, anti-corruption measures, and institutional designs within each member state sheds light on the complexities and nuances that define the governance structures of the BRICS nations. Furthermore, the interplay between ideology and governance underscores the unique challenges and opportunities faced by the bloc. The convergence of these distinctive political ideologies and governance structures necessitates a delicate balance between sovereignty and solidarity. Through a comprehensive understanding of the BRICS bloc's political ideologies and governance structures, we can gain valuable insights into the cooperative strategies, decision-making processes, and policy implementations that shape its collective influence on the global stage.

INITIAL CHALLENGES AND MILESTONES

The early years of the BRICS coalition were marked by a host of challenges that tested the resilience and determination of its member nations. One of the initial hurdles the bloc faced was the diversity of political ideologies and governance structures among its members. While these differences could have hindered cooperation, the leadership of BRICS exhibited a commitment to dialogue and consensus-building, emphasizing mutual respect and understanding. This approach helped overcome initial skepticism and paved the way for forming a cohesive power bloc. Moreover, the geopolitical landscape at the time presented significant obstacles, as existing global power dynamics often overlooked the emerging influence of BRICS. The member countries strategically navigated through this landscape, striving to gain recognition and representation on the world stage.

Amidst these challenges, BRICS also achieved pivotal milestones that strengthened its position as a formidable force in international affairs. The establishment of institutional frameworks for cooperation, such as the New Development Bank and the Contingent Reserve Arrangement, demonstrated the willingness of BRICS members to create alternative mechanisms for financial stability and development assistance. These initiatives not only showcased the collective strength of the bloc but also signified a departure from traditional Western-dominated institutions. Additionally, advancements in trade and investment relationships, coupled with collaborative agreements in areas such as technology transfer and innovation, underscored the proactive efforts of BRICS to foster sustainable growth and development within and beyond their borders.

Furthermore, the ability of BRICS to navigate economic uncertainties and instabilities within the global market marked a significant milestone. Despite external pressures, the collective GDP and trade figures of BRICS member nations exhibited consistent growth, challenging existing narratives of economic hegemony. This resilience in the face of adversity bolstered the confidence of the member countries and solidified their commitment to the principles of fairness, equity, and inclusivity in global economic governance.

In summary, the initial challenges faced by BRICS served as crucibles of unity and resilience, ultimately leading to the achievement of critical milestones that defined its emergence and consolidation as a notable power bloc. The spirit of cooperation and the determination to overcome obstacles continue to exemplify BRICS's ethos, setting the stage for its enduring influence in shaping the future of global politics and economics.

ECONOMIC POLICIES AND GROWTH TRAJECTORIES

The economic policies and growth trajectories of the BRICS countries have been a focal point of global interest and scrutiny since the formation of this powerful bloc. Each member state, namely Brazil, Russia, India, China, and South Africa, has adopted distinct economic policies that have played pivotal roles in shaping their individual growth trajectories and, consequently, influencing the collective economic dynamics of the BRICS coalition. A critical examination of these policies unveils a mosaic of innovative strategies, challenges, and successes that have propelled the economies of the member states and reshaped the global economic landscape. Brazil, for instance, has articulated an economic policy emphasizing market-oriented reforms and infrastructure development to augment its competitiveness in global markets. Meanwhile, Russia's economic trajectory has been shaped by its rich endowment of natural resources and a focus on economic diversification to mitigate vulnerabilities in energy markets. Similarly, India has leveraged its demographic dividend and robust service sector to bolster economic growth despite infrastructure bottlenecks and regulatory complexities. In stark contrast, China's economic policies have pivoted around export-led growth, investments in strategic industries, and initiatives such as the Belt and Road Initiative to foster global connectivity and trade dominance. South Africa, with its historical legacy and mineral wealth, has pursued policies to foster inclusive growth and address socio-economic disparities. Evolving global economic trends, technological advancements, and cooperation with other emerging economies have also influenced the growth trajectories of these nations within the BRICS framework. Exploring economic policies and growth trajectories of BRICS member countries provides deeper insights into the varying strategies adopted in response to local developmental needs and global economic interdependencies. Furthermore, it elucidates how these policies have contributed to shaping the economic transformation of the BRICS bloc as a formidable force in the international arena, shaping the future of global economic governance and cooperation.

STRATEGIC PARTNERSHIPS AND INTERNATIONAL RELATIONS

In international relations, the strategic partnerships formed by BRICS members have contributed significantly to the evolving global order. Shared interests, common goals, and a desire for cooperation in various domains such as politics, economics, security, and culture characterize these partnerships. Brazil, Russia, India, China, and South Africa have strategically engaged with each other and with other nations to enhance their influence and further their collective objectives. One of the defining features of BRICS' international relations strategy is its commitment to upholding principles of sovereignty, non-interference, and mutual respect, which has allowed the bloc to forge alliances based on equitable and inclusive cooperation rather than dominance or subjugation.

At the core of BRICS' strategic partnerships lies a deep understanding of the shifting geopolitical landscape and a conscious effort to diversify their global engagements beyond traditional power centers. The group has fostered ties with various regional organizations such as the Shanghai Cooperation Organization (SCO), Association of Southeast Asian Nations (ASEAN), and the African Union. Through these partnerships, BRICS members have played pivotal roles in shaping regional agendas, promoting stability, and fostering economic development across different continents.

Economically, BRICS has established partnerships with emerging markets and developing nations to foster a more balanced and fair international trade architecture. Establishing institutions like the New Development Bank (NDB) and the Contingent Reserve Arrangement (CRA) reflects the bloc's commitment to providing alternative financing options and strengthening economic resilience for its member countries and beyond. These strategic economic partnerships have sought to challenge existing norms and institutions, advocating for reforms that better represent the interests of developing economies on the global stage.

In security, BRICS collaborations have addressed common challenges, including terrorism, transnational crime, and cybersecurity threats. The bloc has emphasized collective security, encouraging dialogue and cooperation to mitigate regional conflicts and promote peace. Moreover, the collaborative efforts in defense and security initiatives signal a shared commitment to safeguarding common interests and ensuring stability in an increasingly complex and unpredictable world.

Culturally, BRICS members have capitalized on their rich and diverse heritage to forge meaningful partnerships in education, arts, and tourism. By promoting people-to-people exchanges and cultural diplomacy, the bloc has strengthened its soft power and enhanced understanding and goodwill among its populations, paving the way for deeper societal linkages and collaboration.

Through its strategic partnerships and international relations initiatives, BRICS has paved a new path in global governance, emphasizing inclusivity, diversity, and mutual benefit. As the bloc continues to navigate the complexities of the contemporary world, its approach to strategic partnerships will play a pivotal role in shaping the future dynamics of international relations.

BRICS SUMMITS: MAJOR DECLARATIONS AND AGREEMENTS

BRICS summits serve as pivotal junctures where member nations converge to shape the trajectory of global economic and political landscapes through major declarations and agreements. These summits provide a platform for leaders to deliberate on critical issues and formulate collective strategies to foster mutual growth and prosperity while championing multilateralism, inclusivity, and equitable development principles. The BRICS bloc has utilized these gatherings to solidify its stance on key international matters, affirming its commitment to sovereignty, non-interference, and respect for diverse cultural and social systems. Through several declarations, BRICS has emphasized the need to reform global governance institutions to reflect contemporary geopolitical realities better. By leveraging their combined influence, BRICS members have worked to address imbalances in the global financial architecture and advance efforts to democratize decision-making processes in international financial institutions. Furthermore, BRICS summits have signed crucial agreements that bolster economic cooperation, technological exchange, and sustainable development initiatives among member nations. These agreements have underscored the collective resolve to foster innovation, invest in infrastructure, promote trade facilitation, and enhance regional connectivity, laying the groundwork for shared prosperity and progress. In addition, the summits have played a significant role in enhancing cultural ties and people-to-people exchanges, setting the stage for greater understanding and collaboration among the diverse societies represented within the bloc. BRICS summits have also provided a unified voice on global security challenges, with member states reaffirming their commitment to combatting terrorism, cyber threats, and transnational crime. The collective declarations from these summits have positioned BRICS as a formidable advocate for peace, stability, and cooperation in global affairs, offering alternative perspectives on complex geopolitical issues. As the world continues to grapple with evolving geopolitical dynamics, BRICS summits remain integral in driving forward the narrative of mutual respect, cooperation, and shared prosperity, contributing significantly to shaping the future course of international relations.

INFLUENCE ON GLOBAL TRADE AND INVESTMENT FLOWS

The BRICS nations, including Brazil, Russia, India, China, and South Africa, have collectively emerged as significant global trade and investment players. Their combined economic strength and strategic collaborations have fostered a noticeable impact on international commerce and capital deployment patterns. As these nations continue to advance their economic agendas and pursue mutually beneficial partnerships, the ripple effects of their actions reverberate across continents.

One of the key aspects of the BRICS' influence on global trade is their collective market size and demographic diversity. With a combined population of over 3 billion, the BRICS countries represent a substantial consumer base and labor force. This large market potential has attracted the attention of multinational corporations seeking to expand their global footprint. Consequently, this has led to increased cross-border investments and trade activities, shaping the dynamics of international commerce.

Moreover, the BRICS nations have strategically leveraged their rich endowments of natural resources and developed formidable industrial capabilities. This has enabled them to become significant exporters of commodities and manufactured goods, exerting a considerable impact on global supply chains and pricing dynamics. Additionally, the growth of intra-BRICS trade has further solidified the bloc's position as a formidable trading entity, fostering economic interdependence and diversification of trade routes.

Developing collaborative initiatives among BRICS countries, such as the New Development Bank (NDB) and the Contingent Reserve Arrangement (CRA), has also influenced global trade and investment flows. These institutions have provided alternative financing options and risk mitigation mechanisms, reducing reliance on traditional Western-dominated financial structures. Furthermore, by promoting infrastructure development and sustainable projects through joint investment programs, the BRICS have stimulated trade corridors and facilitated more excellent connectivity, particularly in emerging markets.

It is imperative to recognize that the BRICS' influence extends beyond trade in tangible goods, encompassing services and intellectual property as well. Their burgeoning service sectors and advancements in technology and innovation have unleashed new opportunities for cross-border collaborations and investment ventures. Notably, the rise of digital economies and e-commerce platforms within the BRICS has reshaped consumer behavior and market access, pioneering new avenues for global trade and investment diversification.

In conclusion, the BRICS nations' combined impact on global trade and investment flows is not merely confined to incremental growth statistics; it represents a fundamental reorientation of the geopolitical and economic landscape. As these nations continue to align their policies and deepen their integration, their influence will transcend traditional paradigms, shaping the architecture of future international commerce and investment strategies.

CULTURAL EXCHANGES AND SOCIOPOLITICAL COOPERATION

Cultural exchanges and sociopolitical cooperation are vital components of the collaboration of the BRICS (Brazil, Russia, India, China, and South Africa), playing a significant role in shaping this influential alliance's collective identity and character. Understanding each member nation's diverse cultural heritage and societal dynamics is essential for fostering mutual understanding and strengthening cooperation. The appreciation and promotion of cultural diversity, traditions, languages, arts, and customs among BRICS nations serve as pillars for meaningful exchanges that transcend geographical boundaries. Initiatives such as collaborative cultural festivals, art exhibitions, film screenings, and literary exchanges provide avenues for citizens of BRICS countries to engage with, learn from, and celebrate the unique contributions of each other's cultures. These interactions promote intercultural dialogue and contribute to the enrichment and preservation of cultural heritage, fostering a sense of shared identity and unity among member states. Furthermore, sociopolitical cooperation within BRICS extends beyond cultural exchanges to encompass many diplomatic, social, and humanitarian initiatives. The member nations engage in dialogue and collaboration on issues such as education, healthcare, gender equality, human rights, and sustainable development, reflecting their commitment to addressing global challenges collectively. Sociopolitical cooperation also involves joint efforts to promote peace, stability, and security at regional and international levels. By sharing best practices and engaging in constructive dialogue, the BRICS nations demonstrate a collective determination to uphold democratic values, advocate for inclusivity, and support achieving equitable and sustainable development goals. Moreover, through platforms like the BRICS Academic Forum and the BRICS Think Tanks Council, intellectual exchanges and policy dialogues facilitate sharing knowledge, expertise, and experiences, leading to informed decision-making and policy formulation across various sectors. These engagements contribute to pooling resources, expertise, and capacities, ultimately fostering mutual trust, respect, and solidarity among the member nations. In conclusion, cultural exchanges and sociopolitical cooperation are integral elements in strengthening the cohesion and resonance of the BRICS alliance, embracing the richness of cultural diversity and harnessing the collective potential for sociopolitical collaboration to position BRICS as a dynamic force for positive change, fostering a future characterized by shared prosperity, understanding, and mutual respect.

ASSESSMENT OF SUCCESSES AND ONGOING CHALLENGES

As the BRICS alliance continues to evolve, it becomes imperative to assess its achievements and persisting obstacles comprehensively. The successes of the BRICS bloc are evident in various domains. Economically, the combined GDP of Brazil, Russia, India, China, and South Africa accounts for a significant portion of the world's total economic output. This collective economic strength has allowed BRICS member states to assert themselves on the global stage and participate in shaping international financial and trade agendas. Moreover, the cooperative initiatives within BRICS have facilitated cross-border investments, technological collaborations, and infrastructural developments, contributing to the advancement of member nations' economies.

Sociopolitically, BRICS has fostered a platform for cultural exchanges and mutual understanding among member states, promoting people-to-people interactions and enhancing diplomatic ties. The consortium has also addressed common challenges such as poverty, inequality, and sustainable development, emphasizing the need for inclusivity and social progress. Furthermore, BRICS has diversified its strategic partnerships by engaging with other emerging economies and regional alliances, expanding its geopolitical influence beyond its initial framework.

Despite these successes, the BRICS alliance grapples with ongoing challenges that demand attention and resolution. One prominent issue revolves around the disparity in economic development among member countries, which has led to tensions and unequal contributions within the bloc. Additionally, divergent political ideologies, governance structures, and foreign policy priorities complicate aligning concerted efforts toward shared objectives. The capacity to effectively address geopolitical crises and security concerns remains a crucial test for BRICS, especially amid global uncertainties and regional instabilities. Furthermore, navigating through evolving global governance mechanisms and multilateral institutions presents an ongoing challenge for the alliance.

Another critical aspect that requires continuous assessment is the sustainability of BRICS' cooperative agenda amidst shifting global dynamics and power configurations. As competing interests and external pressures shape the geopolitical landscape, BRICS member nations must adapt their strategies and collaboration frameworks to maintain relevance and efficacy. This necessitates a nuanced approach to balancing national priorities with collective aspirations, ensuring that the alliance preserves its unity and purpose while accommodating diverse perspectives and evolving global demands.

In essence, the assessment of BRICS's successes and ongoing challenges reveals a complex interplay of opportunities and impediments. Strategic recalibration and sustained dialogue are essential to harnessing the alliance's potential and addressing persistent hurdles, ultimately steering BRICS towards continued relevance and impactful global engagement.

CHAPTER 4

The Economics of Competition: Analyzing G7 and BRICS Economies

GLOBAL ECONOMIC COMPETITIVENESS

In today's interconnected and interdependent global economy, economic competitiveness plays a pivotal role in shaping the trajectory of nations and regions. It is a multifaceted concept encompassing a range of factors, including productivity, innovation, trade policies, regulatory frameworks, infrastructure, education, and technological advancement. At its core, economic competitiveness reflects a nation's capacity to create and sustain wealth while improving the living standards of its citizens. Furthermore, it influences a country's position in the global marketplace, its ability to attract investment, and its resilience during economic turbulence. The significance of economic competitiveness cannot be overstated, as it directly impacts GDP growth, employment rates, and overall prosperity. Against the backdrop of rapid globalization, understanding the intricacies of economic competitiveness and positioning one's economy for success has never been more crucial. Therefore, this section sets the stage for a comprehensive analysis of global economic competitiveness by delving into the fundamental drivers, challenges, and opportunities that shape the competitive landscape.

By closely examining the factors that contribute to economic success within the G7 and BRICS economies, this analysis seeks to unearth insights that can inform policy decisions, spur reforms, and foster sustainable development on a global scale.

OVERVIEW OF G7 ECONOMIES: MAJOR INDICATORS AND BENCHMARKS

The G7 countries, comprising the United States, Japan, Germany, France, the United Kingdom, Italy, and Canada, are among the world's most developed and influential economies. This section delves into a comprehensive analysis of the major economic indicators and benchmarks that characterize the G7 nations. One of the primary measures of economic health is the Gross Domestic Product (GDP), which reflects the total value of goods and services produced within a country's borders. The GDP of the G7 countries collectively represents a substantial portion of the global economy, exerting significant influence on international trade, investment flows, and financial markets. Additionally, examining key indicators such as unemployment rates, inflation levels, and income distribution provides insight into the socioeconomic conditions within these advanced economies. Another critical benchmark is the level of industrial production, highlighting the manufacturing and output capabilities of the G7 nations. This ties into the overall competitiveness and technological advancement that underpin their economic strength. Financial stability and performance are also key considerations, with metrics such as stock market indices, foreign exchange reserves, and national debt shaping perceptions of economic robustness. Furthermore, the trade balance and current account deficits or surpluses convey information about the G7 countries' engagement in international commerce and their dependence on foreign markets. Beyond quantitative measures, qualitative aspects, including innovation, research and development expenditure, and the quality of infrastructure, are pivotal in understanding these economies' long-term sustainability and adaptability. Lastly, the regulatory environment and ease of doing business indicators shed light on the institutional frameworks that support or impede entrepreneurial activities and investment. Analyzing these major indicators and benchmarks provides a multifaceted perspective of the G7 economies, unraveling their complexities and fundamental drivers of economic influence.

ASSESSMENT OF BRICS ECONOMIES: GROWTH TRAJECTORIES AND CHALLENGES

As we delve into the assessment of BRICS economies, it becomes evident that these nations have emerged as significant players in the global economic landscape. Each member, Brazil, Russia, India, China, and South Africa, exhibits unique growth trajectories and presents challenges that shape their respective economic outlooks. Let's start with a comparative analysis of their GDP growth rates, where China and India stand out with robust expansion, while others witness more moderate growth. The diverse nature of their economies is reflected in their industrial composition. For instance, Brazil is known for its prowess in agriculture and mining, while Russia thrives on energy resources and heavy industries. On the other hand, India has carved a niche in IT services, while China leads in manufacturing and export-oriented industries. Furthermore, the structural reforms undertaken by each nation play a pivotal role in fostering economic growth. Despite their potential, the BRICS economies face challenges related to income inequality, infrastructure deficiencies, and bureaucratic hurdles. Additionally, geopolitical tensions, trade imbalances, and currency fluctuations complicate their economic prospects. It's imperative to recognize that these nations' policy decisions and strategic adaptations will significantly influence their paths ahead. A thorough exploration of their monetary policies, fiscal discipline, and long-term development plans is essential to gain insights into their growth trajectories. Moreover, navigating global economic uncertainties and external shocks demands resilience and agility. By studying the varied approaches adopted by BRICS members to address financial vulnerabilities and spur innovation, we can discern the probable outcomes and anticipate their evolution as key economic powerhouses. In essence, comprehending the growth trajectories and challenges of BRICS economies enables us to grasp the multifaceted nature of global competition. It underscores the significance of their contributions to the evolving economic order.

SECTORAL ANALYSIS: KEY INDUSTRIES DRIVING COMPETITION

The competition between the G7 and BRICS economies is not limited to overall economic performance but extends to specific industries that drive their growth and global competitiveness. In this section, we will delve into the key sectors of these economies and analyze how they contribute to the overall economic landscape. The manufacturing industry plays a pivotal role in the competition between the G7 and BRICS nations. While the G7 countries have historically excelled in advanced manufacturing, including automotive, aerospace, and high-tech equipment production, the BRICS economies have rapidly expanded their manufacturing capabilities, particularly in electronics, pharmaceuticals, and consumer goods. The service sector is another critical component of the competition between these economies. The G7 economies are known for their dominance in financial services, technology, and professional services. At the same time, the BRICS nations have shown remarkable growth in areas such as IT outsourcing, telecommunications, and business process outsourcing. Furthermore, the energy sector is a significant battleground for economic competition. The G7 nations have traditionally led in technology and innovation in the renewable energy sector. At the same time, the BRICS economies have demonstrated a strong focus on traditional energy sources and substantial investments in renewable energy infrastructure. Additionally, the agricultural industry remains a critical factor in economic competition. The G7 countries boast advanced agricultural technologies and high-value crop production, whereas the BRICS nations exhibit vast agricultural land and growing agribusiness opportunities. Moreover, the healthcare and pharmaceutical sectors are key areas of competition. The G7 economies are recognized for cutting-edge medical research and pharmaceutical development, while the BRICS economies are making strides in generic drug manufacturing and R&D investments. Finally, the technology and innovation industry are driving forces in the rivalry between these economies. The G7 nations lead in innovation-driven sectors such as biotechnology, nanotechnology, and artificial intelligence, while the BRICS nations are increasingly investing in technology research and development to bolster their competitive advantage. Analyzing these key industries provides insight into the complex dynamics of economic competition between the G7 and BRICS countries, highlighting their strengths and areas for further development.

FISCAL POLICIES: TAXATION AND GOVERNMENT SPENDING

Fiscal policies play a crucial role in shaping the economic landscape of both the G7 and BRICS economies. Taxation and government spending are key instruments wielded by policymakers to influence economic activities, promote growth, and ensure fiscal stability. In this section, we will delve into the intricate mechanisms of fiscal policies within the context of the G7 and BRICS nations, analyzing their approaches and the impacts of taxation and government spending on their respective economies. Taxation serves as a primary source of revenue for governments, providing the necessary funds for public services, infrastructure development, and social welfare programs. The level and structure of taxation vary across the G7 and BRICS nations, reflecting differing philosophies and priorities. Governments employ progressive, proportional, or regressive tax systems, depending on their socio-economic objectives and principles of equity. Moreover, corporate taxation, capital gains tax, value-added tax (VAT), and personal income tax are critical components influencing economic behavior and resource allocation within these economies. Equally significant is government spending, which encompasses expenditures on defense, healthcare, education, and social welfare, among other areas. The composition and scale of government spending provide insights into national priorities, with defense budgets reflecting geopolitical strategies and social welfare expenditure indicating a commitment to inclusive growth and development. Analyzing how G7 and BRICS economies approach government spending offers valuable perspectives on their governance philosophies and societal values. Moreover, the interplay between taxation and government spending influences economic efficiency, income distribution, and overall macroeconomic stability. As we delve deeper into these nuances, it becomes evident that the divergent approaches to fiscal policies have far-reaching implications for the competitiveness and resilience of the G7 and BRICS economies. Thus, a nuanced understanding of fiscal policies, tax structures, and government spending is imperative for comprehending the economic dynamics and policy frameworks at play within the global arena.

MONETARY STRATEGIES: INFLATION, INTEREST RATES, AND CURRENCY STABILITY

In the complex global economics web, monetary policy significantly influences a nation's economic landscape. This section delves into the intricate dynamics of monetary strategies, focusing on inflation management, interest rate policies, and the crucial aspect of currency stability. Monetary strategies are the operative levers that central banks employ to regulate the availability of money and credit within an economy. By understanding and actively managing these components, nations can seek to achieve optimal economic stability and growth. Inflation, the sustained increase in the general price level of goods and services, is a critical factor influencing consumer purchasing power and investment decisions. Central banks strive to maintain a delicate balance by employing interest rate adjustments and open market operations to control inflationary pressures. These efforts are aimed at preserving the value of the national currency and fostering confidence in the financial system. Moreover, interest rates influence borrowing and spending behaviors, steering economic activities. The meticulous calibration of interest rates impacts various sectors, including housing, manufacturing, and consumer discretionary spending, contributing to overall economic vitality. Maintaining a stable currency is also paramount in fostering international trade and investment. Currency stability directly impacts export competitiveness, exchange rate fluctuations, and the allure of a nation's assets to foreign investors. Consequently, central banks often engage in foreign exchange interventions to mitigate abrupt currency fluctuations and uphold stability. A nuanced understanding of these monetary strategies is essential in comprehending the resilience and adaptability of G7 and BRICS economies amidst the ever-evolving global economic landscape. As the preceding discussions have elucidated, the interplay between fiscal policies, monetary strategies, and trade dynamics collectively shapes nations' economic performance and competitive edge across the G7 and BRICS spectrums.

TRADE DYNAMICS AND BALANCES: EXPORTS VS. IMPORTS

Trade dynamics and balances play a pivotal role in shaping nations' economic strength and stability within the global market. The balance between exports and imports is a critical indicator of a country's overall trade performance and position in the international economic landscape. This section will delve into the intricate mechanisms that govern trade dynamics, exploring the implications of export and import activities on the economies of G7 and BRICS nations.

The concepts of comparative advantage and competitiveness lie at the heart of trade dynamics. Countries leverage their unique capabilities and resources to engage in international trade, seeking to maximize their gains from specialized production and exchange. In this context, exports represent domestic goods and services sold to foreign markets, while imports denote products and services brought in from overseas. Understanding the balance between these two activities is essential in evaluating a nation's commercial relationships with the rest of the world.

For the G7 economies, trade dynamics reflect a mix of advanced industrial capabilities, technological expertise, and diversified export portfolios. With an emphasis on high-value goods and services, G7 nations often maintain trade surpluses, leveraging their strong competitive positions in automotive engineering, pharmaceuticals, and information technology sectors. Furthermore, the G7's significant investments in research and development contribute to continuous innovation and product quality, bolstering their exports across global markets.

Conversely, BRICS economies exhibit a different trade profile focusing on raw materials, natural resources, and labor-intensive manufacturing. These nations often experience trade deficits due to their reliance on imported technologies and high-value goods. However, the robust export of commodities like oil, metals, and agricultural products is a key revenue source for BRICS countries, contributing to their economic growth despite trade imbalances.

The dynamics of trade balances extend beyond mere statistics, influencing currency valuation, national employment levels, and domestic industries' viability. Moreover, trade policies, including tariffs, quotas, and trade agreements, shape the direction of exports and imports, impacting both the domestic economy and international relationships. Understanding the intricate interplay of these factors provides crucial insights into the economic strategies and vulnerabilities of G7 and BRICS member states.

As we navigate the nuances of trade dynamics and balances, it becomes evident that these elements serve as economic health and vitality barometers. A more profound comprehension of how exports and imports influence national economies enables us to forecast future trends, anticipate market behaviors, and implement informed policy interventions. By scrutinizing the complexities of trade balances, we can gain valuable perspectives on the evolving nature of global economic interdependence and the strategic maneuvers of G7 and BRICS economies in pursuing sustainable development and prosperity.

INVESTMENT FLOWS AND FOREIGN DIRECT INVESTMENTS (FDI)

As integral components of the global economic landscape, investment flows, and foreign direct investments (FDI) are pivotal in shaping the competitive dynamics between the G7 and BRICS economies. In recent decades, both groups have actively engaged in cross-border investment activities, seeking to gain strategic footholds in key industries and markets. FDI, in particular, has emerged as a crucial indicator of economic integration and influence on a global scale.

The G7 economies have traditionally been significant sources of FDI, with established multinational companies leading the charge in overseas investments. These investments are driven by the pursuit of market expansion, access to resources, and acquiring technological expertise. Furthermore, implementing favorable trade policies and bilateral agreements has facilitated the outward flow of investments from G7 nations into various sectors worldwide.

In contrast, the BRICS nations have increasingly become attractive destinations for FDI, owing to their robust economic growth, burgeoning consumer markets, and natural resource abundance. The influx of FDI into BRICS countries has propelled their industrial development and solidified their positions as formidable players in the global economy.

Examining the trends in investment flows reveals intricate networks of capital allocation and strategic partnerships between the G7 and BRICS. The diversification of FDI portfolios across different sectors, such as manufacturing, technology, energy, and finance, underscores the multifaceted nature of economic interactions. Moreover, the rise of emerging sectors like renewable energy and digital infrastructure has drawn increasing FDI interest from both groups, indicating a transformative shift in investment patterns.

It is vital to acknowledge the impact of investment flows and FDI on host economies, as they bring with them not only capital but also knowledge transfer, managerial expertise, and employment opportunities. However, concerns over dependency, sovereignty, and ethical considerations necessitate a balanced approach to managing inbound investments. G7 and BRICS nations have strived to create conducive environments for foreign investors, offering incentives, ensuring regulatory transparency, and fostering innovation ecosystems.

Looking ahead, the evolution of investment flows and FDI will continue to shape the economic narratives of the G7 and BRICS, influencing technological advancements, market competitiveness, and sustainable development. Understanding the interplay of these financial currents is imperative for policymakers, businesses, and stakeholders seeking to navigate the complexities of an increasingly interconnected global economy.

ECONOMIC RESILIENCE: RESPONSE TO GLOBAL CRISES

In the face of global crises, whether triggered by financial instability, geopolitical tensions, natural disasters, or health emergencies, the economic resilience of nations within the G7 and BRICS becomes a critical determinant of their ability to withstand and recover from such challenges. This section delves into the multifaceted strategies and responses employed by the member countries of these influential groups to mitigate the impact of global crises on their economies. Economic resilience encompasses a range of factors, including robust fiscal policies, effective monetary measures, proactive trade and investment frameworks, and agile regulatory mechanisms. Each component enhances a nation's capacity to weather turbulent times.

FUTURE OUTLOOK: PREDICTING ECONOMIC TRENDS IN G7 AND BRICS

The future economic outlook for the G7 and BRICS nations is subject to complex dynamics that encompass a broad spectrum of factors. In projecting economic trends, it is essential to consider various variables such as technological advancements, demographic shifts, geopolitical developments, and evolving trade relations. A major factor influencing the economic landscape revolves around developing and adopting advanced technologies. Artificial intelligence, automation, and machine learning are poised to revolutionize industries, altering production processes and reshaping labor markets. Such technological disruptions will profoundly impact the economies of both G7 and BRICS nations, driving innovation, efficiency, and new business models. Moreover, demographic changes, particularly aging populations in some G7 nations, will significantly affect economic growth, labor availability, and social welfare systems. This demographic shift contrasts with the youthful populations of many BRICS nations, presenting distinct opportunities and challenges. Geopolitical developments, including trade disputes, regional conflicts, and international cooperation, will be pivotal in shaping economic trends. The ongoing rebalancing of global power dynamics, especially the rise of China and India, will profoundly affect trade patterns, investment strategies, and currency dynamics. Predictions about economic trends must account for the interplay of domestic and international political and policy decisions. The evolution of trade relations is also critical in understanding future economic trends. Bilateral and multilateral trade agreements, tariff policies, and non-tariff barriers will significantly influence export-import balances and industrial specialization. For G7 nations, the resilience of European economies and the post-pandemic recovery efforts will be focal points in determining long-term economic performance.

Meanwhile, BRICS nations face the challenge of balancing rapid economic growth with structural reforms to ensure sustainable development. Intricate interlinkages exist between these two groups of nations, given the mutual interdependence in global trade and investment flows. Therefore, the future outlook for G7 and BRICS economies necessitates an intricate analysis of intertwined macroeconomic indicators, financial systems, and socioeconomic conditions. By closely examining these diverse factors, policymakers, analysts, and businesses can gain valuable insights into potential economic scenarios and make informed decisions to navigate dynamic and uncertain times.

CHAPTER 5

Geostrategic Interests and Political Dynamics in G7 Nations

UNDERSTANDING GEOSTRATEGIC INTERESTS: AN OVERVIEW

Geostrategic interests play a pivotal role in shaping the international policies of G7 nations. Each member, comprising the United States, Canada, France, Germany, Italy, Japan, and the United Kingdom, identifies and prioritizes its international interests based on a complex interplay of geographical location, historical ties, and economic needs. The geostrategic interests of these nations are deeply rooted in their historical experiences, including colonial legacies, war narratives, and power struggles. Geographical location also significantly influences their geopolitical aims. For instance, with its global military presence and strategic alliances, the United States extends its interests across various continents. As a vast northern nation, Canada bears unique responsibilities in the Arctic and North Atlantic regions while maintaining strong ties with its southern neighbor. France, with historical ties to former colonies and a significant presence in Africa and the Middle East, exhibits a multifaceted set of interests. At the heart of Europe, Germany balances its economic might with diplomatic engagements across the European

Union and beyond. With its strategic Mediterranean positioning, Italy is important in regional stability and migration matters. In an area of heightened regional tensions, Japan navigates its security interests amid territorial disputes and alliance dynamics in the Asia-Pacific.

Meanwhile, with its historical imperial footprint, the United Kingdom seeks to redefine its role in a post-Brexit era, recalibrating its global engagement. Furthermore, economic considerations significantly shape the geostrategic interests of G7 nations. These countries, being among the world's largest economies, utilize their economic leverage to advance their geopolitical agendas. From trade pacts to development aid, investment strategies to currency management, the economic dimensions of their geostrategic interests often intertwine with security concerns, environmental stewardship, and technological innovation. Understanding how each G7 nation identifies and prioritizes its geostrategic interests is essential for comprehending the complexities of international relations and global governance.

MAPPING POLITICAL LANDSCAPES OF G7 NATIONS

As we delve into the complex fabric of geopolitical influence, it becomes imperative to map the intricate political landscapes of G7 nations. The dynamics within these nations have far-reaching implications on global governance and strategic decision-making. Each member country brings its unique historical, cultural, and political context to this alliance, shaping the collective approach to international affairs.

The United States is a pivotal player in global politics and holds a prominent position within the G7. Its expansive military capabilities, economic prowess, and diplomatic reach define the coalition's agenda. The interplay of domestic politics, bipartisan relations, and power struggles within the US government significantly impacts its stance on key global issues.

Moving across the Atlantic, European G7 members bring diverse political systems and ideologies. The relationships among these nations, often rooted in centuries of shared history and conflicts, undergo constant evolutions as they navigate the modern geopolitical landscape. Factors such as the European Union's supranational influence, Brexit repercussions, and individual member-state policies contribute to the nuanced political dynamics within the region.

Canada and Japan witness the fusion of traditional values with progressive global engagement. Each nation's unique approach to diplomacy, trade agreements, and strategic partnerships reflects its geopolitical agenda. Canada and Japan's internal socio-political structures interweave with their international roles, ultimately influencing the cohesive stance of the G7.

Lastly, Italy, Germany, and France each command distinct geopolitical footprints shaped by historical legacies and contemporary challenges. Strategic alignments, economic policies, and foreign relations strategies relevant to global political equilibrium mark their participation in the G7.

To comprehend the intricate web of political landscapes within the G7, we must deconstruct each member nation's internal power dynamics, policy inclinations, and evolving alliances. This exploration lays the foundation for understanding the complexity of decision-making processes and the diverse motivations that underpin international cooperation and competition among these influential nations.

US AND EUROPEAN RELATIONS: THE TRANSATLANTIC ALLIANCE

The transatlantic alliance between the United States and Europe represents a cornerstone of global geopolitics, characterized by a complex interplay of historical, political, economic, and security dynamics. Rooted in the aftermath of World War II, the partnership between the US and European nations has been instrumental in shaping international relations, trade agreements, security pacts, and diplomatic endeavors. At its core, the transatlantic bond is underpinned by shared democratic values, commitment to human rights, and a mutual interest in upholding global stability. Despite occasional strains and differences, the relationship has been vital for global cooperation and progress.

From a geopolitical perspective, the transatlantic alliance has served as a bulwark against adversarial influences and authoritarian regimes, with the US and Europe aligning their foreign policy objectives to pursue common goals. This alignment has been manifest in joint military operations, intelligence-sharing agreements, coordinated diplomatic initiatives, and collaborative efforts in addressing global challenges ranging from terrorism to cybersecurity threats. Moreover, the transatlantic partnership has played an instrumental role in promoting multilateralism and supporting international institutions such as the United Nations, NATO, and the World Trade Organization.

Economically, the US and Europe enjoy extensive trade ties, investment partnerships, and cross-border business collaborations that have fostered economic growth and prosperity on both sides of the Atlantic. The interdependence between these economies not only amplifies their collective influence but also serves as a stabilizing force in the global market. Furthermore, the transatlantic economic relationship enables technological innovation, research exchange, and the harmonization of regulatory standards, laying the groundwork for sustainable development and competitiveness in the digital era.

However, the transatlantic alliance faces contemporary challenges, including divergent policy priorities, trade disputes, and strain in diplomatic relations. Events such as Brexit and shifts in US foreign policy have sparked debates about the future trajectory of the transatlantic partnership. Efforts to navigate these challenges involve extensive dialogue, compromise, and recalibration of strategic approaches to ensure that the alliance remains resilient and adaptive in a rapidly evolving global landscape. Ultimately, the transatlantic alliance embodies a crucial axis of geopolitical influence, demonstrating the enduring significance of transnational cooperation in shaping the world's political, economic, and security architecture.

SHIFTS IN POWER DYNAMICS: BREXIT AND BEYOND

Brexit marked a monumental shift in the power dynamics within the G7 nations, particularly in the relationship between the United Kingdom and the European Union. The decision to leave the EU introduced significant uncertainty and geopolitical ramifications, impacting not just economic ties but also security alliances and foreign policy considerations. As the UK navigates through the complexities of extricating itself from the EU, the nation and the bloc find themselves repositioning on the global stage.

In the aftermath of Brexit, the balance of power and influence among G7 nations has gradually transformed. Traditional dynamics that shaped international relations are being reassessed as the EU recalibrates its partnerships and the UK asserts its newfound independence. This realignment produces ripple effects across multiple spheres, from trade and investment to defense and intelligence collaborations.

The implications extend beyond immediate regional repercussions into the broader geopolitical landscape. The evolving role of the UK outside the EU and the redefined relationship between the UK and the US offer insights into the complex interplay of geostrategic interests. Moreover, considering the historically close ties between the US and the UK, the potential impact on the Euro-Atlantic security framework and defense cooperation mechanisms warrants careful analysis.

At the same time, other G7 members are closely monitoring the developments stemming from Brexit as they weigh the ramifications for their own strategic interests and bilateral relationships. The shifting landscape presents opportunities for diplomatic realignments and economic partnerships while posing challenges in harmonizing divergent national objectives and reconciling competing geopolitical aspirations.

Looking beyond Brexit, the global political dynamics are reshaped by the ongoing power shifts within the G7. As traditional powerhouses seek to consolidate influence and emerging economies assert themselves, the interconnected nature of geopolitical interactions necessitates a nuanced understanding of the evolving power dynamics. Engaging with these intricate changes demands astute geopolitical foresight and strategic insight as G7 nations navigate the uncertainties and opportunities unfolding in this transformative era.

SECURITY CONCERNS AND MILITARY ENGAGEMENTS

Security concerns and military engagements are pivotal aspects of the geostrategic interests of G7 nations. The evolving global landscape has necessitated a reevaluation of security paradigms, with defense and military capabilities playing a central role in safeguarding national interests and upholding international stability. The G7 member countries have historically been at the forefront of addressing security challenges stemming from geopolitical tensions, asymmetric threats, and transnational risks. These nations have continuously adapted their military strategies to counter emergent threats, ranging from conventional warfare scenarios to unconventional forms of aggression, such as cyberattacks and terrorism. Additionally, the broader spectrum of security concerns encompasses maritime security, border protection, and responses to humanitarian crises and natural disasters, highlighting the multidimensional nature of contemporary security dynamics. Military engagements, whether through bilateral or multilateral alliances, reflect the cooperative efforts of the G7 nations in addressing global security challenges. Collaborative military exercises, intelligence-sharing initiatives, and joint peacekeeping operations underscore the commitment of these nations to collective security and defense cooperation.

Furthermore, the G7's coordinated approach towards leveraging military capabilities is a deterrent against potential aggressors and enhances the effectiveness of humanitarian interventions and crisis response. In an increasingly interconnected world, where borders are not insurmountable barriers, transnational security threats demand cohesive and agile responses. The G7 nations recognize the imperative of international collaboration in combating common security challenges, exemplified by their strong support for global peacekeeping missions and coalition efforts in conflict resolution. Beyond traditional military engagements, the G7 nations actively contribute to international peace and security through diplomatic initiatives, promoting arms control measures, and engaging in dialogue with non-state actors to mitigate the impact of asymmetric threats. The interplay between security concerns and military engagements underscores the intricate relationship between geopolitical interests and international stability. The G7 nations must balance assertive deterrence strategies with diplomatic dialogue and conflict resolution mechanisms to foster a secure and stable global environment. In conclusion, security concerns and military engagements are integral to the G7's strategic calculus. They delineate their proactive stance in shaping global security architecture and fortifying their positions as leaders in ensuring international peace and stability.

ECONOMIC LEVERAGING AS A GEOSTRATEGIC TOOL

Economic leveraging has emerged as a crucial instrument in geostrategic maneuvering, where nations utilize their economic prowess to achieve geopolitical objectives and assert influence on the global stage. The intertwining of economic power with strategic interests has significantly reshaped the dynamics of international relations, providing states with an additional dimension to assert dominance and advance their agendas. This chapter delves into the multifaceted ways economic leveraging is employed as a geostrategic tool by G7 nations, highlighting the far-reaching implications of these maneuvers.

At the heart of economic leveraging lies the intricate web of trade policies, tariffs, and economic alliances that nations meticulously weave to bolster their geopolitical standing. Through strategic trade agreements and negotiations, G7 nations leverage their economic capabilities to forge alliances, impose sanctions, or incentivize compliance with desired international norms. Furthermore, the use of economic aid, investment, and development assistance serves as a potent tool for projecting influence and establishing dependencies, shaping the economic landscapes of other nations in a manner conducive to their strategic interests.

Another dimension of economic leveraging involves the utilization of financial instruments and economic sanctions to coerce or dissuade adversarial actions, thereby exerting pressure on target entities and nations. G7 nations deftly wield economic sanctions to penalize noncompliant states, deter aggressive behavior, and alter the calculus of decision-making at the international level. These sanctions are crafted to inflict targeted economic pain while minimizing spillover effects, driving home the message that deviation from preferred strategic trajectories will carry substantial economic consequences. In essence, economic power becomes a lever to incentivize adherence to established norms and punish transgressions, underpinning broader geostrategic goals.

Moreover, the convergence of economic leveraging with technological innovation has opened new frontiers in geostrategic competition. The race for dominance in cutting-edge technologies such as artificial intelligence, quantum computing, and cyber capabilities intertwines economic and security imperatives, where control over critical technologies confers substantial strategic advantage. G7 nations strategically deploy their economic clout to invest in and safeguard technological advancements, reinforcing their geopolitical influence and preempting potential challenges from rival powers. This intersection of economic and technological realms accentuates the centrality of economic leveraging in shaping the contemporary geostrategic landscape.

In conclusion, the adept harnessing of economic resources and capabilities as a geostrategic tool has become indispensable in pursuing national interests and asserting global influence. G7 nations judiciously navigate the complexities of economic leveraging to mold international dynamics in alignment with their strategic ambitions, underscoring the pivotal role of economic power in the contemporary geopolitical arena.

ENERGY DOMINANCE AND RESOURCE POLITICS

Energy dominance and resource politics play a pivotal role in shaping the geostrategic interests of G7 nations. With an increasing global demand for energy resources, the competition for control and access to these vital commodities has become a defining factor in international relations. The quest for energy security and the geopolitical implications of resource abundance or scarcity profoundly impact foreign policy decisions, regional stability, and global alliances. As G7 nations have historically been significant consumers and energy producers, their policies and strategies in this domain significantly influence the dynamics of international politics. The push for renewable energy sources and sustainable practices has also prompted discussions on environmental conservation and climate change mitigation within the framework of resource politics.

Additionally, exploring and exploiting new frontiers in energy production, such as shale gas and deep-sea oil reserves, have raised questions about territorial claims, regulatory frameworks, and potential conflicts over resource extraction. Moreover, the interplay between energy dominance and resource politics intertwines with issues of trade relations, economic dependencies, and technological advancements. The strategic partnerships and rivalries among G7 nations in securing energy supplies reflect complex negotiations and power struggles, often culminating in diplomatic maneuvers and multilateral agreements. Furthermore, the quest to diversify energy sources and routes has led to the development of ambitious infrastructure projects, underlining the significance of geopolitical positioning and regional influence. The competition for control over critical energy transit routes, such as pipelines and maritime corridors, amplifies the strategic importance of these resources and magnifies the impact of resource politics on global geopolitics. As emerging economies within the G7 alliance also vie for energy resources and seek to assert their geopolitical agendas, the dynamics of resource politics continually evolve, providing fertile ground for analyzing the interplay of national interests, global cooperation, and systemic challenges. In conclusion, the nexus of energy dominance and resource politics emerges as a key determinant of international power relations, underscoring the intricate interconnections between energy security, economic stability, and geopolitical influence.

TECHNOLOGICAL INNOVATIONS AND GEOPOLITICAL INFLUENCES

The intertwining of technological innovations and geopolitical influences has become a cornerstone of global power dynamics within the G7 nations. Technology is increasingly shaping international relations and strategic interests, from the advancement of artificial intelligence and quantum computing to cybersecurity and space exploration developments. The race for technological supremacy has significant implications for geopolitics and national security. Unprecedented connectivity through digital infrastructure has led to immense influence and control over data, information flows, and critical infrastructure, pivotal components of modern warfare. As G7 nations continuously pursue breakthroughs in emerging technologies, the competition for dominance is not merely economic but predominantly geopolitical. Technological advancements grant capabilities that can fundamentally alter the balance of power on the international stage. This has led to intricate considerations around data privacy, surveillance, and the protection of intellectual property rights.

Moreover, applying advanced technologies has redefined military strategies, intelligence gathering, and covert operations, thus reshaping traditional notions of conflict and security. The quest for innovation and technological leadership fosters diplomatic ties and partnerships, with countries vying to forge alliances and secure support for their technological agendas. By establishing collaborative ventures and joint research initiatives, G7 nations aim to bolster their influence and leverage across the global technological landscape, particularly to counter the technological advancements of other global powers such as the BRICS nations. The geopolitical implications of these technological pursuits extend beyond conventional warfare and span into economic realms. The control of critical technologies offers a strategic advantage in trade negotiations, market positioning, and industrial dominance.

Furthermore, technological innovations often underpin efforts toward societal transformation and economic productivity, creating immense potential for global soft power influence. Despite the inherent benefits, the volatile nature of technological developments also introduces vulnerabilities and risks regarding cyber threats, supply chain dependencies, and control over emerging industries. Given these considerations, G7 nations must navigate the evolving landscape of technological advancements while actively engaging in responsible governance, ethical considerations, and international collaboration to ensure stability and security in an increasingly tech-driven world.

CULTURAL DIPLOMACY AND INFLUENCE PEDDLING

Cultural diplomacy is a potent instrument for projecting soft power and shaping international perceptions. The cultivation and dissemination of a nation's cultural assets, including language, arts, traditions, and heritage, are deployed strategically to foster goodwill, build bridges, and influence opinions beyond borders. In the context of G7 nations, this approach is meticulously employed to reinforce positive narratives, create lasting impressions, and cultivate partnerships that transcend political and economic agendas. Understanding that cultural diplomacy acts as a force multiplier in international relations, governments invest in promoting their national identities through various channels, such as artistic exchanges, language programs, and cultural showcases. By doing so, they aim to engender mutual respect, trust, and admiration while advancing their foreign policy objectives.

Furthermore, although a sensitive issue, influence peddling underpins the subtle art of leveraging cultural connections for strategic gains. Alongside fostering collaboration and empathy, nations utilize their historical legacies and contemporary cultural expressions to shape global conversations and assert their sway in the diplomatic arena. However, beneath the veneer of cultural harmony lies the complex interplay of power dynamics and political interests, revealing how cultural exchange can become entwined with influence operations. As the boundaries between public diplomacy and propaganda blur, the ethical dimensions of influence peddling come into sharp focus, prompting critical discussions on transparency, authenticity, and reciprocity.

Consequently, pursuing cultural diplomacy demands a delicate balance between promoting shared understanding and safeguarding against exploiting cultural ties for ulterior motives. Looking ahead, it is imperative to recognize the evolving landscape of cultural diplomacy in the digital age, where social media, digital platforms, and virtual experiences present novel opportunities and challenges. Navigating this terrain will require G7 nations to adapt, innovate, and engage with global audiences authentically while mitigating the risks of misinformation, cultural appropriation, and undue influence. Ultimately, the effectiveness of cultural diplomacy and influence peddling hinges on the richness of cultural exchanges and the integrity and sincerity with which these engagements are conducted, underlining the significance of ethical stewardship in an interconnected world.

FUTURE PROJECTIONS: ANTICIPATING CHANGES IN THE POLITICAL FRAMEWORK

As we look to the future, it is imperative to anticipate the changes that will shape the political framework of the G7 nations. The geopolitical landscape continually evolves, driven by many factors, such as economic shifts, technological advancements, and changing global dynamics. In this regard, it is crucial to analyze the potential trajectories that the political framework of these nations might take. One of the key aspects to consider is the impact of growing interconnectedness and interdependence among nations. The political framework will likely witness a trend toward greater collaboration and cooperation as the world becomes increasingly interconnected through trade, communication, and shared challenges. This could manifest in deeper alliances, multilateral agreements, and joint initiatives addressing common issues.

Furthermore, the rise of new powers and the shifting global economic balance will undoubtedly influence the political dynamics within the G7 nations. The emergence of non-traditional powers and rapidly developing economies presents opportunities and challenges for the established political order. It is essential to carefully assess how these changes may impact geopolitical strategies, foreign policies, and alliances among G7 nations. Additionally, demographic shifts and societal changes are poised to shape the future political landscape significantly. With aging populations in certain G7 countries and the rise of younger demographics in others, there will be corresponding implications for policy priorities, social welfare systems, and international engagements.

Moreover, environmental concerns and the imperative to address climate change will increasingly influence political agendas. The need for sustainable practices, renewable energy adoption, and environmental conservation measures will inevitably drive political decision-making and cooperation among G7 nations. It is vital to recognize the potential disruptive influences posed by technological advancements. The rapid pace of artificial intelligence, cybersecurity, and digital governance innovation can introduce transformative changes that will necessitate recalibrations within the political framework. Privacy, surveillance, and the regulation of emerging technologies will assume greater significance in shaping political dynamics and international relations. Ultimately, anticipating changes in the political framework of the G7 nations requires a comprehensive understanding of evolving global trends, regional dynamics, and the interplay of socio-economic, technological, and environmental factors. By closely monitoring these developments and engaging in foresight exercises, policymakers and stakeholders can better prepare for the challenges and opportunities that lie ahead, ensuring the continued relevance and effectiveness of the political framework in an ever-changing world.

CHAPTER 6

The Pivot to Asia: BRICS' Struggle for Influence

BRICS' STRATEGIC SHIFT TOWARDS ASIA

The BRICS nations, comprising Brazil, Russia, India, China, and South Africa, have embarked on a strategic shift towards Asia, driven by various geo-economic motivations to reinforce their global influence and economic prowess. The initial impetus behind this pivot stems from recognizing Asia's burgeoning economic significance, characterized by rapid industrialization, technological advancement, and a burgeoning consumer market. By redirecting their focus towards Asia, the BRICS countries seek to harness the region's growth potential and position themselves as key stakeholders in its economic trajectory. The strategic realignment also underscores the geopolitical imperative for BRICS to establish a more diversified and stable network of economic partnerships beyond their traditional domains. This move represents a proactive effort to mitigate the vulnerabilities associated with over-dependence on Western markets, constituting a fundamental element of their pursuit of economic and political stabilization. As such, through engagement with the Asian continent, BRICS aims to bolster its resilience against global economic fluctuations and enhance its capacity to navigate evolving geopolitical dynamics. Moreover, the pivot toward Asia encapsulates the collective ambition of BRICS to diversify their trade portfolio and reduce reliance on any single economic partner. By establishing deeper roots in the Asian market, the member countries endeavor to fortify their export markets, secure access to vital resources, and forge mutually beneficial economic ties. This diversification strategy is underpinned by a long-term vision of fostering sustainable economic growth and prosperity within the BRICS economies, thereby fostering higher living standards for their citizens and consolidating their positions as global economic powerhouses. Furthermore, the strategic shift towards Asia aligns with the broader aspiration of BRICS nations to foster a multipolar world order by asserting their influence in shaping the geopolitical landscape. Leveraging the opportunities presented by Asia's economic ascent enables BRICS to contribute to the recalibration of global power dynamics, thereby promoting a more equitable and inclusive international system. Consequently, the strategic reorientation towards Asia serves as a means to pursue economic development and stability and as a medium through which BRICS can assert their collective influence on the international stage.

ANALYZING THE GEO-ECONOMIC MOTIVATIONS OF BRICS IN ASIA

As the geopolitical landscape continues to evolve, the BRICS nations have shown a strategic interest in strengthening their presence and influence in the dynamic region of Asia. This pursuit is underpinned by a range of geo-economic motivations that reflect the diverse interests and aspirations of the member countries within the BRICS alliance. The concerted efforts to analyze these motivations offer valuable insights into the collective strategies of BRICS to navigate and thrive in the fast-growing Asian market. At the heart of this analysis lies the understanding of each member's specific economic goals and priorities, which are aligned with the broader vision of enhancing the collective economic foothold in Asia. Moreover, the geo-economic motivations encompass leveraging Asia's burgeoning consumer base, tapping into its robust supply chains, harnessing technological innovations, and accessing key resources critical for sustaining economic growth. Ongoing initiatives such as the Belt and Road Initiative, the Asian Infrastructure Investment Bank, and various bilateral trade agreements underscore BRICS' endeavors to shape Asia's economic narrative actively. Furthermore, regional cooperation on infrastructure development, energy security, and sustainable development reinforces the geo-economic motivations of BRICS, signaling a commitment to fostering mutually beneficial partnerships in Asia. The engagement with Asia also serves as a means for BRICS nations to diversify their trade dependencies, reduce vulnerabilities, and expand their export markets. By assessing these geo-economic motivations, it becomes evident that BRICS aims to strategically position itself as a formidable economic force capable of not only complementing but also challenging the existing economic order in the region. The multifaceted nature of these motivations underscores the complexities and opportunities inherent in BRICS' pursuit of influence in Asia, thus necessitating a nuanced understanding of the historical, cultural, political, and economic realities to effectively analyze and interpret these emerging powers' collective actions and policies.

CHINA'S DOMINANT ROLE AND ITS IMPLICATIONS FOR FELLOW BRICS

As the world's second-largest economy and a significant global power, China holds a dominant role in shaping Asia's economic and geopolitical landscape. Within the context of BRICS, China's ascendancy presents opportunities and challenges for its member nations. Economically, China's significant trade and investment activities within Asia have fueled its rapid growth, serving as an impetus for infrastructural development and connectivity across the region. As the leading trading partner for many Asian countries, China's economic influence has facilitated the integration of regional economies, consolidating its position as a pivotal player in the continent's financial architecture. However, this unparalleled economic prowess also raises concerns among BRICS partners about China's ability to disproportionately wield influence within the group, potentially impacting collective decision-making processes. Geopolitically, China's assertive stance in territorial disputes and strategic initiatives, such as the Belt and Road Initiative, has amplified regional power dynamics, triggering apprehensions among other BRICS members regarding potential power imbalances. Moreover, China's military modernization and expanding presence in the South China Sea have evoked unease among its regional counterparts, necessitating a delicate calibration of strategic postures by fellow BRICS nations. The implications of China's dominance extend to soft power and cultural diplomacy, with its growing influence in reshaping global narratives and perceptions. While recognizing the benefits of collaborating with China, BRICS members are aware of the imperative to preserve their national interests and autonomy in the face of China's expansive reach. Therefore, navigating the complexities of China's dominant role requires a nuanced approach from BRICS, characterized by constructive engagement, mutual respect, and safeguarding the collective interests of the alliance.

INDIA: A COUNTERBALANCE IN REGIONAL DYNAMICS

India plays a pivotal role in the complex dynamics of the Asia region, particularly within the context of BRICS' struggle for influence. India is a vital counterbalance to China's dominance as the second-most populous country globally and a rapidly growing economic power. With its rich history, diverse culture, and strategic position in South Asia, India presents unique opportunities and challenges in shaping the regional landscape. As BRICS seeks to expand its footprint in Asia, it must navigate the intricate web of relationships with India and consider its multifaceted impact on the group's collective ambitions. Geopolitically, India's historical rivalry with China and its evolving partnerships with other Asian nations underscore its significance as a potential mitigating force in the power play within the region. Economically, India's burgeoning market offers immense potential for trade and investment, presenting lucrative opportunities for collaboration within BRICS and beyond. Furthermore, India's commitment to democratic principles and its emphasis on multilateralism further contribute to its role as a stabilizing factor amidst the escalating competition for influence in Asia. India's military prowess and strategic defense capabilities also augment its position as a crucial player in maintaining the regional balance of power. By recognizing India's nuanced role and engaging in proactive dialogue and cooperation, BRICS can harness the strength of India's influence to bolster its standing in the region. Moreover, understanding India's internal dynamics, diverse cultural heritage, and the complexities of its federal structure is essential for formulating effective strategies to leverage India's potential as a counterbalance in the dynamic interplay of regional forces. As BRICS navigates its pursuit of influence in Asia, India's participation and partnership will undeniably shape the collective narrative and define the group's trajectory in the region, making it imperative for BRICS to align its vision with India's interests and aspirations for shared success and mutual growth.

INVESTMENT PATTERNS AND ECONOMIC OPPORTUNITIES IN ASIA

Asia is a vibrant and dynamic region, offering many investment opportunities for the BRICS nations. The economic landscape in Asia, characterized by its diversity and rapid growth, presents an appealing prospect for the member states to expand their economic and political influence. As the global economic center of gravity continues to shift towards this region, it has become increasingly imperative for BRICS nations to position themselves strategically within the burgeoning Asian market.

The investment patterns in Asia exhibit a spectrum of opportunities across various sectors. Manufacturing industries, technological innovation, infrastructure development, and energy resources are among the key areas that have attracted significant interest from BRICS countries. China, in particular, has significantly bolstered its regional presence through extensive investments in infrastructure and strategic acquisitions. Moreover, India's emerging economy and its demographic dividend further underline Asia's potential as a lucrative market for trade and investment.

Amid these investments, the challenges of navigating diverse regulatory frameworks and cultural nuances cannot be overlooked. Understanding the intricacies of business in Asia is crucial for successfully implementing investment strategies. Additionally, the role of multilateral forums, such as the Asian Infrastructure Investment Bank (AIIB) and the Belt and Road Initiative (BRI), has reshaped the investment dynamics in the region, creating both opportunities and complexities for BRICS nations.

The economic opportunities in Asia extend beyond mere financial gains. They also offer prospects for greater collaboration in research and development, knowledge exchange, and human capital advancement. This opens doors for innovation and technological cooperation, enabling BRICS nations to participate in the region's growth trajectory while contributing to its economic and societal development.

The synergies between Asia's economic powerhouses and the BRICS alliance's collective strength lead to a paradigm shift in the global economic order. By aligning their interests with the development narrative of Asia, the member states not only empower their economies but also contribute to the broader economic evolution of the region. The strategic focus on investment patterns and economic opportunities in Asia symbolizes a pivotal frontier for the BRICS nations, fostering mutual growth and prosperity in a rapidly transforming global landscape.

CULTURAL DIPLOMACY AND SOFT-POWER ENHANCEMENTS

Cultural diplomacy has emerged as a key tool in the arsenal of international relations, enabling nations to exert influence and build relationships through the exchange of arts, ideas, language, and traditions. In the context of BRICS' pivot to Asia, cultural diplomacy plays a pivotal role in enhancing the soft power capabilities of member nations. Each BRICS country boasts a rich cultural heritage that can be strategically leveraged to strengthen ties with Asian countries, fostering mutual understanding and goodwill.

Promoting language learning and cultural exchanges forms the cornerstone of BRICS' soft-power enhancements in Asia. Through initiatives such as language training programs, educational scholarships, and cultural events, BRICS nations seek to deepen their cultural footprint in Asia. By showcasing their diverse traditions, literature, music, and cinema, BRICS countries aim to capture the imagination of Asian audiences and create lasting impressions that transcend traditional geopolitical narratives.

Furthermore, the development of cultural institutions and collaborative artistic projects serves as a conduit for fostering meaningful connections between BRICS nations and Asian counterparts. This includes joint exhibitions, artistic performances, and literary festivals that serve as platforms for intercultural dialogue, promoting empathy and insight into both regions' societal values and beliefs. Moreover, establishing cultural centers and exchange programs reinforces the bonds of friendship and promotes the appreciation of shared human experiences, transcending boundaries and enriching the tapestry of global culture.

In addition to cultural showcases, the digital realm has become an increasingly powerful arena for cultural diplomacy. Leveraging social media, digital platforms, and online content, BRICS nations actively engage with Asian populations, enabling the dissemination of cultural products and narratives. The strategic use of digital channels amplifies the reach of cultural diplomacy, creating enduring connections and cultivating a sense of mutual respect and admiration across borders.

BRICS must harness the potential of cultural diplomacy as a means to shape perceptions and win hearts in Asia. By embracing the wealth of their cultural heritage, member nations can forge enduring connections, inspire cross-cultural collaborations, and foster a climate of mutual trust and respect. As BRICS asserts its presence in the Asian landscape, cultural diplomacy is a potent force in advancing the collective soft power of the coalition, paving the way for fruitful engagement and sustainable partnerships in the region.

MILITARY POSTURES AND SECURITY ALIGNMENTS IN THE ASIAN CONTEXT

The military dimensions of BRICS' engagement with Asia carry significant implications for regional security dynamics and global power balances. As each BRICS member maintains a distinct military posture, their collective stance in the Asian context is a subject of growing importance. China's assertiveness in the South China Sea, including its island-building activities and maritime claims, has heightened tensions with neighboring states and elicited responses from other Asian nations and the US. This has prompted even closer military cooperation between Russia and China, with joint exercises and arms trade creating an evolving strategic environment. Additionally, India's traditionally strong ties with Russia have been recalibrated as New Delhi seeks to diversify its defense partnerships and modernize its armed forces. Moreover, Brazil and South Africa have showcased ambitions to elevate their presence in the Indo-Pacific region, underscoring the shared interests and concerns of BRICS in ensuring stability and prosperity. As Asia undergoes rapid military modernization and maneuvering, BRICS faces the challenge of aligning its security policies to safeguard its strategic investments and bolster its influence. The prospects of multilateral security engagements, peacekeeping missions, and joint military drills present opportunities for BRICS to signal their resolve in addressing regional security threats and fostering cooperative measures in the broader Asian arena. Meanwhile, the complex interplay of historical rivalries, territorial disputes, and geopolitical strategies necessitates prudent navigation for BRICS to steer clear of entanglements while contributing to conflict resolution and peacebuilding efforts in Asia. By carefully calibrating their security alignments, BRICS can demonstrate their commitment to upholding stability, respect for international law, and the peaceful resolution of disputes – cornerstones of their collective vision for a multipolar world order. These deliberations underscore the need for BRICS to engage Meaningfully with Asian stakeholders, reinforce mutual confidence-building measures, and promote inclusive security architectures that accommodate the diverse interests of a rapidly evolving continent.

CHALLENGES AND CONTROVERSIES FACED BY BRICS IN ASIA

As BRICS nations intensify their engagement in Asia, they face many challenges and controversies that test the resilience of their strategic initiatives. One of the paramount challenges is navigating the complex web of territorial disputes and historical animosities that persist among several Asian nations. The sensitive nature of these issues demands diplomatic finesse and deft negotiation skills from BRICS leaders to avoid escalating tensions or being embroiled in regional conflicts.

Furthermore, economic rivalries and trade barriers pose significant hurdles to BRICS's quest for influence in Asia. As they seek to establish themselves as key economic players within the region, they encounter resistance from established Asian economic powers and face protectionist policies that impede their access to specific markets. Moreover, the varying levels of development and divergent economic systems among Asian countries add layers of complexity to BRICS' efforts, requiring astute economic strategies and adaptability.

Another controversy faced by BRICS in Asia pertains to human rights and governance standards. As they forge partnerships and engage in extensive investment activities, they must grapple with the ethical implications of collaborating with authoritarian regimes and governments with poor human rights records. This intricate balancing act between national interests and global moral obligations necessitates careful deliberation and transparency.

Cybersecurity threats also loom large as BRICS extends its reach into Asia. The region's digital landscape presents unique vulnerabilities, and malicious cyber activities pose a significant risk to both governmental and corporate entities. Addressing these cybersecurity challenges requires robust collaborative frameworks and sophisticated technological capabilities, demanding considerable investments in cybersecurity infrastructure and expertise.

Moreover, cultural differences and linguistic barriers can hinder effective communication and mutual understanding, presenting an ongoing obstacle for BRICS as they strive to bolster their soft power in the region. Overcoming these barriers necessitates sustained cultural exchange programs and language education initiatives to foster greater cross-cultural appreciation and empathy.

In conclusion, BRICS's challenges and controversies in Asia underscore the complexity of their regional endeavors. By confronting these obstacles with strategic insight, diplomatic dexterity, and a genuine commitment to cooperation, BRICS can surmount these challenges and carve a path toward sustainable influence and collaboration in Asia.

PARTNERSHIPS WITH ASEAN AND OTHER ASIAN ENTITIES

The partnerships between BRICS, the Association of Southeast Asian Nations (ASEAN), and other critical Asian entities have become increasingly crucial in the region's geopolitical landscape. BRICS nations have recognized the strategic importance of engaging with ASEAN, a group of ten rapidly developing Southeast Asian countries, including Indonesia, Malaysia, the Philippines, Singapore, Thailand, Brunei, Vietnam, Laos, Myanmar, and Cambodia. The partnership aims to foster economic relations, promote peace and stability, and address various challenges in the region. Additionally, BRICS' collaboration with other influential Asian entities such as Japan, South Korea, and the Gulf Cooperation Council (GCC) member states has been instrumental in shaping the balance of power in Asia. The multifaceted nature of these partnerships encompasses trade and investment, security cooperation, cultural exchanges, and sustainable development initiatives. Economically, the collaborations seek to deepen trade ties, facilitate investment flows, and enhance economic integration between the respective regions. They also work towards infrastructure development, technology transfer, and capacity-building efforts. Furthermore, security cooperation includes joint military exercises, intelligence sharing, and counterterrorism initiatives to promote regional stability and address common security threats. Cultural exchanges through educational programs, artistic endeavors, and people-to-people initiatives contribute to a deeper understanding and appreciation of each other's histories and traditions. Lastly, sustainable development initiatives focus on environmental conservation, renewable energy projects, and climate change mitigation strategies. Looking ahead, BRICS' future strategy for engagement with ASEAN and other Asian entities will likely prioritize mutually beneficial partnerships that foster inclusive growth, support regional peace and stability, and contribute to addressing global challenges. Leveraging collective strengths and resources, BRICS aims to deepen its engagement with diverse and dynamic Asian entities while upholding the principles of mutual respect, non-interference, equality, and shared benefits. By bolstering these partnerships, BRICS seeks to play a proactive and constructive role in shaping the evolving regional architecture and promoting a more inclusive and interconnected world.

PROJECTIONS AND FUTURE STRATEGY OF BRICS' INFLUENCE IN ASIA

As the global geopolitical landscape continues to evolve, the BRICS nations have strategically recalibrated their influence in Asia, recognizing the region's growing economic significance and political clout. The future strategy of BRICS in Asia is poised to be a dynamic interplay of economic cooperation, strategic partnerships, and diplomatic maneuvers. Projections indicate that BRICS will leverage its collective economic weight to forge deeper ties with key Asian entities, fostering a mutually beneficial environment for trade, investment, and technological collaboration. The group aims to expand its influence beyond traditional spheres of engagement and establish itself as a pivotal player in shaping the future of Asia.

One of the central tenets of BRICS' future strategy in Asia lies in capitalizing on the region's burgeoning middle class and rapidly urbanizing population. By identifying opportunities for infrastructure development, sustainable urbanization, and technology transfer, BRICS aims to contribute significantly to the socio-economic progress of Asian nations while simultaneously solidifying its foothold in the region. Moreover, the collective emphasis on innovation, research, and development is anticipated to propel BRICS into becoming a catalyst for technological advancement, which will further augment its influence in Asia.

Furthermore, BRICS's future strategy in Asia entails a nuanced approach to regional security and stability. By enhancing military-to-military cooperation and fostering dialogue mechanisms on regional security issues, BRICS seeks to demonstrate its commitment to promoting peace and security in the region. Additionally, collaborative efforts in countering transnational threats such as terrorism, cyber warfare, and maritime security challenges are expected to feature prominently in the BRICS' agenda for the region.

In alignment with its future strategy, BRICS also envisions comprehensive engagement with ASEAN and other influential Asian bodies to bolster its regional presence and impact. By cultivating strategic partnerships with these entities, BRICS aims to navigate the complex geopolitical currents of Asia and shape regional governance structures that reflect a multipolar world order. This proactive outreach will involve harnessing soft power resources, cultural exchanges, and people-to-people connections to foster greater understanding and trust among the nations of Asia.

Overall, the future projection of BRICS' influence in Asia underscores the group's aspirations to emerge as a pivotal force in driving the economic, political, and security dynamics of the region. As the global spotlight increasingly turns towards Asia, BRICS seeks to position itself as a key architect of the continent's future, contributing to sustainable development, peace, and prosperity for the benefit of all stakeholders involved.

CHAPTER 7

Technological Advancements and Their Impact on Global Dominance

THE INTERSECTION OF TECHNOLOGY AND GLOBAL POWER

The intersection of technology and global power has catalyzed profound shifts in the geopolitical landscape, delineating a contemporary era where innovation and influence are inexorably entwined. As nations strive to assert dominance on the world stage, technological prowess has emerged as an indispensable tool, reshaping the traditional paradigms of power dynamics. This symbiotic relationship between technology and global power leverages scientific advancements, digital infrastructure, and strategic economic investments to secure strategic advantages and propel national interests. Undeniably, the ubiquitous integration of cutting-edge technologies has not only redefined the parameters of national security but has also permeated sectors such as trade, energy, and communication, solidifying its status as a transformative force on the global canvas. Embracing the imperatives of this digital age, nations are fervently vying for supremacy in emerging technological domains, evoking a fierce contestation that underscores the vital correlation between technological innovation and geopolitical ascendancy. The pervasiveness of artificial intelligence, quantum computing, space exploration, and biotechnology has infused new dimensions into global prowess, representing frontier arenas where nations seek to bolster their strategic footing and unfurl their ambitions. Consequently, this chapter embarks on an immersive journey through technological advancements and international influence, probing the intricate tapestry that reflects the coalescence of science, diplomacy, and power play.

HISTORICAL OVERVIEW OF TECHNOLOGICAL IMPACT ON SUPERPOWERS

The historical interplay between technological advancements and global dominance is a captivating narrative that has significantly shaped human history. From the Industrial Revolution to the present digital transformation era, technological innovations have been pivotal in determining the rise and fall of superpowers. In the early modern period, the development of steam power and mechanized manufacturing processes fueled the ascendancy of nations such as Britain and, later, the United States. This period marked a shift from agrarian economies to industrial powerhouses, establishing a new paradigm of global influence. The impact of innovation was further underscored by the emergence of telecommunications and transportation networks, enabling rapid dissemination of information and efficient connectivity across continents.

The 20th century witnessed the profound impact of the technological arms race during periods of geopolitical tension, most notably in the Cold War between the United States and the Soviet Union. The space race, nuclear capabilities, and advancements in computing showcased these superpowers' technological prowess and underscored the instrumental role of cutting-edge technology in asserting dominance on the global stage. With the dawn of the digital age, the landscape of global power dynamics underwent a paradigm shift. The rise of the internet, data analytics, and the proliferation of mobile technologies transformed how societies functioned, opening new avenues for economic and military supremacy. Notably, the tech revolution brought tremendous communication, trade, and intelligence gathering changes. As we stand on the cusp of the fourth industrial revolution, characterized by artificial intelligence, robotics, and nanotechnology, the historical overview of technological impact on superpowers is crucial for understanding the symbiotic relationship between innovation and global dominance. The trajectory of nations has been inexorably intertwined with their technological capabilities, emphasizing the indispensable nature of harnessing cutting-edge advancements to secure strategic advantages and maintain leadership in an ever-evolving global order.

INNOVATION ECOSYSTEMS: A COMPARATIVE ANALYSIS

Innovation ecosystems are the interconnected, interdependent networks of institutions, firms, and individuals that collectively drive technological progress and economic growth. In the context of global dominance, understanding and comparing these innovation ecosystems is critical to comprehending the prowess of superpowers. The United States, as a traditional powerhouse in technological advancement, has fostered an ecosystem that thrives on entrepreneurial spirit, academic research, and venture capital. It boasts renowned technology hubs such as Silicon Valley and Route 128, where startups, industry giants, and research institutions collaborate to push the boundaries of innovation. On the other hand, countries within the BRICS alliance have been rapidly evolving their innovation ecosystems, with China emerging as a formidable force. The Chinese government's strategic investments in research and development and a culture of mass entrepreneurship have propelled its tech sector to unprecedented heights. Additionally, India's tech industry, known for its prowess in software development and IT services, has transformed into an innovation juggernaut, attracting global attention. Conversely, Russia, while historically strong in scientific research, faces challenges in sustaining a robust innovation ecosystem due to geopolitical and economic factors. Brazil and South Africa have also made significant strides, each with its unique strengths and challenges in fostering innovation. Key factors such as funding mechanisms, regulatory frameworks, access to talent, and collaboration between academia and industry must be evaluated when comparing these ecosystems. Furthermore, the role of government policies and international partnerships cannot be overlooked. Recognizing the symbiotic relationship between innovation ecosystems and global dominance is essential for anticipating shifts in power dynamics. As the lines between technological leadership and geopolitical influence continue to blur, a deep dive into these ecosystems illuminates the strategies and mechanisms that underpin the race for global supremacy.

ARTIFICIAL INTELLIGENCE AND MACHINE LEARNING: PIONEERS AND DOMINATORS

Artificial intelligence (AI) and machine learning (ML) have emerged as pivotal technologies reshaping global power dynamics. In the contemporary geopolitical landscape, nations deploying and mastering AI and ML are positioned as pioneers and dominators in various strategic domains. The transformative potential of AI and ML extends across military capabilities, economic competitiveness, healthcare advancements, cybersecurity resilience, and societal governance.

Countries with robust research and development ecosystems are at the forefront of AI and ML innovation, where public-private partnerships foster cross-sector collaborations and knowledge dissemination. Notably, the United States and China are pioneers in this realm, leveraging their substantial investments in AI and ML to propel technological advancements and gain a competitive edge in varied sectors.

The strategic deployment of AI and ML also has profound implications for national security and defense capabilities. Autonomous systems, predictive analytics, and cognitive computing revolutionize military operations, intelligence gathering, and cybersecurity strategies. The ability to harness vast amounts of data and derive actionable insights has become a critical determinant of military superiority and resilience against evolving threats.

In addition to military applications, AI and ML are pivotal in driving economic growth and fostering innovation. Countries that effectively integrate these technologies into their industries and services benefit from enhanced productivity, optimized resource allocation, and disruptive business models. Moreover, the race to lead in AI and ML development reflects broader ambitions for economic dominance and influence in future global markets.

Furthermore, integrating AI and ML in healthcare systems holds immense promise for personalized medicine, disease prediction, and drug discovery. Nations implementing AI-driven healthcare solutions are committed to improving public welfare and enhancing their healthcare infrastructure, solidifying their standing as pioneers in the global health sector.

As AI and ML continue to permeate critical spheres, such as finance, education, and urban planning, the geopolitical landscape is witnessing a reconfiguration of power dynamics. The rise of AI-enabled smart cities, digital financial ecosystems, and intelligent educational platforms further cements the influence of pioneering nations as dominators in shaping the future of societies and economies.

The race to become pioneers and dominators in AI and ML signifies more than technological prowess; it embodies a quest for global influence and ascendancy across multifaceted domains. As emerging and established powers alike navigate this transformative landscape, the ramifications of AI and ML leadership on global dominance are poised to redefine international relations and shape the contours of tomorrow's world.

QUANTUM COMPUTING AND ITS GEOPOLITICAL IMPLICATIONS

Quantum computing represents a paradigm shift in information processing, promising unprecedented computational power that could revolutionize various industries. In the geopolitical landscape, the development and deployment of quantum technologies have far-reaching implications for national security, economic competitiveness, and strategic dominance. As nations race to achieve quantum supremacy, the global balance of power is being redefined. Quantum computing possesses the potential to solve complex problems at an exponential speed compared to classical computers. This capability is significant for cryptography, code-breaking, and secure communication methods, critical components of modern warfare and intelligence operations. The ability to decrypt sensitive information or create unbreakable encryption can provide a significant advantage to state actors. Consequently, the quest for quantum technology has become intertwined with traditional power struggles and espionage activities. Governments and multinational corporations compete fiercely to lead the quantum revolution, recognizing its transformative capacity to maintain technological superiority. The development of quantum computing also raises concerns about its disruptive impact on existing economic structures. With the potential to render current encryption methods obsolete, quantum technology challenges the established norms and protocols governing global finance, trade, and cybersecurity. As a result, countries are strategically positioning themselves to harness the economic benefits and mitigate the risks posed by quantum computing. Moreover, the geopolitical implications extend to scientific collaboration and intellectual property rights. International alliances and partnerships are being forged to pool resources and expertise in quantum research while the race to secure patents and proprietary knowledge intensifies. These endeavors reflect the broader competition for influence and leadership in the quantum domain, shaping the dynamics of global innovation and knowledge dissemination. Furthermore, the implications of quantum computing on emerging technologies such as artificial intelligence, materials science, and communication networks amplify its geopolitical relevance. The convergence of these fields amplifies the potential for transformative breakthroughs and disruptive change, necessitating proactive and adaptive strategies from governments and industry players. In summary, the rapid advancement of quantum computing is poised to redefine power structures, economic frameworks, and diplomatic relations on a global scale. Understanding its geopolitical implications is imperative for navigating the complexities of an increasingly interconnected and technologically driven world.

SPACE EXPLORATION AND SATELLITE TECHNOLOGIES

The race for dominance in space exploration and satellite technologies has become a defining feature of global geopolitics. With potential applications ranging from telecommunications and navigation to surveillance and scientific research, the control and utilization of space assets have profound implications for national security and economic advantage. This section delves into the multifaceted domain of space technology and its impact on the global balance of power.

Historically, space exploration has been symbolic of superpower competition, exemplified by the Space Race between the United States and the Soviet Union during the Cold War. This rivalry has evolved into a more complex landscape, with an increasing number of countries and private entities staking their claims in outer space. The deployment of satellite constellations, lunar missions, and ambitious plans for Mars colonization reignite the fervor for space dominance.

Satellite technologies, in particular, have revolutionized various sectors, including communication, weather forecasting, environmental monitoring, and military surveillance. These capabilities enhance the global flow of information and enable governments and corporations to expand their influence and maintain strategic superiority. Additionally, the burgeoning field of satellite-based remote sensing provides invaluable data for agriculture, disaster management, and urban planning, contributing to sustainable development and security.

Furthermore, the militarization of space presents a formidable dimension of geopolitical tension as nations strive to protect their assets and establish space-based defense systems. The potential weaponization of space and the risks associated with debris accumulation in orbit underscore the need for international cooperation and regulatory frameworks. As such, discussions around space governance and preventing conflicts in outer space are gaining prominence within diplomatic circles.

It is imperative to acknowledge the indispensable role of space diplomacy and the collaboration between government agencies, private enterprises, and international organizations in advancing peaceful and beneficial uses of space. Initiatives such as the Artemis Accords and the intergovernmental regulation of space debris mitigation reflect the concerted efforts to promote responsible space activities and avert escalating rivalries.

Ultimately, the trajectory of space exploration and satellite technologies will profoundly shape the global order, necessitating a comprehensive approach to equitable access, sustainability, and security in the space domain. By understanding the evolving dynamics and harnessing the potential of space endeavors, nations can cultivate innovation, address pressing challenges, and forge collaborative pathways toward a prosperous future.

BIOTECHNOLOGY AND ITS INFLUENCE ON HEALTH AND AGRICULTURE

Biotechnology has rapidly emerged as a transformative force in health and agriculture, reshaping the landscape of global dominance. In the field of health, biotechnological advancements have revolutionized the way diseases are diagnosed, treated, and prevented. From personalized medicine to gene editing technologies like CRISPR, biotechnology promises to provide tailored, precision-based solutions for a myriad of medical conditions. This has led to an unprecedented shift towards individualized healthcare, where treatments and interventions are increasingly customized to a patient's genetic makeup and specific needs. Furthermore, biotechnology has paved the way for significant pharmaceutical breakthroughs, with the development of novel drugs and therapies targeting previously untreatable diseases.

Biotechnology has played a pivotal role in addressing global food security challenges in agriculture. Genetically modified organisms (GMOs) have been at the forefront of this revolution, offering crops more resilient to pests, diseases, and environmental stressors. Additionally, biotechnological innovations have enabled the production of biofortified crops with enhanced nutritional value, thereby combating malnutrition and deficiencies in vulnerable populations. The advent of precision agriculture, driven by biotechnology, has empowered farmers to optimize crop yields while minimizing resource inputs, contributing to sustainable and efficient food production.

Moreover, biotechnology has led to the emergence of agri-biotech companies, fostering the development of cutting-edge solutions such as biological pest control agents, disease-resistant crops, and environmentally friendly agricultural practices. Agricultural productivity has been significantly enhanced through biotechnology, playing a critical role in meeting the escalating demands of a growing global population.

The ethical considerations surrounding biotechnological interventions in health and agriculture continue to be subjects of extensive debate and scrutiny. Questions regarding genetic privacy, informed consent, environmental impacts, and equitable access to biotechnological advancements remain pertinent. Additionally, navigating regulatory frameworks and ensuring biotechnology's responsible and safe deployment is imperative to mitigate potential risks and maximize its societal benefits.

As biotechnology continues to unfold, its influence on health and agriculture can redefine global power dynamics, shaping the future of human well-being, food security, and economic stability.

DIGITAL CURRENCY AND BLOCKCHAIN: ECONOMIC SHIFTS

Digital currencies and blockchain technology are reshaping the global economic landscape as the world becomes increasingly interconnected. The rise of cryptocurrencies, led by Bitcoin and Ethereum, has sparked a paradigm shift in traditional financial systems, presenting opportunities and challenges for policymakers, businesses, and consumers.

Blockchain, the underlying technology behind digital currencies, enables secure and transparent peer-to-peer transactions without the need for intermediaries. This decentralized finance approach can potentially reduce transaction costs, streamline cross-border payments, and foster financial inclusion for underserved populations.

Governments and central banks are grappling with the implications of digital currencies on monetary policy, financial stability, and regulatory oversight. While some nations have embraced cryptocurrencies to spur innovation and attract investment, others have raised concerns about potential illicit activities, market volatility, and consumer protection.

Moreover, the emergence of central bank digital currencies (CBDCs) has added a new dimension to the digital currency landscape. CBDCs, issued and backed by national authorities, offer the prospect of a digitized sovereign currency that could enhance payment efficiency and provide greater monetary policy control.

The broader adoption of digital currencies and blockchain technology disrupts traditional business models across industries. From supply chain management and logistics to identity verification and intellectual property rights, integrating blockchain solutions is revolutionizing data integrity, transparency, and security.

Furthermore, smart contracts, self-executing agreements coded on blockchain platforms, have the potential to automate and enforce complex contractual arrangements, thereby reducing reliance on intermediaries and expediting commercial transactions.

However, the rapid evolution of digital currencies and blockchain technology raises pertinent legal and regulatory considerations. The protection of intellectual property rights in blockchain-based innovations, the enforcement of contractual obligations in smart contract environments, and the governance of decentralized autonomous organizations (DAOs) present intricate challenges that require adaptive legal frameworks and international cooperation.

The symbiotic relationship between digital currencies, blockchain technology, and traditional financial systems will continue to influence economic paradigms, investment strategies, and global trade dynamics. Understanding the transformative impact of digital currency and blockchain on economic shifts is essential for fostering technological innovation, ensuring financial stability, and navigating the complexities of the evolving global economy.

TECHNOLOGY TRANSFER AND INTELLECTUAL PROPERTY RIGHTS

The exchange of technological knowledge and innovations across national borders has become increasingly prevalent in the contemporary global landscape. This phenomenon, known as technology transfer, is pivotal in driving economic growth, fostering innovation, and addressing societal challenges internationally. However, with the fluidity of information and the rapid pace of technological advancements, the intricate realm of intellectual property rights has emerged as a critical focal point in technology transfer. This section delves into the multifaceted dynamics of technology transfer and its intersecting relationship with intellectual property rights, elucidating the complexities and implications involved. Technology transfer encompasses the movement of cutting-edge ideas, inventions, and expertise from one entity to another, spanning diverse domains such as scientific research, manufacturing processes, and technological applications. It operates within global value chains, spurring cross-border collaborations and contributing to the diffusion of knowledge-intensive assets. Concurrently, intellectual property rights serve as the legal and ethical framework that safeguards the rights of innovators, creators, and organizations regarding their proprietary innovations and original works. These rights encompass patents, trademarks, copyrights, and trade secrets, offering exclusivity and protection against unauthorized usage or replication. The nexus between technology transfer and intellectual property rights engenders a dialectic tension, encapsulating opportunities and challenges. On one hand, technology transfer facilitates the dissemination of breakthrough technologies, fostering mutual progress and shared prosperity among nations. It empowers developing economies to leapfrog barriers and leverage advanced solutions, paving the way for sustainable development and capacity building. Conversely, concerns surrounding intellectual property rights infringement, misappropriation, and exploitation often overshadow technology transfer processes. Patent infringement, copyright violations, and trade secret misappropriation can disrupt collaborative endeavors, erode stakeholder trust, and hinder the equitable distribution of technological benefits. Furthermore, the disparity in intellectual property regimes across nations amplifies the complexities associated with technology transfer. Variations in patent laws, enforcement mechanisms, and regulatory frameworks pose formidable obstacles to seamless knowledge exchange and innovation diffusion. Moreover, the emergence of open-source movements, collaborative innovation models, and alternative licensing approaches add layers of intricacy to the intersection of technology transfer and intellectual property rights. Striking a balance between incentivizing innovation through intellectual property protections and ensuring wider accessibility to transformative technologies remains a pressing global imperative. This necessitates concerted efforts to harmonize intellectual property standards, foster transparent licensing practices, and fortify mechanisms for resolving disputes arising from technology transfer. Moreover, upholding ethical principles, respecting indigenous knowledge systems, and promoting responsible technology sharing are indispensable in navigating the intricate terrain of global innovation and intellectual property governance. As the international community grapples with the evolving demands of technological leadership, fostering an environment conducive to principled technology transfer, ethical intellectual property management, and inclusive innovation ecosystems is paramount for shaping a harmonious and progressive global landscape.

CONCLUSION: SHAPING FUTURE GEOPOLITICAL LANDSCAPES THROUGH TECHNOLOGICAL LEADERSHIP

The preceding exploration into technology transfer and intellectual property rights underscores the critical role that technological leadership plays in shaping future geopolitical landscapes. As we stand on the cusp of unprecedented technological advancement, it is clear that nations and alliances that prioritize innovation, research, and development will exert significant influence in the global arena. The competition for technological dominance is not merely about economic prosperity; it also affects national security, strategic alliances, and overall geopolitical power dynamics. In conclusion, our analysis reveals that the path to future geopolitical supremacy runs through the corridors of technological leadership. As such, countries and alliances must prioritize investment in R&D, fostering innovation ecosystems, and ensuring robust intellectual property protections to secure their positions on the global stage. The interplay between technology, geopolitics, and power is intricately woven, and the choices made today will undoubtedly shape the landscape of international relations for decades. Achieving technological leadership requires a comprehensive approach encompassing education, regulatory frameworks, incentivizing private-sector innovation, and international collaboration. Through a concerted effort to embrace emerging technologies responsibly and ethically, nation-states can establish themselves as preeminent players in the global order. Policymakers, industry leaders, and academics must recognize that technological leadership goes beyond mere economic gains; it is a cornerstone of shaping the geopolitical narratives of the future. By heeding this call and embracing the challenges and opportunities presented by burgeoning technologies, countries, and alliances can carve a path toward a more stable, prosperous, and harmonious world order. Pursuing technological leadership is not a zero-sum game but a collective endeavor that necessitates cooperation and dialogue among nations, transcending traditional geopolitical rivalries and fostering a new era of innovation-driven diplomacy.

CHAPTER 8

Energy Resources and Environmental Policies in BRICS vs. G7

ENERGY LANDSCAPES

The global energy landscape is an indispensable pillar of modern civilization, underpinning economic activities, technological advancement, and societal well-being. As the world grapples with ever-increasing energy demands, it becomes paramount to comprehend the intricacies of energy resource management within a broader geopolitical and environmental context. How nations harness, distribute, and consume energy resources has far-reaching implications, not only for their internal development but also for the overall stability and sustainability of the planet. Recognizing that energy forms the backbone of industrialization and human progress, understanding the global energy dynamics is essential for policymakers, industry leaders, and citizens. Moreover, the increasing interconnectivity of global economies means that no country operates in isolation, making managing energy resources a truly international affair. Hence, this introductory discussion aims to set the stage for a comprehensive exploration of energy policies in G7 and BRICS nations by delving into the broader global context of energy resource management. The quest for sustainable energy sources, the geopolitics of fossil fuels, the impact of energy consumption on climate change, and the innovations in energy technologies all form integral components of the intricate energy landscape. In light of mounting environmental concerns, transitioning towards cleaner and renewable energy sources has become a critical imperative for governments worldwide. Furthermore, fierce competition over access to and control of energy reserves has emerged as a defining feature of contemporary geopolitics, shaping international relations and strategic alliances. As such, this section seeks to underscore the gravity of energy landscapes within global socio-economic development and ecological preservation framework. It is within this multifaceted milieu that the historical evolution and contrasting strategies of G7 and BRICS nations in managing their energy resources will be thoroughly scrutinized, shedding light on their respective policy trajectories, successes, and challenges.

HISTORICAL OVERVIEW OF ENERGY POLICIES IN G7 AND BRICS NATIONS

Energy policies in the G7 and BRICS nations have been shaped by historical, geopolitical, and socioeconomic factors that have contributed to diverse approaches and priorities. The G7 countries, historically developed economies with a long-standing reliance on traditional energy sources such as coal, oil, and natural gas, have undergone significant shifts in their energy policies over time. Following the oil shocks of the 1970s, G7 nations initiated efforts to enhance energy efficiency, reduce dependence on imported oil, and diversify their energy mix. This led to the development of strategic alliances, investment in alternative energy sources, and stringent environmental regulations to mitigate the impacts of energy consumption. In contrast, the BRICS nations, comprising emerging economies with burgeoning energy demands, have pursued aggressive energy policies to secure access to resources, expand energy infrastructure, and promote economic growth. As major producers and consumers of fossil fuels, BRICS nations have prioritized energy security and self-sufficiency while seeking international partnerships to bolster their energy capabilities. Throughout history, both G7 and BRICS nations have faced challenges in balancing their energy needs with environmental considerations, leading to varying levels of commitment to renewable energy adoption and sustainable practices. While G7 nations have increasingly focused on decarbonization and transitioning towards low-carbon economies, BRICS nations have grappled with balancing economic development with environmental stewardship. These contrasting approaches reflect the complex interplay between historical trajectories, economic imperatives, and geopolitical realities that continue to shape energy policies in these influential blocs. By examining the historical evolution of energy policies in G7 and BRICS nations, we gain insights into the divergent pathways that have influenced their current energy landscapes and paved the way for potential areas of cooperation and competition in the global energy arena.

COMPARATIVE ANALYSIS OF RENEWABLE ENERGY INITIATIVES

In comparing the renewable energy initiatives of the G7 and BRICS nations, it is evident that both groups have made significant strides in diversifying their energy portfolios to include renewable sources. The G7 nations, comprising some of the world's most developed economies, have been at the forefront of promoting renewable energy to combat climate change and reduce dependence on fossil fuels. This has resulted in substantial investments in solar, wind, hydroelectric, and biomass energy projects, coupled with ambitious targets for integrating renewable energy into their national grids. On the other hand, the BRICS nations, characterized by their rapid industrialization and growing energy demands, have also recognized the importance of renewable energy. They have strongly focused on harnessing solar and wind power, capitalizing on their abundant natural resources to drive sustainable energy initiatives. While the G7 nations have taken a more coordinated approach to renewable energy development through collaborative research and technological innovation, the BRICS nations have pursued independent strategies, leveraging their specific regional strengths in renewable energy production. Moreover, the differences in economic structures and resource endowments between the G7 and BRICS have influenced their respective approaches to renewable energy implementation. The G7's emphasis on high-technology and capital-intensive renewable projects contrasts with the BRICS' adoption of scalable, cost-effective solutions tailored to their unique socioeconomic landscapes. Both groups face challenges integrating intermittent renewable sources into their energy grids and addressing policy and regulatory barriers hindering widespread adoption. Furthermore, despite the increasing momentum towards renewable energy, fossil fuel subsidies and vested interests continue to present obstacles to the comprehensive transition to clean energy. As such, a deeper understanding of the nuances and implications of renewable energy initiatives within the G7 and BRICS contexts is crucial in shaping future global energy policies and sustainability efforts.

FOSSIL FUELS DEPENDENCY AND REDUCTION STRATEGIES

Fossil fuels have long been the cornerstone of global energy production, powering industrialization, transportation, and modern living. The G7 and BRICS nations have historically relied heavily on fossil fuels to meet their energy needs, leading to environmental degradation and concerns over long-term sustainability. However, as the imperative to combat climate change becomes increasingly urgent, a paradigm shift towards renewable energy sources and reducing fossil fuel dependency has taken center stage in international policy discourse.

The G7 nations, comprising some of the world's most advanced economies, have substantially reduced their reliance on fossil fuels. Aggressive investments in renewable energy infrastructure, coupled with innovative policies promoting energy efficiency and conservation, have contributed to a gradual decline in the share of fossil fuels in the overall energy mix. Moreover, stringent regulatory frameworks to curb carbon emissions and air pollution have been instrumental in incentivizing a transition towards cleaner energy alternatives.

Conversely, the BRICS nations, characterized by rapid industrialization and growing energy demands, continue to grapple with high levels of fossil fuel dependency. While efforts have been made to diversify energy portfolios and boost renewable energy capacity, sustaining economic growth often necessitates continued utilization of coal, oil, and natural gas. This problem between economic development and environmental stewardship presents a complex challenge for BRICS policymakers, requiring a delicate balance between fostering industrial expansion and mitigating ecological repercussions.

In addressing this dilemma, both the G7 and BRICS nations have implemented reduction strategies to mitigate the environmental impact of fossil fuel usage. Initiatives such as carbon pricing mechanisms, investment incentives for clean energy technologies, and collaborative research and development efforts have emerged as pivotal tools for navigating the transition from fossil fuels. Furthermore, international partnerships and multilateral agreements focusing on emission reduction targets and sustainable development goals have provided a framework for cooperation and shared responsibility in combating climate change.

Reducing fossil fuel dependency remains paramount as the global community aligns its efforts to combat climate change and achieve carbon neutrality. The convergence of interests among G7 and BRICS nations in pursuing cleaner energy solutions signals a promising trajectory toward a more sustainable and resilient energy landscape. However, continued commitment to innovation, investment, and policy coordination will be essential in steering the world towards a future less reliant on fossil fuels and more attuned to the imperatives of environmental preservation and energy security.

NUCLEAR ENERGY: DIVERGENT PATHS

Nuclear energy, often a controversial topic, has witnessed divergent paths of development and utilization within the G7 and BRICS nations. The G7 countries have largely opted for a cautious approach towards nuclear energy, emphasizing stringent safety regulations and risk mitigation strategies following the tragic events at Chernobyl and Fukushima. In contrast, BRICS nations have pursued ambitious nuclear energy programs as part of their more considerable energy diversification and security strategies, seeking to harness the potential of nuclear power to meet their growing energy demands. This approach divergence reflects differing risk perceptions, regulatory frameworks, and technological capabilities. Moreover, the varying trajectories of nuclear energy in these blocs also illustrate contrasting priorities regarding sustainable development and environmental stewardship. Specifically, while some G7 nations have moved towards phasing out nuclear power in favor of renewable alternatives, certain BRICS members view nuclear energy as a crucial component of their low-carbon energy mix. Furthermore, geopolitical considerations, such as access to technology and international cooperation, play a significant role in shaping the nuclear energy landscapes within these blocs. As the global community grapples with the imperative to address climate change and achieve energy security, the contrasting approaches to nuclear energy by the G7 and BRICS nations hold paramount importance in shaping the future of the global energy sector. It is essential to critically analyze the strategic implications, technological advancements, and regulatory frameworks driving the divergent paths of nuclear energy adoption and to assess the broader implications for global energy security, non-proliferation efforts, and environmental sustainability. By delving into the multidimensional aspects of nuclear energy, this comparative analysis aims to provide insights into the complex interplay of economic, political, and environmental factors that underpin the evolving dynamics of nuclear energy utilization within the G7 and BRICS nations.

IMPACT OF ENERGY POLICIES ON GLOBAL ENVIRONMENTAL GOALS

Energy policies play a pivotal role in shaping the global environmental landscape. Through their respective energy strategies, both the G7 and BRICS nations have been instrumental in setting the tone for environmental goals. The impact of these policies resonates across various dimensions, ranging from climate change mitigation to biodiversity conservation. The commitment to reducing greenhouse gas emissions, promoting sustainable development, and transitioning towards cleaner energy sources is critical in determining the future state of our planet.

G7 nations have championed initiatives such as the Paris Agreement, emphasizing stringent targets for emission reduction and embracing renewable energy transitions. Collaborative efforts in developing advanced technologies and sharing best practices have been central to fostering an environment-focused approach within the G7 bloc. On the other hand, BRICS countries have prioritized economic development while grappling with the challenge of environmental sustainability. Balancing rapid industrialization with environmental protection remains a key concern for these nations. Utilizing emerging technologies and establishing environmental standards are pivotal steps taken by BRICS to align their energy policies with global environmental goals.

The interplay between energy policies and environmental objectives extends beyond national boundaries. The decisions made by G7 and BRICS nations reverberate globally, influencing the trajectory of climate change, ecological balance, and resource management. Both blocs must address the pressing need to minimize the ecological footprint of their energy consumption and production patterns. Moreover, integrating environmental impact assessments into energy policy formulation and implementation is imperative to ensure a harmonious coexistence of economic progress and environmental preservation.

The realization of global environmental goals hinges upon the collaborative efforts and mutual accountability of G7 and BRICS nations. Synergizing policies, sharing technological innovations, and advocating for sustainable energy utilization are vital elements in mitigating the adverse impacts of energy-related activities on the environment. Aligning national energy strategies with internationally agreed environmental frameworks will signify a strategic shift towards fostering a greener and more sustainable planet for present and future generations.

INNOVATION IN ENERGY TECHNOLOGIES: G7 VS. BRICS

In the race towards a sustainable energy future, both the G7 and BRICS nations have been at the forefront of innovation. The G7 countries, with their long history of technological advancement and significant investments in research and development, have led the way in developing cutting-edge renewable energy technologies. From advanced solar panels to innovative wind turbines and grid-scale energy storage solutions, G7 nations have made remarkable progress in harnessing clean and efficient energy sources.

On the other hand, BRICS nations have also made substantial strides in energy technology innovation, leveraging their growing economies and vast natural resources. With a particular focus on advancing clean coal technologies, exploring unconventional oil and gas reserves, and investing in large-scale hydropower projects, BRICS countries have demonstrated a commitment to expanding their energy technology capabilities.

A key area of difference lies in the approaches G7 and BRICS nations adopt towards energy technology innovation. While G7 nations prioritize sustainability and environmental responsibility, often leading to higher energy production costs, BRICS nations tend to prioritize cost-efficiency and energy accessibility, sometimes at the expense of environmental concerns. This fundamental distinction reflects the varying priorities and challenges faced by these two blocs.

Furthermore, collaboration and competition in energy technology innovation differ significantly between G7 and BRICS nations. G7 countries often collaborate, sharing expertise and resources to accelerate green technology development. In contrast, BRICS nations primarily compete in the global energy market, striving to achieve energy independence and technological self-sufficiency. This creates a dynamic landscape of innovation driven by diverse strategies and priorities.

When analyzing energy technology innovation in G7 and BRICS nations, government policies and regulations cannot be overlooked. G7 countries tend to have more stringent environmental regulations and incentives for clean energy research and development, fostering a conducive environment for innovation. On the other hand, BRICS nations often navigate a complex landscape of regulatory frameworks, balancing economic growth with environmental conservation while ensuring energy security and accessibility for their rapidly growing populations.

As we move into an era of an urgent need for sustainable energy solutions, understanding and comparing the innovation trajectories of G7 and BRICS nations becomes crucial. Both blocs have unique strengths and face distinctive challenges, shaping their pathways towards a greener, more sustainable energy future.

ENERGY SECURITY AND POLITICAL IMPLICATIONS

Energy security is a critical concern for both G7 and BRICS nations, as it encompasses the ability to reliably source and access affordable energy resources essential for economic growth and national security. The political implications of energy security are far-reaching, potentially influencing diplomatic relations, regional stability, and global power dynamics. As G7 countries strive to diversify their energy mix and reduce dependency on fossil fuels, often emphasizing renewable energy sources and technological innovations, they face intricate geopolitical negotiations and strategic partnerships to secure access to crucial resources. Conversely, BRICS nations, endowed with extensive natural resource reserves, seek to leverage their energy abundance to bolster their regional influence and challenge the established global order. This pursuit of energy self-sufficiency amplifies geopolitical rivalries and necessitates complex diplomatic maneuvers. Energy infrastructure projects and long-term supply contracts are wielded as foreign policy tools, shaping alliances and conflicts in the international arena. The control and transportation routes of energy resources become focal points of contention, driving military posturing and intergovernmental disputes. Furthermore, energy security intertwines with broader concerns such as environmental sustainability, climate change, and socioeconomic development. The pursuit of energy independence often clashes with global efforts to mitigate carbon emissions and transition towards greener energy solutions. These conflicting priorities create friction in international cooperation and collectively complicate efforts to address environmental challenges. Additionally, energy access and affordability disparities can exacerbate inequalities within and between nations, heightening social tensions and fostering asymmetrical power dynamics. Geopolitical strategies around energy security also intersect with human rights, governance, and transparency considerations, particularly in regions with sensitive energy resources. The quest for secure energy sources necessitates a delicate balance between national interests, regional stability, and global collaboration. Moreover, the rise of non-traditional energy producers and technological disruptions in the energy sector further complicate the geopolitical landscape, introducing new players and altering traditional power structures. As such, navigating the nexus of energy security and politics requires astute diplomacy, anticipatory policies, and adaptive multilateral frameworks to manage the diverse and interconnected challenges of the evolving energy landscape.

FUTURE TRENDS IN ENERGY CONSUMPTION AND RESOURCES

The future of energy consumption and resources presents a complex landscape influenced by shifting global dynamics, technological advancements, and evolving environmental concerns. As we progress, it becomes increasingly evident that the energy sector will undergo significant transformations impacting both G7 and BRICS nations.

One key trend that is expected to shape the trajectory of energy consumption is the rise of renewable energy sources. The increasing emphasis on sustainability and climate change mitigation has spurred substantial investments and developments in solar, wind, and hydroelectric power. Both G7 and BRICS countries strive to harness these renewable sources to diversify their energy mix and reduce reliance on fossil fuels. The potential for innovation in energy storage techniques and grid infrastructure will be crucial in maximizing the efficacy of renewable energy integration.

Simultaneously, a notable trend in energy consumption pertains to the demand from emerging economies within the BRICS bloc. Rapid industrialization, urbanization, and population growth in BRICS countries are expected to drive a substantial surge in energy demand. This necessitates reevaluating infrastructural capabilities and formulating policies to ensure reliable and sustainable energy access for burgeoning populations.

Moreover, advancements in energy technology, such as electric vehicles and smart grids, are poised to revolutionize energy consumption patterns. The transition towards electric mobility and the proliferation of intelligent energy distribution systems present opportunities to enhance energy efficiency and decrease reliance on conventional transportation fuels. This shift requires strategic planning, substantial investments in charging infrastructure, and grid modernization to accommodate the growing transportation electrification.

Furthermore, the exploration and exploitation of unconventional energy resources, including shale gas and methane hydrates, are anticipated to impact the global energy landscape. While these resources offer newfound potential for energy security and diversification, they pose environmental and geopolitical considerations that necessitate prudent management and regulation.

In conclusion, forecasting future energy consumption and resource trends demands comprehensive analyses incorporating technological, economic, and environmental dimensions. Both G7 and BRICS nations will confront the imperative to adapt their energy policies and infrastructures to align with upcoming shifts in consumer behaviors, international regulations, and resource availability. Embracing renewable energy, addressing mounting demand from emerging economies, and leveraging technological innovations will be pivotal in shaping tomorrow's energy mix and steering global energy policy.

SUMMARY AND IMPLICATIONS FOR INTERNATIONAL POLICY

In summary, examining future trends in energy consumption and resources within the context of BRICS and G7 nations reveals several key implications for international policy. Both G7 and BRICS countries are projected to experience significant growth in energy demand, driven by population expansion, urbanization, and industrial development. These increasing energy needs will require a strategic approach to resource management and environmental sustainability on a global scale.

One notable implication is the pressing need for enhanced international cooperation and collaboration in addressing energy challenges. With growing interdependence in the global energy market, the relevance of multilateral agreements and frameworks becomes paramount. Developing common strategies for energy diversification, efficiency improvements, and clean technology deployment is essential to mitigate geopolitical tensions and ensure long-term energy security.

Furthermore, the transition towards renewable energy sources presents joint investment and technological innovation opportunities between G7 and BRICS nations. By leveraging each other's strengths in research and development, as well as sharing best practices in policy implementation, countries can accelerate the shift towards sustainable energy systems. This collaboration could also facilitate the transfer of green technologies to emerging economies, promoting inclusive and equitable access to clean energy.

From a policy perspective, international institutions and governing bodies must integrate energy considerations into broader diplomatic and trade discussions. Energy security, climate change, and environmental protection should be central themes in international negotiations, reinforcing the interconnectedness of economic prosperity and ecological preservation. Encouraging responsible energy governance through robust regulatory frameworks and transparent accountability measures will foster mutual trust and stability among nations.

Moreover, the ethical dimensions of energy policies cannot be overlooked when shaping international relations. Balancing economic aspirations with environmental stewardship and social equity demands a reevaluation of values and responsibilities at the global level. Promoting ethical and sustainable energy practices requires a collaborative approach that transcends geopolitical divides and prioritizes the welfare of present and future generations.

In conclusion, the evolving landscape of energy resources and consumption presents challenges and opportunities for international policy. Recognizing the shared interests and interconnected fates of G7 and BRICS nations, concerted efforts towards cooperative energy governance can pave the way for a more secure, inclusive, and environmentally conscious global future.

CHAPTER 9

Cultural Diplomacy and Soft Power: Contrasting Approaches

CULTURAL DIPLOMACY

Cultural diplomacy is a cornerstone of international relations, employing cultural resources to build bridges between nations and shape global perceptions. This multifaceted practice seeks to foster mutual understanding, cooperation, and respect across diverse societies. Embracing the idea that culture is a powerful instrument for forging connections, cultural diplomacy recognizes the influence of arts, traditions, language, literature, and ideologies in enriching international dialogue.

The fundamental objective of cultural diplomacy is to promote a nation's values, ideas, and ethos beyond its borders, thereby establishing enduring relationships on an interpersonal level. By leveraging cultural assets, governments and institutions aim to cultivate goodwill and trust, paving the way for deeper collaboration in various areas such as trade, education, and technology. Moreover, cultural diplomacy endeavors to mitigate intercultural tensions and prejudice by highlighting commonalities and celebrating differences, all while reinforcing the concept of global citizenship and unity.

Cultural diplomacy encompasses various activities, from art exhibitions, music festivals, and film screenings to educational exchanges, language programs, and historical heritage preservation initiatives. Additionally, it extends to the digital realm, encompassing social media campaigns, virtual tours, and interactive platforms designed to facilitate cross-cultural engagement.

At its essence, cultural diplomacy strives to transcend geopolitical disputes and narrow national interests, seeking instead to foster meaningful and lasting connections grounded in shared intellectual and emotional experiences. This enhances a country's international standing and contributes to developing a more interconnected and harmonious global community. Through thoughtful utilization of soft power and cultural diplomacy, nations can project their identity and ideals onto the world stage, influencing perceptions and forging enduring bonds that transcend traditional diplomatic channels.

DEFINING SOFT POWER IN THE INTERNATIONAL ARENA

Soft power, a term coined by political scientist Joseph Nye, has become a pivotal concept in international relations, offering a compelling framework for understanding the dynamics of global influence. Unlike hard power, which relies on military and economic coercion, soft power operates through attraction and persuasion, shaping preferences and behaviors without force or payment. At its core, soft power emanates from a nation's culture, political values, foreign policies, and institutions, exerting a profound impact on the global stage. It encompasses a broad spectrum of assets, including but not limited to a country's diplomatic prowess, education system, popular culture, and societal values. Soft power allows nations to wield influence by projecting an appealing image, prompting other actors to align with their objectives willingly. Recognizing the significance of soft power is essential for comprehending the complexities of modern diplomacy and global interactions.

Analyzing the concept involves delving into how states harness their cultural, ideological, and normative resources to shape perceptions and outcomes. Furthermore, the multifaceted nature of soft power compels scholars and practitioners to explore the intricate interplay between national narratives, public diplomacy initiatives, and international engagement strategies. By examining how soft power operates within different contexts, one gains insight into the underlying mechanisms that enable nations to assert influence in an increasingly interconnected world. The ability to effectively wield soft power can have far-reaching implications, affecting everything from trade and commerce to security dynamics and geopolitical alignments. As such, studying and understanding how nations leverage their soft power capabilities is crucial for deciphering the nuances of contemporary global affairs. In this section, we will delve deep into the various dimensions of soft power, elucidating its role in shaping the behavior of states and non-state actors and exploring the ethical and strategic considerations associated with its use in pursuing national interests.

HISTORICAL EVOLUTION OF CULTURAL DIPLOMACY IN G7 NATIONS

Cultural diplomacy has been an integral aspect of international relations, with its roots extending deep into the historical evolution of the G7 nations. Cultural expression and artistic exchange as a means of international engagement date back centuries, with various soft powers employed to influence foreign policies and public perceptions. Throughout history, the G7 nations have utilized cultural diplomacy to convey their values, ideals, and societal norms to the global community, shaping narratives and fostering mutual understanding.

The aftermath of World War II marked a significant period in the utilization of cultural diplomacy by G7 nations to rebuild relationships and promote peace. Programs such as the Marshall Plan, which focused on economic assistance and cultural exchanges, sought to strengthen ties between nations and cultivate a sense of collaboration and shared values. These initiatives laid the foundation for ongoing cultural diplomacy efforts to nurture alliances and promote democracy.

In the following decades, the Cold War era saw the G7 nations engaging in cultural competition with the Soviet bloc, utilizing art, literature, music, and other cultural exports to demonstrate the vitality and appeal of Western ideals. This period also witnessed the emergence of institutions like the British Council, Goethe-Institut, and Alliance Française, which promoted language learning, cultural exchange, and intellectual discourse, further bolstering diplomatic ties and enhancing cross-cultural appreciation.

The late 20th century and early 21st century brought about a profound transformation in cultural diplomacy as G7 nations embraced digital technologies and popular culture to extend their global influence. For example, the proliferation of American films, music, and television series became powerful tools for projecting the nation's image and shaping global perceptions. Additionally, establishing cultural centers, festivals, and educational programs abroad allowed G7 nations to showcase their diverse heritage and foster connections with international audiences.

Moreover, the G7 nations have consistently leveraged cultural diplomacy to address pressing global challenges such as climate change, human rights, and socio-economic development. Through collaborative cultural initiatives and artistic engagements, they have endeavored to inspire change, forge solidarity, and advocate for universal values, positioning themselves as champions of progress and innovation. As cultural diplomacy continues to evolve, the G7 nations remain committed to harnessing the transformative power of soft power to build enduring partnerships and promote mutual respect on the world stage.

BRICS: EMERGING STRATEGIES IN SOFT POWER USAGE

As the world continues to shift in global power dynamics, the BRICS nations—Brazil, Russia, India, China, and South Africa—have emerged as crucial players in international relations and cultural diplomacy. With their growing economic prowess and rich cultural heritage, these nations have begun to strategically leverage their soft power resources to expand their influence on the world stage. The concept of soft power, popularized by political scientist Joseph Nye, emphasizes the ability of nations to sway others through attraction and persuasion rather than coercion or force. In this context, the BRICS countries employ innovative approaches to exert their soft power internationally. One notable strategy is the promotion of their diverse cultural identities, art, cuisine, traditions, and language on a global scale. Through cultural initiatives such as film festivals, art exhibitions, music performances, and language exchange programs, the BRICS nations actively engage with international audiences to foster mutual understanding and goodwill, enhancing their global appeal. Moreover, they are harnessing digital platforms and social media to amplify their cultural narratives and values, effectively reaching a widespread audience and shaping perceptions about their societies. This digital outreach has enabled the BRICS nations to build bridges with individuals and communities worldwide, transcending geographical and linguistic barriers. Another aspect of their soft power usage involves educational and academic exchanges. By facilitating scholarships, research collaborations, and university partnerships, the BRICS countries are nurturing intellectual networks and building human capital, positioning themselves as hubs for knowledge exchange and innovation. Furthermore, investment in tourism and hospitality bolsters their soft power as visitors experience the unique charms and hospitality of BRICS nations, fostering positive associations. These multifaceted strategies underscore the evolving nature of soft power utilization within the BRICS bloc, reflecting a deliberate and coordinated effort to project a compelling and attractive image globally. However, challenges persist, including the need to address internal diversity and inequality and effectively counter existing narratives that may hinder their soft power objectives. Nevertheless, the emerging strategies in soft power adoption by the BRICS nations mark a significant trend in reshaping international relations and cultural diplomacy, serving as a testament to their ambition and potential impact on the future global landscape.

METHODS AND MEDIA IN GLOBAL CULTURAL EXCHANGE

Global cultural exchange is a multifaceted endeavor involving various methods and media to promote cross-cultural understanding and appreciation. In today's interconnected world, the dissemination of cultural expressions is facilitated by various platforms and channels, spanning traditional and digital mediums. Utilizing these diverse tools is critical in fostering dialogue, empathy, and mutual respect among nations and peoples. Cultural diplomacy initiatives often leverage several key methods to engage global audiences, including but not limited to arts and entertainment, educational exchanges, language programs, and digital platforms. Arts and entertainment serve as compelling vehicles for cultural exchange, as they transcend linguistic barriers and communicate universal themes. Through exhibitions, performances, and film festivals, diverse artistic expressions contribute to a shared global identity, highlighting the beauty and intricacies of different cultures. Educational exchanges are pivotal in cultivating mutual understanding and goodwill between nations. By facilitating student and faculty exchanges, academic collaborations, and research partnerships, institutions harness the power of knowledge and learning to bridge cultural divides. Language programs also play a crucial role in promoting intercultural communication and understanding. Initiatives that offer language courses, translation services, and linguistic immersion experiences facilitate meaningful interactions and effective communication across borders. Moreover, the digital landscape has significantly transformed cultural exchange, enabling unprecedented reach and immediacy. Social media, online forums, streaming platforms, virtual reality, and interactive websites have become invaluable tools for transcending geographical boundaries and connecting individuals worldwide. These digital platforms allow for the instantaneous dissemination of cultural content while enabling real-time interaction and engagement. The strategic use of media in global cultural exchange is fundamental to amplifying the impact of cultural diplomacy efforts. Leveraging print, broadcast, and digital media outlets helps amplify cultural narratives, broaden audience reach, and foster meaningful dialogues. Collaborations with journalists, content creators, and influencers further enhance the visibility and resonance of cultural messages. Cultural diplomacy practitioners must stay abreast of evolving media landscapes and effectively adapt their strategies to leverage emerging trends. Ultimately, the diverse methods and media used in global cultural exchange collectively contribute to building bridges of understanding and respect, enriching the fabric of international relations, and nurturing a more harmonious and interconnected world.

CASE STUDIES OF EFFECTIVE CULTURAL DIPLOMACY

Cultural diplomacy is a multifaceted tool nations utilize to foster positive relationships, enhance understanding, and project soft power globally. Through the strategic employment of cultural assets, countries have achieved remarkable success in influencing perceptions and building bridges across diverse societies. In this section, we delve into illuminating case studies that exemplify the effectiveness of cultural diplomacy in achieving foreign policy objectives.

One profound example of effective cultural diplomacy is the British Council's work promoting British culture and values across the globe.

The British Council has played a pivotal role in strengthening the UK's international influence by organizing cultural events, supporting English language education, and facilitating artistic collaborations. The council's programs have showcased the richness of British heritage and facilitated dialogues, paving the way for enhanced bilateral relations and increased cooperation in areas such as education and trade.

Another notable case study is the Alliance Française, a non-profit organization that promotes French language and culture worldwide. Through its global network, the Alliance Française has been instrumental in fostering mutual understanding and collaboration. The organization has successfully projected France's soft power by offering language courses, organizing cultural events, hosting art exhibitions, and fostering enduring ties and partnerships with numerous countries.

Moving eastward, the Confucius Institute, China's initiative for promoting Chinese language and culture internationally, has emerged as a pivotal player in shaping perceptions about China. By establishing centers in various countries and offering Chinese language courses, cultural performances, and academic exchanges, the Confucius Institute has significantly heightened global interest in Chinese culture and language. Furthermore, it has contributed to building people-to-people connections, thereby enhancing China's global influence.

The above case studies reflect the pivotal role played by cultural diplomacy in furthering national interests. These initiatives illustrate how leveraging cultural resources can profoundly impact international relations, transcending linguistic and geographical barriers. As we examine these successful endeavors, it becomes evident that cultural diplomacy is a linchpin in shaping perceptions, bridging differences, and cultivating lasting friendships between nations.

EVALUATING IMPACT: SOFT POWER METRICS AND MEASUREMENTS

Soft power, as a concept, relies on the ability to shape the preferences of others through attraction rather than coercion. Effectively evaluating the impact of soft power initiatives requires a sophisticated understanding of cultural, economic, and political dynamics. In practical terms, the evaluation of soft power influence involves the measurement of a nation's attractiveness, credibility, and the resonance of its values and policies in the international arena. This process encompasses both qualitative and quantitative assessments, requiring a multifaceted approach. Quantitative measures may include analyzing trends in tourism, trade, foreign direct investment, and international student numbers to gauge the appeal and influence of a country's cultural output. Qualitative assessments involve examining opinion polls, media coverage, and cultural diplomacy initiatives to assess the perception and reception of a nation's soft power efforts. Additionally, tracking social media engagement, cultural exchanges, and the reach of educational and cultural programs can provide valuable insights into the effectiveness of soft power strategies. Nevertheless, the complexity of evaluating soft power impact lies in capturing the nuanced shifts in perceptions and attitudes towards a nation over time. This necessitates the development of innovative methodologies that can adapt to the evolving landscape of global communication and cultural exchange. Furthermore, as soft power extends beyond governmental actions to encompass the role of civil society, academia, and private sector actors, comprehensive evaluation frameworks must also consider the contribution of non-state entities in shaping international narratives and perceptions. Challenges in assessing soft power impact arise from the inherent subjectivity of attractiveness and influence. Cultural nuances, historical legacies, and regional variations can significantly impact the reception of soft power initiatives, making it challenging to create universally applicable metrics. Moreover, the intangible nature of soft power means that traditional metrics used to evaluate hard power capabilities, such as military strength or economic output, are not directly transferable. Developing standardized metrics for comparing different nations' soft power capacities remains a contentious issue within international relations. Despite these challenges, the importance of evaluating the impact of soft power cannot be overstated. By understanding the effectiveness of cultural diplomacy and soft power initiatives, nations can refine their strategies, allocate resources judiciously, and cultivate relationships that contribute to their global standing. The ability to quantitatively and qualitatively measure the influence of soft power is essential for informed policy-making and diplomatic decision-making, ultimately shaping the contours of international relations in an increasingly interconnected world.

CHALLENGES AND PITFALLS IN CULTURAL DIPLOMACY INITIATIVES

One of the most critical aspects of cultural diplomacy initiatives is a thorough understanding of the intricate challenges and potential pitfalls that may hinder their success. While using soft power through cultural means can be highly impactful, it is not without its obstacles. One of the primary challenges arises from the diversity and complexity of cultures across different nations. What may be viewed as culturally appealing in one country might be perceived differently or even cause offense in another. This potential for misunderstanding underscores the importance of thoroughly researching and respecting local customs and traditions before implementing cultural diplomacy initiatives. Additionally, the ever-evolving digital landscape presents a challenge in effectively reaching global audiences. Navigating social media, online platforms, and digital content distribution while maintaining authenticity and cultural sensitivity requires adept management and strategy. Another significant challenge is the risk of cultural appropriation or misrepresentation. To avoid such pitfalls, practitioners of cultural diplomacy must ensure that their initiatives are based on respect, collaboration, and mutual benefit rather than exploitation or dominance. Furthermore, the inherent influence of political interests in cultural diplomacy efforts poses a substantial challenge. Negotiating the balance between government agendas and genuine cultural exchange demands careful diplomacy and transparency. Moreover, ensuring long-term sustainability and impact beyond short-lived impressions and superficial engagements is a persistent challenge. Successful cultural diplomacy initiatives require ongoing commitment, investment, and stakeholder engagement to foster enduring relationships and promote lasting positive perceptions. Finally, the logistical and financial constraints of implementing large-scale cultural diplomacy programs present factual challenges that must be navigated creatively and strategically. The effective allocation of resources, securing sustainable funding, and managing logistical complexities amid geopolitical shifts can significantly impact the success of cultural diplomacy initiatives. Understanding and addressing these challenges and pitfalls is essential for the strategic development and execution of culturally sensitive and influential diplomatic initiatives.

COMPARATIVE ANALYSIS BETWEEN G7 AND BRICS APPROACHES

Cultural diplomacy has emerged as a critical tool in international relations, allowing nations to exert influence and shape perceptions by promoting their cultural values and heritage. As we delve deeper into the comparative analysis between G7 and BRICS approaches to cultural diplomacy, it becomes evident that both blocs adopt distinct strategies and face unique challenges in pursuing soft power. Firstly, the G7 nations, comprising advanced industrial economies, have historically utilized cultural diplomacy to reinforce their global dominance, often leveraging their rich artistic traditions, films, and educational exchanges to project a positive image internationally. In contrast, the BRICS nations, characterized by their rapid economic growth and cultural diversity, have increasingly emphasized cultural diplomacy to showcase their vibrant societies and challenge prevailing Western narratives.

This dichotomy underscores the divergent objectives and methods the two groups employ in their cultural outreach efforts. Moreover, while G7 nations typically possess well-established cultural institutions and global media presence, BRICS countries have sought to leverage their burgeoning creative industries and digital platforms to amplify their cultural influence on the world stage. Despite these differences, G7 and BRICS nations face challenges, including balancing authenticity with tailored messaging, navigating cultural sensitivities, and ensuring inclusivity in their diplomatic engagements. Additionally, the evolution of communication technologies and social media has necessitated innovative approaches to engage global audiences effectively, further complicating cultural diplomacy for both groups. A comprehensive comparative assessment of G7 and BRICS cultural diplomacy illustrates the intricate interplay between historical legacies, economic contexts, and geopolitical aspirations that shape their respective soft power strategies. Understanding these nuances is crucial for policymakers, diplomats, and scholars seeking to navigate the complex landscape of cultural diplomacy and its implications for contemporary international relations.

FUTURE DIRECTIONS IN CULTURAL DIPLOMACY

As a crucial component of international relations, cultural diplomacy is continually evolving to adapt to the ever-changing global landscape. Looking ahead, future directions in cultural diplomacy will be shaped by several key factors that warrant careful consideration and strategic planning. Firstly, technological advancements and the digital revolution are expected to play an increasingly significant role in shaping the practice of cultural diplomacy. As the world becomes more interconnected through social media, streaming platforms, and virtual reality, cross-border cultural exchanges and interaction opportunities are poised to expand. Furthermore, harnessing the potential of emerging technologies such as artificial intelligence and augmented reality presents new avenues for enhancing cultural outreach and understanding between nations. It will be imperative for policymakers and practitioners of cultural diplomacy to leverage these tools effectively to foster mutual respect and appreciation across diverse societies. Secondly, the shifting demographic trends and multicultural dynamics within societies demand a nuanced approach to cultural diplomacy. As globalization continues to blur traditional boundaries, recognizing and celebrating diversity become pivotal in promoting inclusive cultural relations. Future strategies in cultural diplomacy should prioritize initiatives that embrace and highlight the richness of various cultural traditions while promoting intercultural dialogue and understanding. A proactive effort to engage with marginalized communities and empower voices from underrepresented backgrounds will be essential in fostering a truly inclusive global cultural landscape. Thirdly, the environmental and sustainability challenges facing the world call for reimagining cultural diplomacy efforts. In the coming years, environmentally conscious practices and eco-friendly initiatives are expected to be integrated into cultural exchange programs and events. Emphasizing sustainability and environmental stewardship in cultural diplomacy engagements can effectively address shared global concerns while fostering collaboration among nations. Moreover, promoting the preservation of cultural heritage and indigenous knowledge in tandem with sustainable development goals presents an opportunity for cultural diplomacy to contribute meaningfully to the broader agenda of global sustainability. Finally, the fusion of arts, entertainment, and cultural expressions with diplomatic endeavors will continue to shape the future landscape of cultural diplomacy. Leveraging the universal language of music, film, literature, and other artistic forms has proven to be a compelling tool for building bridges between nations. Integrating creative industries and cultural productions into diplomatic activities holds immense potential for forging enduring connections and influencing perceptions on a global scale. As cultural diplomacy evolves, embracing innovative approaches that leverage the influence of creative arts will catalyze deeper cross-cultural engagement and mutual understanding. In essence, the future directions in cultural diplomacy will be intricately tied to embracing technological advancements, championing diversity and inclusion, addressing environmental imperatives, and harnessing the profound impact of creative expressions. Navigating these pathways with foresight and adaptability will be essential in shaping a more interconnected and harmonious global community through cultural diplomacy.

CHAPTER 10

Military Alliances and Defense Postures: A Comparative Study

MILITARY ALLIANCES AND DEFENSE POSTURES

Military alliances play a pivotal role in shaping the contemporary geopolitical landscape, serving as essential mechanisms for countries to ensure their security, deter aggression, and advance their strategic interests. These alliances are formed based on shared security concerns, common military objectives, and a mutual commitment to collective defense. As the global balance of power continues to evolve, the significance of military alliances in maintaining stability and deterring potential threats cannot be overstated. In an era characterized by complex security challenges, including asymmetric warfare, cyber threats, and regional conflicts, the interplay of military coalitions has become increasingly intricate and crucial. The historical context of military alliances provides valuable insights into their evolution and impact on international relations. Understanding how these alliances have shaped the geopolitical dynamics within the G7 and BRICS can offer profound perspectives on their present significance and future trajectories. Furthermore, with advancements in technology and changes like warfare, the defense postures of nations have undergone notable transformations, influencing the rationale behind their participation in military alliances. This section delves into the multifaceted dimensions of military alliances and defense postures, examining their contributions to global security, their complexities, and the implications for international stability and cooperation.

HISTORICAL OVERVIEW OF MILITARY COALITIONS IN G7 AND BRICS

The historical evolution of military coalitions within the G7 and BRICS is a fascinating narrative marked by geopolitical rivalries, ideological differences, and strategic alignments. The foundations of military alliances within the G7 can be traced back to the aftermath of World War II when the United States formed security pacts such as NATO to counter the perceived threat posed by the Soviet Union and its allies. This marked the beginning of a cohesive military bloc aimed at deterring aggression and preserving the balance of power in the post-war era. Conversely, the BRICS nations, comprising Brazil, Russia, India, China, and later South Africa, have a more complex history of military cooperation. Despite shared geopolitical ambitions and aspirations for multipolarity, the BRICS countries have historically maintained a degree of strategic autonomy and refrained from forming formal military alliances akin to those in the G7. Instead, they have focused on fostering diplomatic ties and economic collaboration to advance their collective interests while avoiding overt military entanglements. The historical context of these military coalitions underscores the differing approaches to security and defense adopted by the G7 and BRICS nations, reflecting contrasting geopolitical imperatives and historical experiences. It also sets the stage for a comparative analysis of the underlying principles, decision-making processes, and strategic objectives that have shaped the military postures of these influential global blocs.

THEORIES OF DEFENSIVE ALIGNMENT AND OFFENSIVE REALISM

Defensive alignment and offensive realism are two prominent theories that shape the military alliances and defense postures of nations within the G7 and BRICS. Defensive alignment theory posits that states form alliances primarily to counterbalance the threats posed by rival nations, seeking security through collective defense agreements. This approach emphasizes the importance of maintaining a solid defensive capability to deter potential adversaries and ensure mutual protection within the alliance.

In contrast, offensive realism contends that states engage in alliances and military posturing to pursue power and expand influence. According to this theory, nations are driven by the imperative to maximize their relative power and attain hegemony, often leading to aggressive international strategies and competitive behavior. Offensive realists argue that such actions are necessary for survival in a world characterized by anarchy and constant competition among states.

These theories have significant implications for the military alliances and defense postures of G7 and BRICS nations. The historical application of defensive alignment theory can be observed in the formation of NATO and the collective security measures taken by G7 countries during the Cold War. Conversely, the principles of offensive realism have influenced the assertive military strategies pursued by certain BRICS members as they seek to expand their global influence and secure access to strategic resources.

Furthermore, the interplay between these two theories has contributed to the complex geopolitical landscape, where defensive and offensive motivations shape the decisions and actions of nations within the G7 and BRICS. Understanding these theoretical underpinnings is essential for comprehending the evolving dynamics of global military alliances, the adoption of defense postures, and the intricate balance of power in international relations.

As the international community navigates through an era marked by shifting geopolitical alignments and emerging security challenges, the nexus between defensive alignment and offensive realism continues to shape the strategies and interactions of G7 and BRICS nations. It is imperative to analyze and evaluate the practical application of these theories in contemporary military and defense policies to anticipate the potential implications for global stability and regional security arrangements.

CURRENT MILITARY ALLIANCES WITHIN THE G7: STRUCTURE AND CHALLENGES

The structure of military alliances within the Group of Seven (G7) reflects the complex geopolitics and historical relationships among member countries. The North Atlantic Treaty Organization (NATO) is a cornerstone of military cooperation within the G7, serving as a primary forum for collective defense and security. NATO's structure promotes mutual assistance and deterrence in the face of potential threats, fostering interoperability and coordination among member states' armed forces. However, the challenges of NATO and other G7 military alliances are multifaceted. One significant challenge lies in reconciling member states' diverse national interests and strategic priorities, which can sometimes lead to differing perspectives on the nature and scope of collective defense efforts. Additionally, evolving security threats, such as cyber warfare, asymmetric conflicts, and non-state actors, present new challenges that demand innovative responses from G7 military alliances. Furthermore, debates over burden-sharing and defense spending persist within the G7, reflecting varying levels of commitment and capabilities among member nations. These discussions often highlight the need for equitable distribution of responsibilities and resources to ensure the effectiveness of collective defense initiatives. Moreover, the dynamic geopolitical landscape, including shifts in global power dynamics and the rise of new security concerns, compels G7 military alliances to adapt their structures and strategies to remain relevant and responsive to emerging threats. The interconnected nature of contemporary security challenges underscores the importance of fostering deeper cooperation and coordination within the G7, leveraging the strengths of individual member states to address shared security imperatives. As such, navigating the structural and operational challenges facing G7 military alliances requires sustained diplomatic efforts and strategic vision to uphold the principles of collective defense while confronting the evolving nature of global security.

DEFENSE STRATEGIES AND ALLIANCES WITHIN BRICS

The defense strategies and alliances within the BRICS (Brazil, Russia, India, China, South Africa) bloc represent a complex interplay of geopolitical interests, historical relationships, and evolving security dynamics. Each member nation brings unique challenges, opportunities, and priorities to the collective defense posture of BRICS.

With its vast borders and natural resources, Brazil has historically focused on bolstering its defense capabilities to protect its territorial integrity and economic interests. The country has pursued strategic partnerships with neighboring nations while engaging in regional security initiatives to combat transnational threats.

With its history of superpower status and extensive military-industrial complex, Russia plays a central role in shaping the defense posture of BRICS. The nation's assertive foreign policy stance and modernization of its armed forces have contributed significantly to the collective security framework within the bloc.

As a nuclear-armed power with diverse security challenges, India emphasizes a balanced approach to national defense, encompassing conventional military strength, nuclear deterrence, and counter-terrorism capabilities. Its regional ambitions and aspirations for global influence further shape the strategic calculus within BRICS.

China's rapid military modernization, expansion of its naval capabilities, and assertive territorial claims have redefined the security landscape in the Asia-Pacific region. As the most populous and economically dominant member of BRICS, China's defense policies and alliances significantly affect the bloc's collective security.

While not as prominent in the global arms trade or power projection as some of its BRICS counterparts, South Africa is vital in enhancing the African continent's security architecture. Its contributions to peacekeeping operations, counter-terrorism efforts, and maritime security complement the broader defense strategies and alliances within BRICS.

The evolving nature of defense alliances within BRICS is characterized by a delicate balance of cooperation, political sensitivities, and diverging strategic objectives. As the member nations navigate their respective security challenges and global aspirations, the collective defense posture of BRICS continues to evolve, influencing regional and global security dynamics.

NATO AND ITS ROLE IN SHAPING G7 MILITARY POLICIES

The North Atlantic Treaty Organization (NATO) has played a pivotal role in shaping the military policies of the G7 nations by fostering a collective defense strategy and providing a platform for cooperation and coordination among its member states. Founded in 1949 as a response to the new security challenges arising from the aftermath of World War II, NATO has continued to evolve in alignment with shifting global dynamics. With a core principle of mutual defense, NATO has been instrumental in influencing the defense postures, strategies, and capabilities of G7 countries.

One of NATO's key contributions to shaping G7 military policies is promoting interoperability and standardization among its members. By establishing common standards for equipment, communication systems, and operational procedures, NATO has facilitated greater military cooperation and integration among G7 armed forces. This has enhanced the collective defense capability of the G7 nations and fostered a sense of unity and solidarity in addressing common security challenges.

Furthermore, NATO is a forum for strategic discussions and policy coordination, providing a platform for G7 members to exchange intelligence, assess threats, and deliberate on joint military actions. The alliance's integrated command structure, which allows for rapid decision-making and force deployment, enables G7 nations to demonstrate a unified front in response to emerging security threats and crises.

NATO's role in shaping G7 military policies extends beyond its immediate membership. Through partnerships and outreach programs, NATO engages with non-member G7 nations, offering avenues for dialogue, capacity-building, and joint exercises. This engagement widens NATO's influence on G7 military strategies and fosters a more cohesive approach to security challenges at a global level.

Moreover, NATO's evolution and adaptation to contemporary security concerns, including cyber attacks, hybrid warfare, and terrorism, have influenced the G7's strategic outlook and defense planning. The alliance's commitment to collective defense and deterrence has underscored the importance of preemptive measures and preparedness within the G7 framework, shaping their military doctrines and resource allocation.

In summary, NATO has been a significant force in shaping the military policies of the G7 nations, promoting interoperability, providing a platform for strategic coordination, engaging with non-member states, and adapting to evolving security dynamics. As NATO continues to navigate new challenges, its role in influencing the defense postures of the G7 is likely to remain indispensable in safeguarding shared security interests.

COMPARATIVE ANALYSIS OF MILITARY SPENDING AND RESOURCE ALLOCATION

In examining the military capabilities of the G7 and BRICS nations, conducting a thorough comparative analysis of their military spending and resource allocation is essential. Military spending encompasses the budgetary allocation towards defense, which includes expenses related to personnel, equipment, research, and development, as well as operations and maintenance. This criterion is a critical indicator of a nation's commitment and capability to build and maintain a strong defense posture. The G7 countries, with the United States at the forefront, have historically been the world's largest military spenders. Their defense budgets are reflective of their global responsibilities and power projection capabilities.

Conversely, the BRICS nations have significantly increased their military spending in recent years, aiming to bolster their defense capabilities and assert themselves as influential geopolitical players. As part of the comparative analysis, it is imperative to delve into the specific areas where military resources are allocated within each group of nations. For the G7 countries, substantial investments are directed towards advanced military technologies, intelligence gathering, and cyber warfare capabilities, aligning with their focus on modern warfare tactics. On the other hand, the BRICS nations prioritize enhancing their conventional military capabilities, with a significant emphasis on ground forces, naval fleets, and air superiority. Additionally, both groups place considerable importance on research and development activities, albeit with differing objectives - the G7 nations emphasize technological innovations for asymmetric warfare and precision strike capabilities. In contrast, the BRICS nations concentrate on indigenous defense production and technological self-reliance.

CASE STUDIES: SUCCESSFUL AND FAILED MILITARY ALLIANCES

In examining the landscape of military alliances, it is essential to delve into specific case studies that highlight successful and failed endeavors within the G7 and BRICS. One illuminating example is the NATO alliance, formed after World War II as a collective defense mechanism against the Soviet Union. NATO's success is evident in its longevity and ability to adapt to evolving global security challenges. Conversely, the Warsaw Pact, established by the Soviet Union and its satellite states, serves as a cautionary tale of a failed military alliance, ultimately dissolved amidst internal and external pressures.

Shifting our focus to the BRICS nations, the strategic partnership between Russia and China presents an intriguing case study. This alliance, characterized by mutual defense agreements and extensive military cooperation, underscores the evolving geopolitical dynamics and power structures within the BRICS bloc. On the contrary, the attempts at forging a cohesive defense posture among the BRICS countries have faced substantial hurdles stemming from differing national interests and historical rivalries.

Further insights emerge by examining joint military operations led by G7 members, such as the campaign against ISIS in the Middle East. The collaborative efforts and interoperability demonstrated in this context signify successful military coalitions. Conversely, the failure to establish a unified defense strategy during the 2003 Iraq War reflects the challenges of aligning diverse national interests and policy objectives within the G7 framework.

The case studies illustrate the critical factors contributing to military alliances' success or failure. These encompass geopolitical unity, mutual trust among member states, the coherence of military doctrines, and the capacity for coordinated decision-making. Moreover, the ever-changing global security landscape necessitates continuous adaptation and preparedness, highlighting the significance of lessons gleaned from historical case studies. By comprehensively analyzing these examples, policymakers and strategists can garner valuable insights to inform future defense postures and military alliances, fostering greater cohesion and efficacy in addressing emergent security challenges.

FUTURE TRENDS IN GLOBAL DEFENSE STRATEGIES

Amidst the evolving geopolitical landscape, the future of global defense strategies is poised to witness notable shifts and transformations. As technological advancements continue to reshape the nature of warfare, nations must adapt their defense postures to anticipate and counter emerging threats. One key trend shaping the future of defense strategies is the growing prominence of asymmetric warfare, where non-state actors and cyber warfare capabilities pose significant challenges to traditional military structures. This necessitates a reevaluation of strategic priorities and resource allocations to combat these unconventional threats effectively. Additionally, the increasing fusion of conventional military capabilities with artificial intelligence, autonomous weapons systems, and space-based assets underscores nations' need to invest in cutting-edge technologies and modernize their defense arsenals.

Furthermore, the growing interconnectedness of global supply chains and critical infrastructure introduces new vulnerabilities that necessitate a holistic approach to defense, encompassing not only conventional military strength but also cybersecurity and resilience against hybrid threats. The future will likely witness a paradigm shift towards more agile and adaptable alliances, frameworks, and coalitions that swiftly respond to dynamic threats and crises in international security cooperation. As the spectrum of security challenges broadens to include environmental degradation, pandemics, and disinformation campaigns, defense strategies will increasingly incorporate multi-dimensional approaches that address traditional and non-traditional security concerns. Moreover, the ethical and legal dimensions of warfare, including regulating emerging technologies and protecting civilian populations, will feature prominently in future defense strategies. In an era of rapid technological innovation, anticipatory governance, and ethical considerations will play pivotal roles in shaping the trajectory of global defense strategies. Overall, the future landscape of global defense strategies will be defined by a dynamic interplay of technological, geopolitical, and societal factors, necessitating proactive adaptations and collaborative approaches to ensure international peace and security.

SUMMARY OF KEY FINDINGS AND POLICY RECOMMENDATIONS

Examining future trends in global defense strategies has provided invaluable insights into the evolving nature of military alliances and defense postures in the contemporary international landscape. As the geopolitical and security environments continue to undergo rapid transformations, policymakers, defense experts, and strategic analysts must discern the critical findings from this comprehensive analysis, which can serve as a foundation for formulating practical policy recommendations.

One of the study's central conclusions is the increasing significance of asymmetric warfare and non-traditional security threats, including cyberattacks, terrorism, and hybrid warfare, that transcend conventional military paradigms. Consequently, a critical need exists for multilateral cooperation and information-sharing mechanisms among G7 and BRICS nations to collectively confront these emerging challenges.

Moreover, the assessment revealed that the proliferation of advanced technologies, such as artificial intelligence, unmanned aerial vehicles, and autonomous weapon systems, is reshaping the dynamics of modern warfare. This underscores the necessity for comprehensive regulatory frameworks and ethical guidelines to govern the development and application of these technologies within international security.

The comparative analysis of military spending and resource allocation underscored the disparities in defense investments between the G7 and BRICS countries. While the former exhibit higher defense budgets and sophisticated arsenals, the latter emphasize leveraging regional alliances and diplomatic initiatives to bolster their defense capabilities. Recognizing this dichotomy is paramount in devising equitable mechanisms to address global security concerns while respecting the diverse strategic priorities of nations within these coalitions.

Furthermore, the exploration of successful and failed military alliances illuminated the intricate interplay of diplomatic, economic, and security factors underpinning defense partnerships' efficacy. Drawing from these case studies, it is evident that fostering mutual trust, transparency, and a shared strategic vision are pivotal determinants of successful military coalitions, thereby necessitating sustained dialogue and confidence-building measures among member states.

Building upon these critical findings, the following policy recommendations are proposed: Firstly, there ought to be a concerted effort to enhance interoperability and joint military exercises between G7 and BRICS nations to foster mutual understanding and readiness for potential cooperative endeavors. Secondly, investing in capacity-building programs and defense infrastructure in vulnerable regions can fortify the resilience of allied nations against regional threats and crises. Thirdly, promoting responsible arms control and disarmament initiatives and confidence-building measures can engender a climate of stability and trust amongst global actors. Finally, advocating for the integration of gender perspectives and diversity in defense policies and prioritizing civilian-military coordination in humanitarian interventions can ensure more inclusive and effective security strategies.

In conclusion, this chapter's exhaustive evaluation of future defense trends and the ensuing policy prescriptions underscores the criticality of adaptability, agility, and inclusivity in navigating the complex web of global security challenges. World leaders and defense stakeholders can pave the way for a more resilient, cooperative, and secure international order by heeding these findings and enacting the recommended policy measures.

CHAPTER 11

New Alliances: Shifting Powers in the 21st Century

As we progress into the 21st century, the global landscape of power and influence is significantly transforming. Traditional alliances and partnerships are evolving, and new configurations are emerging to reflect our world's changing geopolitical and economic dynamics.

The traditional G7 powerhouses are facing increasing competition and are being forced to adapt to the rise of new players, such as the BRICS nations and other emerging economies. This shift in power dynamics is reshaping the global order and prompting a reevaluation of traditional diplomatic and economic alliances.

The evolving nature of global power is fueled by a confluence of factors, including rapid technological advancements, the growing interconnectedness of economies, and the rise of non-state actors as influential players in international affairs. These changes contribute to a more complex and multipolar world, where traditional power structures give way to a more diffuse distribution of influence and authority.

Economic Realignment and New Alliances One key driver behind the formation of new alliances is the changing economic landscape. The rise of emerging economies, particularly in Asia, has reconfigured global trade and investment patterns. Nations seek to form strategic partnerships to leverage the economic potential of these rapidly growing markets, leading to new economic alliances and regional trade agreements.

For example, the Belt and Road Initiative (BRI), spearheaded by China, has established new trade and infrastructure partnerships across Asia, Africa, and Europe. This ambitious project has the potential to reshape the economic and geopolitical dynamics of these regions, offering participating countries opportunities to benefit from enhanced connectivity and trade. The Comprehensive and Progressive Agreement for Trans-Pacific Partnership (CPTPP) also represents a significant trade agreement among 11 Pacific Rim countries, demonstrating the proliferation of new economic alliances in a shifting global economic landscape.

Furthermore, the economic realignment is also fueled by the advent of new technological frontiers, such as artificial intelligence, renewable energy, and advanced manufacturing. As nations compete and cooperate in these cutting-edge industries, new economic partnerships and alliances are being forged to harness the potential of these emerging technologies and drive economic growth and innovation.

Security Dynamics and Strategic Alliances Shifting security dynamics are also influencing geopolitical realignment. Traditional security alliances, such as NATO, are being tested by new global security challenges, including cyber threats, terrorism, and the proliferation of weapons of mass destruction. As a result, nations are forging new security partnerships to address these evolving security threats, diversifying security alliances and cooperation frameworks.

In the security realm, the Quad, comprising the United States, Japan, India, and Australia, has emerged as a strategic partnership to promote a free and open Indo-Pacific region. This alliance reflects the growing concerns over regional security and the need to preserve maritime security and the rule of law in the Indo-Pacific. Additionally, the African Union and the G5 Sahel Joint Force represent collaborative security efforts to address the complex security challenges in the Sahel region of Africa, showcasing the emergence of new strategic alliances in response to regional security threats.

Furthermore, non-traditional security challenges, such as climate change and pandemics, shape security alliances. The increasing recognition of the interconnectedness of these global threats is prompting nations to form new alliances focused on resilience, preparedness, and collective action to address these common challenges.

Ideological and Cultural Affinities Additionally, ideological and cultural affinities play a role in forming new alliances. Nations increasingly seek partnerships with like-minded countries with shared values and principles, leading to new ideological alliances based on shared political systems, cultural ties, and social norms.

The European Union, for instance, represents a unique alliance of nations with a shared commitment to democracy, human rights, and the rule of law. This alliance promotes economic and political integration and serves as a bastion for promoting democratic values and norms in international relations. Moreover, cultural and linguistic alliances, such as La Francophonie, which brings together French-speaking nations, serve as platforms for cultural exchange and cooperation among member countries with shared cultural heritage, language, and values.

The implications of these shifting alliances are profound, impacting the dynamics of global governance, international cooperation, and conflict resolution. The rise of new powers and alliances is challenging the dominance of traditional power centers and necessitating a reevaluation of global governance structures to better accommodate the interests of a more diverse array of stakeholders.

At the same time, forming new alliances presents opportunities for enhanced collaboration and dialogue among nations. By embracing the diversity of interests and perspectives represented by these new alliances, the international community can work towards addressing global challenges more effectively and fostering greater understanding and cooperation on a global scale.

In conclusion, the shifting powers in the 21st century are reshaping the global order, necessitating a reexamination of traditional alliances and a reorientation of international cooperation frameworks. By understanding and adapting to these changes, nations can navigate the complexities of a multipolar world and work towards building a more inclusive, equitable, and peaceful global order.

CHAPTER 12

Trade Wars and Economic Sanctions: The Weapons of Choice

TRADE WARS AND ECONOMIC SANCTIONS

In international relations, deploying trade wars and economic sanctions has become a defining feature of modern geopolitical strategy. Nations wield these tools to exert influence, pursue strategic objectives, and respond to perceived threats in the global economic landscape. At the heart of this approach lies the recognition that economic power is not merely an instrument of prosperity but also a potent lever for advancing national interests and shaping the behavior of other states. Historical precedence attests to the enduring significance of these measures, with trade conflicts and sanctions tracing back centuries as means of projecting authority, coercing adversaries, and safeguarding domestic industries. Against this backdrop, contemporary trade wars and economic sanctions must be understood as pivotal instruments in pursuing geopolitical advantage and protecting national sovereignty. The intersection of politics, economics, and international relations converges in trade disputes and punitive economic measures, underscoring their critical role in shaping the global order.

HISTORICAL OVERVIEW OF TRADE CONFLICT

Trade conflicts have a long and storied history, dating back to ancient civilizations and continuing into the present day. Throughout history, nations and empires have engaged in trade disputes, often resulting in economic turmoil, political tensions, and even armed conflicts. The earliest recorded trade dispute dates back to the Peloponnesian War between Athens and Sparta, where economic sanctions and trade embargoes were utilized as strategic tools. Fast forward to the modern era, trade conflicts have significantly evolved with the rise of global interdependence and complex supply chains. The Age of Exploration brought fierce competition for natural resources and trade routes, leading to conflicts such as the Anglo-Dutch Wars and the Seven Years' War. The industrial revolution intensified trade rivalries, culminating in protectionist policies and tariff wars among major powers. The devastating impact of the Great Depression in the 1930s exacerbated trade tensions, ultimately contributing to the outbreak of World War II. The post-war period saw the establishment of international institutions like the GATT and, later, the WTO to foster cooperation and resolve trade disputes through diplomacy and multilateral negotiations. However, trade conflicts persisted despite these efforts, which was evident in the US-Japan trade friction during the 1980s and early 1990s. More recent examples include trade disputes between the United States, China, and the European Union. These conflicts have impacted the involved economies and reverberated across the global market, affecting businesses and consumers worldwide. Understanding the historical evolution of trade conflict is crucial in comprehending the complexities of the contemporary trade landscape. Historical perspectives provide valuable insights into the root causes, patterns, and mechanisms of trade conflicts, paving the way for informed policymaking and strategic decision-making in the face of present-day challenges.

THE MECHANISM OF SANCTIONS: LEGAL AND ECONOMIC DIMENSIONS

Sanctions represent a crucial instrument in international relations, utilized by nations to impose restrictions on targeted entities, often as a response to perceived threats or violations of international norms. The imposition of sanctions is guided by a complex web of legal and economic dimensions, requiring careful consideration and precise execution. From a legal perspective, the authorization and implementation of sanctions typically stem from national legislation or international agreements. These measures must adhere to established legal frameworks, ensuring compliance with domestic and international laws. At the same time, economic dimensions play a pivotal role in shaping the impact and effectiveness of sanctions. Economic penalties can significantly disrupt trade, investment, and financial transactions, exerting pressure on the targeted entities. This two-pronged approach intertwines legal legitimacy with economic leverage, creating a potent tool for signaling disapproval and compelling behavioral change. The enforcement of sanctions mandates close collaboration between government bodies, regulatory authorities, and international organizations to deploy a multifaceted approach. This may involve freezing assets, restricting access to global financial systems, imposing export/import limitations, and instituting tariffs to curtail the targeted entity's economic activities. However, the collateral damage from these measures necessitates a balanced assessment of their potential humanitarian implications. Careful evaluation of the intended impact and unintended consequences is critical to mitigate adverse effects on innocent populations and vulnerable demographic segments. Comprehensive monitoring and periodic reassessment are essential to minimize the humanitarian toll while achieving the desired policy outcomes. Furthermore, coordinating sanctions with diplomatic initiatives remains imperative to avoid protracted conflicts and foster avenues for dialogue. Effective communication channels and intermediary mediation efforts can de-escalate tensions and create windows for constructive engagement. In the contemporary geopolitical landscape, the mechanics of sanctions exemplify a delicate interplay between legal prerogatives and economic imperatives, demanding prudence, precision, and foresight in their application.

CASE STUDIES: NOTABLE TRADE WARS IN THE 21ST CENTURY

In the 21st century, trade wars have become powerful tools for nations to assert their economic and political agendas. One of the notable trade conflicts in recent history is the ongoing trade war between the United States and China. The escalation of tariffs and retaliatory measures between these two economic giants has significantly impacted global markets. Imposing tariffs on billions of dollars worth of goods has disrupted supply chains and created uncertainty for businesses worldwide. The trade dispute has not only affected the economies of the US and China but also sent ripples across other countries reliant on their trade relationships. Another significant case study is the trade tensions between the US and the European Union (EU). Disputes over subsidies to aircraft manufacturers and disagreements on import tariffs have led to retaliatory tariffs on various products, including steel, aluminum, and agricultural goods. This conflict has strained transatlantic relations and raised concerns about the stability of the global trading system. Additionally, the impact of Brexit on trade relations between the UK and the EU serves as a pertinent case study. The negotiations surrounding the departure of the UK from the EU and the subsequent trade arrangements have posed challenges for both parties. Uncertainty over future trade agreements, particularly in financial services and agriculture, has added complexity to an intricate process. These case studies exemplify the complexities and far-reaching consequences of trade wars in the contemporary era. They underscore the necessity of diplomatic dialogue and negotiated resolutions to mitigate the adverse effects on global economies and international relations.

IMPACT OF SANCTIONS ON GLOBAL ECONOMIES

Sanctions have become a powerful tool in international relations, frequently used to pressure target countries and influence their behavior. However, the impact of sanctions extends far beyond the intended targets, often creating significant ripple effects across the global economy. One of the most immediate impacts of sanctions is felt in the financial markets, where uncertainty and risk aversion can lead to volatility and disruptions. Investors may become wary of engaging with sanctioned entities or countries, leading to capital flight and destabilization of currency markets. Furthermore, sanctions can disrupt established trade relationships, causing supply chain disruptions and price fluctuations for essential goods. This, in turn, can affect businesses and consumers worldwide, leading to increased costs and potential shortages. The energy sector is particularly susceptible to the impact of sanctions, as restrictions on oil and gas exports can lead to shifts in global energy prices and geopolitical tensions. Moreover, sanctions can hinder technological advancement and innovation by restricting access to critical components and knowledge sharing. This can impede progress in various industries and slow down global technological development. Notably, the humanitarian impact of sanctions cannot be overlooked. They can exacerbate poverty and lead to shortages of essential goods, affecting the most vulnerable populations in the target countries. Moreover, the effectiveness of sanctions in achieving their objectives is a subject of debate. While they may impose economic hardships on targeted nations, they can also galvanize domestic support for governments and foster a siege mentality among populations. In some cases, sanctions have led to the emergence of black market economies and illicit networks, undermining the intended impact. The international community must consider these multifaceted consequences when resorting to sanctions as a foreign policy tool. A comprehensive understanding of the impact of sanctions on global economies is crucial for policymakers and stakeholders to navigate complex international dynamics and mitigate unintended repercussions.

POLITICAL OBJECTIVES BEHIND TRADE WARS

Trade wars and economic sanctions are not merely tools of economic policy; they are often strategic instruments employed by nations to pursue political objectives on the global stage. Behind the rhetoric of protecting domestic industries or ensuring fair trade lies a complex web of geopolitical ambitions and power play. Firstly, it is essential to recognize that geopolitical motives fundamentally drive trade wars. Nations engage in trade conflicts to protect their economic interests and exert influence over regional or global economic dynamics. This can include leveraging tariff impositions or market access restrictions to pressure rival nations into complying with diplomatic or geopolitical demands. For example, a country may impose tariffs on specific imports to pressure another nation to alter its foreign policy stance or secure advantageous terms in bilateral negotiations. Additionally, trade wars are a tool for asserting dominance and shaping the global economic order within excellent power competition. Major powers may strategically deploy tariffs, export controls, or embargoes to weaken adversaries economically, bolstering their geopolitical position. Furthermore, political objectives behind trade wars extend beyond immediate economic gains. These conflicts are often initiated to enforce behavioral changes in target countries, such as limiting intellectual property theft, addressing currency manipulation, or coercing adherence to international norms. Moreover, leaders may use trade wars to garner domestic political support or deflect public scrutiny from other issues. Governments seek to project strong leadership and assert control over economic narratives by framing trade disputes as battles to defend national interests. It is crucial to recognize the interconnectedness of politics and international trade. When examining the motivations behind trade wars, it becomes evident that economic considerations cannot be divorced from geopolitical strategies and national interests. Acknowledging these political underpinnings provides a more comprehensive understanding of the complexities of global trade dynamics and is a critical foundation for informed decision-making and effective diplomacy.

SHORT-TERM AND LONG-TERM EFFECTS ON DOMESTIC MARKETS

Trade wars and economic sanctions have far-reaching implications for domestic markets, affecting short-term and long-term economic stability. In the short term, the imposition of tariffs and trade barriers can lead to disruptions in supply chains, increased input costs for businesses, and higher consumer prices. This often results in market volatility, reduced investor confidence, and heightened uncertainty within the domestic economy.

Furthermore, trade conflicts can lead to retaliatory measures from targeted nations, escalating tensions and creating a hostile business environment. As a result, domestic industries may experience decreased exports, diminishing their competitiveness in international markets. This can harm the profitability and viability of businesses, particularly those heavily reliant on global trade.

In the long term, the effects of trade wars and economic sanctions can be more profound, influencing the structural composition of domestic markets. Industries may undergo significant restructuring as they adapt to new trade conditions and seek alternative markets. This restructuring process can lead to layoffs, relocations, and business consolidation, potentially altering the employment landscape and regional dynamics.

Moreover, prolonged trade conflicts can impede economic growth and innovation by limiting access to foreign technologies, resources, and expertise. This can hinder the development of domestic industries and weaken the nation's overall competitiveness in the global arena. Trade barriers and sanctions may also incentivize increased protectionism, leading to a distortion of market mechanisms and hindering efficiency.

Amidst these challenges, governments often implement interventionist policies to mitigate the negative impacts of trade wars and economic sanctions. These may include subsidies, support programs for affected industries, and efforts to diversify trading partners. However, such interventions can also introduce distortions into the market, potentially creating dependencies and inefficiencies.

Ultimately, the short-term and long-term effects on domestic markets stemming from trade conflicts underscore the intricate interplay between geopolitics and economics. These repercussions necessitate strategic planning and adaptive resilience from businesses, industries, and policymakers as they navigate the complexities of international trade dynamics.

RESPONSES AND STRATEGIES: HOW NATIONS NAVIGATE SANCTIONS

When confronted with economic sanctions, nations must strategically navigate the complex international relations and economic interdependencies. A typical response to sanctions is the reorientation of trade patterns and partnerships. By diversifying their trade networks, countries aim to offset the detrimental effects of sanctions on their economies. This often involves forging new alliances and strengthening ties with alternative trading partners to mitigate the impact of restricted access to key markets. Additionally, nations may resort to internal policy reforms to boost self-sufficiency and reduce dependency on sanctioned goods. Such measures could include incentivizing domestic production, investing in technological innovation, and enhancing infrastructure to support local industries. However, these strategies require substantial financial resources and time to yield tangible results. Moreover, targeted nations may engage in diplomatic efforts to garner support from international organizations and sympathetic allies. By leveraging multilateral platforms, they aim to voice their grievances and seek relief from punitive measures. Furthermore, some countries employ retaliatory tactics to counteract sanctions, escalating tensions and leading to a tit-for-tat cycle of economic reprisals. In contrast, a more conciliatory approach involves dialogue and negotiations to find mutually agreeable solutions. Through skilled diplomacy and compromise, nations can potentially alleviate the severity of sanctions or negotiate their gradual easing. Conversely, certain nations may opt for non-compliance and defiance, seeking to withstand the economic pressures exerted by sanctions and projecting resilience on the global stage. Ultimately, the choice of response hinges on carefully evaluating the national interest, weighing short-term hardships against long-term strategic objectives. As geopolitical dynamics continue to evolve, the efficacy of these responses will play a pivotal role in shaping the outcomes of future economic sanctions.

ECONOMIC SANCTIONS AND HUMAN RIGHTS CONSIDERATIONS

Economic sanctions are crucial in international relations and are often used to enforce compliance with global norms and regulations. However, implementing such sanctions raises complex ethical questions, particularly concerning their impact on human rights. The imposition of economic sanctions can have wide-ranging effects on the civilian population of targeted countries, often leading to deprivation of basic needs such as food, medicine, and access to essential services. Despite efforts to design targeted sanctions to minimize collateral damage, the unintended humanitarian consequences cannot be ignored. It is imperative for policymakers to carefully assess the potential human rights implications of imposing economic sanctions. In many cases, sanctions disproportionately affect vulnerable communities, exacerbating poverty and suffering. Moreover, the long-term consequences of economic hardship resulting from sanctions may undermine the principles they seek to uphold, including promoting human rights and dignity. As we navigate the complexities of international diplomacy and geopolitical strategy, balancing achieving policy objectives and safeguarding fundamental human rights is crucial. This necessitates robust mechanisms for monitoring the humanitarian impact of sanctions and ensuring that they remain consistent with international human rights standards. Additionally, engaging in constructive dialogue with affected populations and relevant stakeholders is essential to understanding the real-life repercussions of economic sanctions. Furthermore, the interconnected nature of the global economy underscores the need for comprehensive assessments of how sanctions can reverberate beyond national borders, affecting regional stability and the broader international community. As we confront the intricate interplay between economics and human rights, critically examining the ethical dimensions of economic sanctions is indispensable for shaping responsible and effective foreign policy. By integrating human rights considerations into economic sanctions discourse, we can strive towards a more sustainable and morally grounded approach to advancing global peace and security.

FUTURE OUTLOOK: THE ROLE OF DIPLOMACY IN TRADE CONFLICTS

As the global landscape continues to evolve, the inherent interconnectedness of nations is increasingly shaping the direction of economic policy. In the realm of trade conflicts, diplomacy is paramount in steering the course towards mutual understanding and resolution. The future outlook on diplomacy in trade conflicts encompasses multifaceted dimensions—from fostering dialogue and negotiation to building sustainable frameworks for dispute resolution. Leveraging diplomacy as a tool for conflict mitigation requires a comprehensive approach that integrates economic, political, and cultural considerations.

One crucial aspect of the future outlook involves reimagining traditional diplomatic practices to address the complexities of modern trade conflicts. Nations must adapt to the changing dynamics of economic interdependence and recognize the necessity of proactive engagement in constructive dialogue. By embracing a forward-looking mindset, diplomatic efforts can focus on fostering collaboration rather than confrontation, aiming to build bridges across diverse interests and objectives.

Furthermore, the future of diplomacy in trade conflicts necessitates a concerted effort to integrate emerging technological advancements. Digital diplomacy, leveraging digital channels and platforms, enhances communication and promotes transparency in the negotiation process. The utilization of big data analytics and artificial intelligence also holds the potential to provide analytical insights that can inform diplomatic strategies in navigating complex trade disputes.

Another critical consideration in the future outlook is the role of multilateral diplomatic initiatives in addressing trade conflicts. Collaborative approaches through regional and international forums offer enhanced cooperation and consensus-building opportunities. By upholding the principles of inclusivity and shared responsibility, such platforms can effectively mediate trade conflicts and establish common ground for equitable solutions.

Moreover, the future of diplomacy in trade conflicts hinges on cultivating a robust network of professional expertise and knowledge exchange. Investing in diplomatic training and capacity-building programs tailored to the intricacies of trade negotiations can empower diplomats with the requisite skills to navigate the evolving landscape of global commerce. Emphasizing continuous learning and cross-cultural competence equips diplomatic representatives to navigate nuanced economic dynamics and foster sustainable resolutions adeptly.

In summary, the future outlook on diplomacy's role in trade conflicts calls for proactive adaptation, technological integration, multilateral collaboration, and strategic capacity-building. By embracing these principles and leveraging diplomatic acumen, nations can aspire to mitigate trade conflicts and chart a course toward harmonious economic relationships rooted in mutual benefit and cooperation.

CHAPTER 13

Public Opinion and Media Influence in Shaping International Policy

UNDERSTANDING PUBLIC OPINION AND MEDIA DYNAMICS

Understanding public opinion and media dynamics is imperative in comprehending the intricacies of shaping international policy. The interplay between these two components plays a crucial role in influencing decision-making processes at both national and global levels. Public opinion, as a collective representation of individual sentiments, beliefs, and preferences, holds significant sway over policymakers as it reflects the pulse of society. Conversely, media serves as the primary conduit through which public opinion is disseminated, amplified, and sometimes even molded. Recognizing the symbiotic relationship between public opinion and media influence is pivotal in navigating the complex international policy formulation and implementation landscape.

Furthermore, the proliferation of digital platforms and social media has accelerated the interconnectedness of public opinion and media influence, amplifying their impact on the global stage. An in-depth analysis of this dynamic relationship is essential for policymakers and stakeholders operating within international relations. By examining historical precedents, contemporary case studies, and theoretical frameworks, one can gain insights into the intricate mechanisms that underpin the reciprocal interaction between public opinion and media influence. In doing so, it becomes evident that quantitative and qualitative methodologies are indispensable for gauging public sentiment and understanding media dynamics. Additionally, the ethical dimensions of information dissemination, including issues related to bias, manipulation, and propaganda, demand meticulous examination to comprehend the true nature of the forces at play. Hence, the journey to comprehensively grasp the nuances of public opinion and media dynamics begins with acknowledging their dual significance in shaping international policy discourse. This section delves deeply into the multifaceted nature of public opinion and media influence, offering a comprehensive vantage point for readers to appreciate their profound implications in international relations.

THEORETICAL FRAMEWORKS: LINKING PUBLIC OPINION TO POLICY MAKING

Public opinion shapes the foundation upon which policies are formulated and implemented, making it imperative to understand the theoretical frameworks that underpin this critical relationship. The linkage between public sentiment and policymaking has been a subject of extensive academic inquiry in political science. One prominent framework is the 'mandate theory,' which posits that elected representatives derive their authority from the consent of the governed, thereby reflecting the people's will in their policy decisions. This framework emphasizes the importance of public approval as a mandate for policy action, establishing a direct correlation between public opinion and government actions. The 'agenda-setting theory' also postulates that mass media can shape public perception by determining the issues that capture the public's attention, subsequently influencing the policy agenda. This theory highlights the pivotal role of media in framing the discourse and setting the tone for public discourse, which affects policy priorities. Another significant framework is the 'pluralist model', which asserts that diverse interest groups and stakeholders compete to influence policy decisions, reflecting the complex interplay of competing public opinions in the policy-making process. This model considers public opinion as one of many voices shaping policy outcomes, suggesting a nuanced understanding of how public sentiment interacts with other influential factors.

Furthermore, the 'elitist theory' contends that a small, privileged elite holds substantial influence over policy-making, with public opinion viewed as having a limited impact on the decisions of those in power. This theory raises pertinent questions about how public opinion drives policy formulation and implementation, prompting a critical examination of the power dynamics at play. As we delve into these theoretical frameworks, it becomes evident that the relationship between public opinion and policymaking is multifaceted and subject to dynamic influences. By elucidating these frameworks, we gain invaluable insight into the intricate mechanisms through which public sentiment intertwines with the policy landscape, ultimately shaping the course of governance and international relations.

ROLE OF TRADITIONAL MEDIA IN SHAPING PUBLIC OPINION

Traditional media has long been recognized as a pivotal force in shaping public opinion and influencing policy decisions at both national and international levels. Print, broadcast, and radio have historically been primary channels for disseminating information and framing public discourse. The editorial discretion exercised by traditional media outlets plays a significant role in setting the agenda and shaping public perceptions on various issues of global significance. Moreover, through in-depth investigative reporting and journalistic analysis, traditional media can provide nuanced perspectives that influence how audiences interpret complex geopolitical events. The symbiotic relationship between traditional media and policymaking cannot be overstated, as it is often through these channels that governments communicate their policies and initiatives to the public, aiming to garner support and validation. Traditional media also acts as a watchdog, holding governing bodies accountable and scrutinizing their actions to ensure transparency and ethical governance. However, the influence of traditional media is not without its drawbacks. Biases, sensationalism, and selective reporting can distort public opinion and hinder balanced discourse. Furthermore, the emergence of digital media platforms has disrupted the traditional hegemony of print and broadcast media, necessitating a reevaluation of the role and impact of traditional media in the contemporary landscape. Therefore, understanding the historical significance and evolving dynamics of conventional media is imperative in comprehending the intricate interplay between media influence and international policy shaping.

IMPACT OF DIGITAL PLATFORMS AND SOCIAL MEDIA

The impact of digital platforms and social media on shaping public opinion and influencing international policy cannot be overstated. With the advent of digitalization, the global landscape of information dissemination has undergone a profound transformation. Digital platforms and social media have become powerful tools for shaping narratives, mobilizing public opinion, and influencing policy decisions on a global scale. Their pervasive influence extends beyond national borders, transcending traditional limitations and reaching a diverse, interconnected audience that spans continents.

Digital platforms and social media have redefined the dynamics of public discourse, providing a platform for individuals, organizations, and governments to engage with audiences in real-time. This fosters an environment where opinions are expressed, disseminated, and amplified at an unprecedented pace. The immediacy and virality of content on these platforms directly impact how international events are perceived and interpreted by the global populace, thereby shaping public sentiment and influencing policymakers.

Furthermore, democratizing information through digital platforms and social media has empowered individuals and marginalized voices, enabling greater participation in public discourse and offering an alternative space for nuanced discussions on international policy issues. This increased accessibility has also enabled grassroots movements and civil society organizations to mobilize support, raise awareness, and advocate for policy changes, exerting tangible influence on government decision-making processes.

However, the unfiltered nature of information dissemination on digital platforms and social media presents challenges in discerning credible sources from misinformation, disinformation, and propaganda. The proliferation of fake news, echo chambers, and algorithmic biases has contributed to the polarization of public opinion and presented significant obstacles in crafting well-informed, evidence-based international policies.

Moreover, the transnational nature of digital platforms and social media necessitates a reevaluation of regulatory frameworks and enforcement mechanisms to address issues of cyber sovereignty, data privacy, and the spread of harmful content. As such, the increasing influence of digital platforms and social media on shaping international policy underscores the need for proactive measures to safeguard the integrity of public discourse while upholding the principles of freedom of expression and information access in alignment with democratic values.

In conclusion, the impact of digital platforms and social media on shaping public opinion and influencing international policy is a multifaceted phenomenon that warrants comprehensive analysis and strategic considerations. While empowering voices and amplifying advocacy efforts, these platforms also present formidable challenges that require collaborative, multi-stakeholder solutions to navigate effectively in the global arena.

CASE STUDIES: MEDIA INFLUENCE ON POLICY DECISIONS

In the complex landscape of international policymaking, media plays a pivotal role in influencing and shaping decisions taken by governments and international organizations. The impact of media on policy decisions is evidenced by numerous case studies that highlight the direct correlation between media discourse and subsequent policy outcomes. One such illustrative case study is the role of media in shaping public opinion and spurring policy actions during the global climate change negotiations. The extensive coverage of environmental issues by media outlets has increased public awareness, thereby creating pressure on governments to take decisive action on climate change through policy initiatives and international agreements. Another compelling case study revolves around portraying conflicts and humanitarian crises in the media, which often prompts interventionist policies by countries or international bodies. The dissemination of powerful imagery and narratives through various media channels can evoke public outcry, resulting in political leaders being compelled to address these concerns through policy interventions and diplomatic efforts.

Additionally, the influence of media in shaping trade agreements and economic policies cannot be understated. Case studies have demonstrated how media coverage of trade negotiations and economic developments has affected public sentiment and consequently influenced the direction of policy decisions. Moreover, the advent of social media platforms has further intensified the impact of media on policy decisions, enabling real-time dissemination of information and the amplification of public discourse. Case studies analyzing the impact of social media movements on policy decisions, such as the Arab Spring or the #MeToo movement, provide compelling evidence of how online activism can translate into tangible policy changes. Furthermore, the interconnectedness of traditional media and digital platforms has given rise to a multifaceted approach to understanding the influence of media on policy decisions. By examining these case studies, it becomes evident that media holds tremendous power in shaping public opinion and consequently steering the course of policy decisions at both national and international levels. As we delve deeper into these case studies, it becomes increasingly clear that media influence on policy decisions is a dynamic and evolving phenomenon that necessitates critical examination and consideration within international relations and governance.

PUBLIC OPINION POLLS AND THEIR ACCURACY

Public opinion polls and their accuracy are critical when examining the influence of public sentiment on international policy. They are widely used tools to gauge the viewpoints and preferences of a population regarding various socio-political issues. These polls significantly shape policy decisions, providing valuable insights into the prevailing public attitudes and perceptions. However, the accuracy and reliability of these polls have been a subject of debate and scrutiny.

One fundamental consideration in assessing the accuracy of public opinion polls is the methodology employed in conducting the surveys. The sampling method, sample size, and demographic representation are essential factors that influence the credibility of the poll results. Pollsters must ensure that the sample accurately reflects the diversity and composition of the population to avoid biased or skewed outcomes.

Furthermore, the framing of survey questions and the timing of data collection can significantly impact the accuracy of public opinion polls. Biased or leading questions and the context in which the questions are presented can inadvertently influence respondents' answers, compromising the poll's accuracy. Additionally, fluctuations in public opinion over time necessitate continuous monitoring and frequent polling to capture evolving sentiments effectively.

Acknowledging the margin of error associated with opinion polls is also crucial. Statistical calculations determine the margin of error, representing the range within which the actual population value is likely to lie. Understanding and interpreting this margin of error is vital for accurately assessing the significance of poll results and minimizing misinterpretation.

Media outlets and analysts' interpretation and reporting of poll results further contribute to the public's perception and understanding of the data. Sensationalism, selective reporting, or misrepresenting survey findings can distort the public's perception of prevalent opinions and contribute to a miscalculated understanding of public sentiment.

Moreover, the influence of social desirability bias, where respondents may tailor their responses to align with societal norms or expectations, challenges the accuracy of public opinion polls. This phenomenon underscores the complexity of capturing genuine, uninfluenced viewpoints, particularly on sensitive or controversial issues.

In conclusion, while public opinion polls serve as valuable instruments in elucidating public sentiment, their accuracy hinges on methodological rigor, ethical conduct, and transparent reporting. Recognizing the nuances involved in conducting and interpreting these polls is imperative for policymakers and the public alike to comprehend and leverage the true extent of their impact on shaping international policy.

MEDIA OWNERSHIP AND BIAS: GLOBAL PERSPECTIVES

Media ownership and bias are critical factors that significantly influence public opinion and shape international policy across the globe. The interconnected nature of media conglomerates and their ownership structures often raises concerns about biased reporting, lack of diversity in viewpoints, and the influence of corporate interests on editorial decisions. In many countries, a few media organizations dominate the market, potentially homogenizing news content and perspectives. This issue becomes even more pronounced when these media entities are affiliated with or controlled by political or corporate interests, raising questions about the objectivity and independence of the information they disseminate.

Media bias manifests in various forms, including selective reporting, narrative framing, and editorial slants that align with the vested interests of the owners or stakeholders. Such biases can be subtle and nuanced, making it challenging for audiences to discern the underlying agenda behind the presented information. Moreover, diverse voices and marginalized communities may find their perspectives underrepresented or misrepresented in mainstream media, further accentuating the issue of bias.

When examining global perspectives on media ownership and bias, it becomes evident that different regions grapple with unique challenges and regulatory frameworks. Some countries have implemented regulations to limit monopolistic practices and ensure a more balanced representation of opinions in the media landscape. However, the effectiveness of these measures varies, and issues related to censorship, self-censorship, and government control continue to pose significant obstacles to achieving a truly independent and impartial media environment.

Furthermore, the rise of digital media platforms has introduced a new dimension to media ownership and bias discourse. Tech giants wield substantial influence over the dissemination of information, and concerns have been raised about algorithmic biases, echo chambers, and the spread of misinformation amplified by these platforms. As a result, the intersection of traditional and digital media landscapes further complicates the evaluation of ownership and bias, necessitating comprehensive regulatory frameworks that address the evolving nature of media consumption.

In light of these complexities, fostering transparency, promoting media literacy, and advocating for diverse ownership structures are critical steps toward mitigating the influence of bias in the media. Additionally, strengthening ethical guidelines and standards for journalistic integrity can contribute to cultivating a more informed and discerning public, reducing susceptibility to biased narratives. Ultimately, understanding the global panorama of media ownership and bias is indispensable in informing effective policymaking and reinforcing democratic principles that uphold the plurality of voices in the public sphere.

GOVERNMENT RESPONSE TO MEDIA AND PUBLIC SENTIMENT

In an age where media narratives can swiftly influence public sentiment, government response to such trends plays a critical role in shaping domestic and international policies. As the fourth estate continues to evolve with the advent of digital media and social platforms, governments face a double-edged sword – the need to address public concerns while maintaining national interests. Thus, governments must adopt a proactive approach towards media and public sentiment. This involves monitoring media discourse and engaging in transparent communication with the public. Governments must be responsive to genuine public concerns and demonstrate accountability through effective policy measures. This responsiveness may include addressing public grievances discussed in the media, clarifying misconceptions, and outlining strategies to address societal challenges. Ultimately, striking a balance between public sentiment and national interests is a delicate task that requires astute leadership and effective communication strategies. Governments must navigate through the complex web of media influence while upholding democratic values and ensuring the integrity of information dissemination. These efforts are essential for enhancing trust in governance and fostering a constructive relationship between the government, media, and the public.

CHALLENGES IN NEUTRAL REPORTING AND INFORMATION INTEGRITY

Neutral reporting and information integrity are fundamental pillars of a transparent and accountable media landscape, crucial in shaping public opinion and influencing international policy. However, achieving neutrality and upholding information integrity faces numerous challenges in today's complex socio-political milieu. Firstly, the prevalence of sensationalism and clickbait in modern journalism poses a significant threat to impartial reporting. The pursuit of high ratings and digital engagement often leads to the prioritization of captivating headlines over factual accuracy, thereby compromising the credibility of news sources. Additionally, the rise of fake news and disinformation campaigns propagated through social media platforms further erodes trust in traditional media institutions. The ease with which false narratives can be disseminated and amplified online presents a formidable obstacle to maintaining information integrity. Moreover, the politicization and polarization of news outlets exacerbate the challenge of neutral reporting. Media organizations often align themselves with partisan interests, leading to biased coverage and the perpetuation of ideological divides within society.

Furthermore, the evolving nature of media ownership and corporate influence introduces complexities in maintaining editorial independence and unbiased reporting. Consolidation of media conglomerates and the vested interests of influential stakeholders can overshadow journalistic integrity, raising concerns about the potential manipulation of public discourse. Beyond these internal challenges, external pressures, such as government censorship and suppression of dissenting voices, pose significant obstacles to neutral reporting and information integrity. Journalists operating in authoritarian regimes or under repressive legislation often face intimidation, persecution, or even imprisonment for attempting to uphold journalistic standards. These constraints inhibit the free flow of information and curtail the public's right to access diverse viewpoints. As technological advancements reshape the media landscape, ensuring neutral reporting and information integrity demands innovative solutions and heightened vigilance. Embracing transparency in sourcing, fact-checking, and reporting processes is imperative to rebuild public trust. Collaborative efforts between media organizations, civil society, and regulatory bodies can establish industry-wide standards to counter disinformation and safeguard the integrity of information dissemination.

Additionally, promoting media literacy and critical thinking skills among the populace is essential in fostering a discerning audience that can scrutinize and evaluate the integrity of news content. Upholding the principles of ethical journalism and holding media outlets accountable for breaches in professional conduct are pivotal steps toward mitigating challenges to neutral reporting and information integrity. Ultimately, the preservation of these values not only serves the public interest but contributes to the advancement of informed decision-making at the international policy level.

STRATEGIC COMMUNICATION AND POLICY PROMOTION

Strategic communication is pivotal in shaping public opinion and influencing policy outcomes in international relations. As nations navigate global governance's complexities, effectively communicating policies and initiatives becomes indispensable. This section delves into the multifaceted nature of strategic communication and its significant implications for fostering understanding and garnering support from diverse stakeholders worldwide.

At the core of strategic communication is the alignment of messaging with overarching policy objectives. Whether it pertains to trade agreements, security arrangements, or climate action, governments and international organizations must articulate their positions and tailor their messages to resonate with different audiences. Moreover, using various communication channels, including traditional media, social platforms, and diplomatic channels, becomes crucial in reaching global citizens, policymakers, and opinion leaders. While disseminating information, a nuanced approach considering cultural sensitivities and linguistic diversity ensures broader accessibility and relevance of policy narratives.

One formidable challenge in strategic communication lies in countering misinformation and disinformation propagated by malign actors. In an era characterized by information overload and pervasive digital connectivity, the spread of false or misleading content can significantly distort perceptions and undermine the credibility of policy initiatives. To mitigate these risks, governments and international bodies employ sophisticated strategies that encompass fact-based rebuttals, targeted interventions, and proactive engagement with media outlets to uphold the integrity of their messages.

Furthermore, strategic communication extends beyond mere dissemination of information; it encompasses proactive policy promotion aimed at garnering public support and engendering goodwill. Leveraging storytelling techniques and impactful visuals, governments make concerted efforts to humanize policy implications and illustrate their positive impact on people's lives. The use of compelling narratives, success stories, and real-life examples helps bridge the gap between complex policy formulations and individuals' everyday experiences, thereby fostering greater resonance and empathy.

In an interconnected world, where public sentiment and global perceptions hold considerable sway, strategic communication assumes an even more critical role. A coherent, consistent, compelling narrative helps build trust, enhance transparency, and strengthen diplomatic ties. It enables nations to present their policies and actions that align with universal values, ethical standards, and the aspirations of humanity. Through strategic communication, the intricate web of international relations is woven with threads of understanding, concord, and cooperation, paving the way for informed decision-making and sustainable global progress.

CHAPTER 14

Emerging Markets and Future Economic Leaders: Projections for 2050

EMERGING MARKETS

Emerging markets have played an increasingly influential role in the global economy, challenging the dominance of traditional economic powerhouses. These markets, also called developing or growth markets, encompass diverse nations exhibiting rapid industrialization, modernization, and economic progress. Historically, emerging markets were primarily associated with the BRICS nations – Brazil, Russia, India, China, and South Africa. However, the concept has expanded in recent years to include a broader array of countries across Asia, Latin America, Africa, and the Middle East. The evolution of emerging markets has been fueled by a combination of factors, including shifts in geopolitical dynamics, surges in foreign direct investment, technological advancement, and demographic changes. These markets are characterized by their distinct attributes, such as dynamic consumer bases, burgeoning middle classes, resource richness, and untapped potential.

Moreover, their contributions to global trade, innovation, and the overall economic landscape cannot be underestimated. As we delve into this exploration, it is crucial to acknowledge the heterogeneity within emerging markets. Each nation possesses unique socio-economic challenges, structural impediments, and development trajectories. From frontier economies striving for basic infrastructure upgrades to export-driven powerhouses seeking diversification, the spectrum of aspirations and ambitions across these markets is extensive. Recognizing these complexities is pivotal in comprehending the multifaceted nature of economic leadership in the coming decades. Consequently, evaluating emerging markets' prospects as future economic leaders necessitates a nuanced approach that factors in historical legacies, institutional frameworks, policy initiatives, and societal transformations. Through this lens, we aim to assess the evolving dynamics of international finance, trade, and investment in shaping the contours of the global economy. As we chart the course toward 2050 and beyond, understanding the variegated landscape of emerging markets is indispensable for discerning the forces that will propel them toward economic leadership.

DEFINING THE CRITERIA FOR ECONOMIC LEADERSHIP

As the global economic landscape continues to evolve, the criteria for economic leadership in the 21st century are increasingly complex and multidimensional. While traditional markers such as GDP growth and industrial output remain significant, newer parameters have gained prominence in assessing a country's economic leadership potential. One crucial factor is technological advancement, which encompasses the ability to innovate and the capacity to adopt and adapt cutting-edge technologies across various sectors. Furthermore, human capital development has emerged as a critical criterion, focusing on education, skill development, and workforce diversity. Sustainable and inclusive economic policies that consider environmental impact, social equity, and ethical business practices are also recognized as fundamental for long-term economic leadership. Another pivotal aspect is geopolitical influence, including a nation's role in international alliances, regional partnerships, and diplomatic initiatives. Financial stability, transparent governance, and regulatory frameworks that foster innovation and entrepreneurship are critical in determining a country's economic leadership. The ability to navigate global trade dynamics, secure access to resources, and build resilient supply chains further define a nation's economic standing.

Moreover, resilience in the face of economic shocks, pandemics, and geopolitical tensions is becoming an essential criterion for economic leadership. Finally, the capacity for cultural diplomacy, soft power projection, and global engagement is increasingly relevant in shaping a nation's economic leadership trajectory. In essence, economic leadership in the 21st century demands a comprehensive approach that integrates traditional economic indicators with new dimensions such as technological prowess, human capital development, sustainable practices, geopolitical influence, financial stability, resilience, and cultural diplomacy.

TECHNOLOGICAL INNOVATION AS A DRIVER OF ECONOMIC SHIFTS

Technological innovation has been a primary catalyst for transforming the global economic landscape, reshaping industries, and driving profound shifts in economies' operations. In today's interconnected world, technological advancement has accelerated unprecedentedly, influencing emerging markets and incumbent economic leaders' competitive dynamics. The relentless pursuit of innovation has spurred the evolution of existing industries and fostered the emergence of entirely new sectors, revolutionizing traditional business models and creating fresh growth opportunities. Key technological advancements, including artificial intelligence, machine learning, automation, and the Internet of Things, have engendered disruptions across various sectors, from manufacturing and finance to healthcare and transportation.

These advancements have not only propelled efficiency gains but also redefined the skills required for the future workforce.

Furthermore, the rapid proliferation of digital technologies has facilitated the global integration of markets, enabling the seamless flow of information, capital, and talent across borders. This interconnectedness has amplified the impact of technological innovations, fueling economic transformations on a global scale. As emerging markets harness these technological advancements to leapfrog traditional stages of development, they are increasingly posing formidable challenges to established economic powerhouses. The ability of emerging economies to leverage technology for inclusive growth, coupled with their agility in adapting to these transformative changes, has positioned them as dynamic contenders for future economic leadership. Moreover, the collaborative potential of technology has paved the way for cross-border innovation partnerships, enabling knowledge exchange and capacity building among nations. However, technological advancement also presents challenges, including data privacy, cybersecurity, and the displacement of specific job categories due to automation. Therefore, as we delve into the relationship between technology and economic shifts, navigating the dualities and complexities accompanying this progress becomes imperative, ensuring that the benefits of technological innovation are equitably distributed and harnessed for sustainable economic development. By understanding the pervasive influence of technological innovation on economic dynamics, we can gain valuable insights into the evolving global economic order and the potential realignment of future economic leaders.

DEMOGRAPHIC CHANGES AND THEIR ECONOMIC IMPLICATIONS

Demographic shifts play a pivotal role in shaping nations' economic landscapes. As populations evolve, so do the demands for goods, services, and labor. Understanding how demographic changes impact economies is crucial for policymakers, businesses, and investors seeking to anticipate future trends. Many developed economies are experiencing aging populations, leading to a decline in labor supply and increased pressure on social security and healthcare systems. On the other hand, several emerging markets are characterized by youthful demographics, presenting both opportunities and challenges. In such regions, a burgeoning workforce can fuel economic growth and provide adequate employment opportunities and investment in education and skill development. However, rapid population growth risks straining resources and infrastructure if not managed effectively.

Furthermore, urbanization trends are reshaping the economic dynamics of countries. As people migrate from rural areas to cities for better job prospects and amenities, urban centers become hubs for economic activity, innovation, and consumer markets. This shift requires substantial investments in urban infrastructure, housing, and transportation to support the growing urban populations. The rise of megacities presents unique economic opportunities and challenges related to congestion, pollution, and inequality.

In addition to the age and urban-rural composition of populations, changing household structures and family dynamics have implications for consumption patterns, savings behavior, and demand for housing and childcare services. For example, dual-income households often have different spending habits than single-income households, impacting the retail and service sectors. Moreover, an aging population may drive demand for healthcare services, while young families might prioritize education and childcare-related expenditures. These shifts in consumer behavior influence the composition of industries and sectors that experience growth or decline.

Global demographic changes also have international ramifications, particularly in migration and talent mobility. The movement of people across borders influences labor markets, cultural diversity, and consumption patterns. Countries experiencing brain drain due to the emigration of skilled workers face challenges in maintaining innovation and competitiveness. At the same time, immigration can contribute to labor force growth and the enrichment of skills within a nation. Managing these demographic transitions requires a comprehensive understanding of the economic implications and proactive policies to harness the potential benefits while mitigating risks.

Overall, demographic changes are integral to the narrative of economic progress and transformation at national and global levels. Embracing the opportunities presented by evolving demographics and addressing the associated challenges will be imperative for countries aiming to position themselves as future economic leaders in a rapidly changing world.

GOVERNMENT POLICIES AND MARKET LIBERALIZATION

Government policies and market liberalization play a pivotal role in shaping the economic landscape of emerging markets. As these economies strive for growth and integration into the global marketplace, the decisions made by their governments have far-reaching implications. Understanding the impact of government policies and market liberalization is essential for foreseeing these economies' trajectory. One of the key aspects of government policies is the implementation of economic reforms that encourage competition, efficiency, and innovation. This often involves deregulation and privatization of state-owned enterprises, aimed at reducing bureaucratic hurdles and fostering a more conducive environment for business development.

Moreover, fiscal policies such as tax reforms, investment incentives, and public expenditure management are crucial in steering economic activities toward sustainable growth. Market liberalization, on the other hand, entails removing trade barriers, reducing import tariffs, and facilitating foreign investments. These measures attract capital inflows, promote healthy competition, and stimulate the domestic economy. Additionally, encouraging entrepreneurship and small businesses through supportive policies can create jobs and economic dynamism.

However, balancing liberalization and protecting local industries from unfair competition is a delicate task for governments.

Furthermore, legal and regulatory frameworks must be established or reformed to ensure fair practices, protection of intellectual property rights, and transparent governance. This fosters trust among investors and strengthens the rule of law within these economies. An effective judiciary system is vital for enforcing contracts and resolving commercial disputes, providing stability for economic activities to thrive. Successful examples of market liberalization and sound government policies can be seen in countries like China, India, and Brazil, where strategic reforms have propelled them onto the global stage. Nevertheless, challenges persist, and ethnopolitical complexities, corruption, and lack of institutional capacity may hinder the efficient execution of policies. Therefore, assessing the impact of government policies and market liberalization requires a nuanced understanding of each country's unique socio-political context. Finally, international cooperation and knowledge sharing can aid emerging markets in developing and implementing effective policies while learning from the experiences of others.

INFRASTRUCTURE DEVELOPMENT IN EMERGING ECONOMIES

Infrastructure development plays a critical role in emerging economies' economic growth and sustainability. As these countries strive to position themselves as future economic leaders, the need for robust infrastructure becomes increasingly apparent. The term 'infrastructure' encompasses many physical assets and facilities, including transportation networks, energy systems, telecommunications, and water and sanitation facilities. Investment in infrastructure enhances domestic connectivity and efficiency and contributes to these economies' overall attractiveness to foreign investors. One of the primary areas of focus in infrastructure development is transportation. Developing modern and efficient transportation networks, such as roads, railways, ports, and airports, is essential for facilitating trade, connecting remote areas with urban centers, and improving accessibility for both businesses and citizens. In addition to transportation, the energy sector is of paramount importance. Access to reliable and sustainable energy sources is crucial for powering industrial growth, supporting urbanization, and driving technological advancements. This involves investment in power generation, transmission, and distribution infrastructure and promoting renewable energy sources to ensure long-term sustainability. Equally significant is the expansion and enhancement of telecommunications infrastructure. In today's digital age, a strong and resilient telecommunications network is indispensable for fostering innovation, enabling e-commerce, and connecting individuals and businesses within and beyond national borders.

Furthermore, addressing the population's basic needs through adequate water supply and sanitation infrastructure is fundamental for improving public health, enhancing quality of life, and promoting social development. The efficient management and development of infrastructure in emerging economies require coordinated efforts between the public and private sectors and strategic planning and regulatory frameworks that promote transparency, accountability, and long-term sustainability. Furthermore, innovative financing mechanisms, such as public-private partnerships and specialized infrastructure funds, are pivotal in mobilizing the capital for large-scale infrastructure projects. Emerging economies must prioritize infrastructure development to bolster their competitiveness, attract investments, and foster inclusive growth. Failure to address infrastructure gaps may impede their ability to capitalize on their demographic dividends and maneuver the challenges of global economic integration.

INVESTMENT TRENDS AND FOREIGN DIRECT INVESTMENT FLOWS

The evolving landscape of global investment trends and foreign direct investment (FDI) flows has become critical in shaping future economic leaders and emerging markets. As the world economy continues to integrate, the patterns of FDI flows have undergone significant transformations, reflecting the changing dynamics of geopolitical, technological, and demographic factors. This section explores the intricate web of investment trends, highlighting the key drivers, challenges, and implications for investing nations and recipient economies.

The global investment landscape has witnessed a notable shift towards emerging markets and developing economies in recent years. These regions are increasingly attracting substantial FDI inflows due to their vast growth potential, expanding consumer markets, and favorable regulatory reforms to ease restrictions on foreign investments. This trend indicates international investors' confidence in the long-term prospects of these economies, which are perceived as the new frontier for profitable business ventures.

Furthermore, the nature of FDI flows has diversified, encompassing various industries, including technology, renewable energy, infrastructure, and manufacturing. This diversification underscores emerging markets' growing maturity and sophistication, making them attractive destinations for capital deployment across various sectors. Analyzing the sectoral distribution of FDI inflows and identifying the areas where emerging economies exhibit comparative advantages, thus offering lucrative opportunities for foreign investors seeking sustainable returns on their investments, is imperative.

Addressing the associated challenges and complexities is crucial amidst the unprecedented surge in FDI flows. Political instability, regulatory uncertainties, and macroeconomic vulnerabilities pose inherent risks for foreign investors, necessitating a comprehensive risk assessment framework. Moreover, the management of FDI inflows requires adept policy frameworks that strike a balance between promoting economic development and safeguarding national interests. Striking the right equilibrium ensures that FDI contributes to sustainable growth, technology transfer, job creation, and overall societal welfare within the recipient countries.

The intersections between investment trends and geopolitical interests are a compelling dimension to this discourse. The strategic motivations underlying FDI flows can often intersect with broader geopolitical objectives of fostering alliances, securing access to key resources, and exerting influence in pivotal regions. Understanding the geopolitical nuances embedded within FDI flows is indispensable for comprehending the evolving power dynamics in the global economic arena, particularly within the context of emerging markets vying for leadership positions.

In conclusion, scrutinizing the trajectories of investment trends and FDI flows provides invaluable insights into the shifting dynamics of global economic leadership. By meticulously examining international investments' patterns, motivations, and ramifications, stakeholders can gain a nuanced perspective on the interplay of financial prowess, global governance, and strategic positioning. Ultimately, navigating the complex terrain of investment trends is essential for predicting the ascendancy of future economic leaders and identifying the synergies that underpin a more interconnected and prosperous world economy.

ROLE OF EDUCATION AND WORKFORCE DEVELOPMENT

Education and workforce development play pivotal roles in shaping the economic trajectory of nations, particularly in emerging markets. A well-educated and skilled workforce is fundamental for sustainable economic growth, innovation, and global competitiveness.

Education is the bedrock for building human capital, empowering individuals with the knowledge, skills, and capabilities necessary to adapt to evolving market demands. Emerging economies, recognizing the critical link between education and economic prosperity, have invested substantially in expanding educational access and improving curriculum quality. Governments are formulating long-term strategies to enhance primary, secondary, and tertiary education, aiming to equip the population with a diverse set of skills that align with the needs of modern industries and technologies.

Moreover, workforce development programs bridge the gap between academic learning and practical industry requirements. Vocational training initiatives, apprenticeship schemes, and continuing education opportunities contribute to nurturing a skilled workforce that can drive innovation and productivity. In many emerging markets, public-private partnerships are instrumental in designing industry-relevant training programs, ensuring that the workforce possesses the technical proficiencies employers seek.

The globalization of labor markets further accentuates the importance of education and workforce development. As emerging economies integrate into the global supply chain, the demand for a versatile and adaptable workforce becomes increasingly apparent. Cross-cultural competence, fluency in multiple languages, and exposure to international business practices are becoming prerequisites for thriving in a globalized economy. Education systems must respond to these demands by instilling technical competencies and a broader understanding of global contexts and intercultural communication.

In conclusion, education and workforce development cannot be overstated in the context of emerging markets' ascent toward becoming future economic leaders. Governments, educational institutions, and businesses must collaborate in creating comprehensive and forward-looking strategies that nurture human capital, foster continuous learning, and propel the workforce to meet the challenges and opportunities of a rapidly evolving global economy.

EMERGING LEADERS: CASE STUDIES FROM ASIA, AFRICA, AND LATIN AMERICA

In the landscape of global economics, the emergence of new leaders is reshaping the traditional power dynamics. In this section, we delve into case studies from three key regions – Asia, Africa, and Latin America – to identify the standout economies and their potential for leading the world economy in 2050. China is a prime example of an emerging economic giant, starting with Asia. The Chinese economy has experienced unprecedented growth over the past few decades, with a focus on technological innovation and infrastructure development. India, too, presents a compelling case, with its burgeoning population and thriving tech sector positioning it as a future leader. Turning to Africa, Nigeria's vast natural resources and youthful population place it on the path to becoming a significant economic force. South Africa's robust financial sector and strategic regional influence also mark it as a key player in the continent's economic rise. In Latin America, Brazil's diverse economy and industrial prowess position it as a frontrunner in the region, while Mexico's trade connections and manufacturing capabilities signal its potential for global economic leadership. These case studies underscore the diversity and dynamism inherent in emerging markets, highlighting the multifaceted nature of future economic leadership. As we analyze these cases, it becomes evident that these regions are not only engines of growth but also sources of innovation, investment, and talent. By understanding the unique strengths and challenges of each emerging leader, we can gain valuable insights into the future landscape of the world economy.

PROJECTIONS FOR 2050: WHO WILL LEAD THE WORLD ECONOMY?

As we envision the global economic landscape in 2050, it becomes ever more apparent that the rise of emerging markets is poised to redefine the dynamic. Projections indicate a significant shift in the balance of economic power, with countries from Asia, Africa, and Latin America playing pivotal roles. China's robust economic growth and technological advancements make it a formidable contender for a leading role in the world economy. Additionally, India's burgeoning population and rapid urbanization are set to propel it to the forefront of the global stage. These countries' demographic dividends and investments in education and innovation are expected to have a transformative impact on the international economic order.

Turning our gaze towards Africa, the continent's abundant natural resources and youthful population are catalysts for its potential ascension as an economic powerhouse. As African nations focus on infrastructure development and regional economic integration, they will likely emerge as key players in shaping the future world economy. Moreover, with their rich biodiversity and expanding middle class, Latin American countries are positioned to wield substantial influence in the global market. Their emphasis on sustainable development and diversification of industries presents promising prospects for economic leadership.

The convergence of these factors raises thought-provoking questions about the nature of global economic governance in the coming decades. Will traditional Western economies experience a relative decline in influence? How will geopolitical alliances evolve in response to these transformative shifts? As these emerging economies gain momentum, forging mutually beneficial partnerships and fostering economic cooperation will be imperative for sustainable global development. The reconfiguration of trade routes, energy dynamics, and technological innovation is anticipated to reframe the contours of economic supremacy.

Moreover, the concept of economic leadership itself may undergo a paradigm shift. A more diverse and inclusive approach to global economic governance, reflective of the multifaceted contributors to economic progress, may come to the fore. Collaborative frameworks prioritizing equitable participation and balanced representation could replace entrenched hierarchies, leading to a more interconnected and resilient global economy.

In light of these projections, fostering understanding and dialogue among nations will be critical in navigating the complexities of this evolving economic order. Furthermore, nurturing a mindset of adaptability and openness to new ideas will be essential for countries and organizations seeking to thrive amidst these transformative tides. Ultimately, the world economy in 2050 is poised to be shaped by various influences, each contributing its unique hues to the canvas of global prosperity.

CHAPTER 15

Cybersecurity Challenges in a Digitally Connected World

CYBERSECURITY IN THE MODERN ERA

Cybersecurity has become a critical priority in our modern, interconnected world. The evolution of technology and the increasing reliance on digital networks have significantly expanded the threat landscape, making it imperative for individuals, organizations, and nations to safeguard their data and systems from cyber-attacks. Digital transformation has fundamentally altered how we conduct business, communicate, and access information in recent decades. This unprecedented shift has given rise to new vulnerabilities and risks that necessitate a redefined approach to cybersecurity. The growing interconnectivity of devices through the Internet of Things (IoT), the adoption of cloud-based services, and the proliferation of mobile technologies have accentuated the complexity of cyber threats. As a result, the traditional security paradigms have been replaced by dynamic, adaptive models that continuously respond to emerging dangers.

Furthermore, the widespread integration of artificial intelligence and machine learning has enhanced cyber adversaries' capabilities and revolutionized defensive strategies, creating a constant race between security measures and sophisticated attacks. Consequently, understanding the foundational importance of cybersecurity is crucial in addressing these challenges. The linchpin upholds digital assets' integrity, confidentiality, and availability, underpinning the trust essential for online interactions. Ultimately, the strength of our digital future is contingent upon our ability to fortify our cyber defenses, adapt to evolving threats, and foster a culture of proactive resilience against malicious activities.

THREAT LANDSCAPES IN GLOBAL DIGITAL NETWORKS

In today's interconnected digital world, threat landscapes have evolved significantly, presenting immense challenges and complexity for cybersecurity professionals and organizations. The proliferation of digital platforms, internet-of-things (IoT) devices, and cloud computing has expanded the attack surface, making it increasingly difficult to defend against emerging threats. Cybercriminals leverage sophisticated techniques such as social engineering, ransomware, and phishing attacks to infiltrate networks and steal sensitive data. Moreover, nation-state actors engage in cyber espionage and sabotage activities, targeting critical infrastructure and strategic assets. These multifaceted threats underscore the need for a comprehensive approach to cybersecurity. Organizations must proactively assess their vulnerabilities, recognize potential threat vectors, and continually adapt their defenses to mitigate risks.

Furthermore, the advent of advanced persistent threats (APTs) poses a grave danger to global digital networks. APTs are stealthy and continuous in nature, often orchestrated by well-resourced adversaries with specific motives. They can bypass traditional security measures and remain undetected within systems for extended periods, exfiltrating valuable information or disrupting operations. Additionally, the growing interconnectedness between physical and digital systems, as seen in smart cities and industrial control systems, introduces new points of vulnerability. The convergence of IT and operational technology (OT) amplifies the potential impact of cyber-physical attacks, posing unprecedented risks to critical infrastructure and public safety.

The rise of decentralized autonomous organizations (DAOs) and blockchain technology also introduces unique security considerations. While blockchain offers robust cryptographic mechanisms, smart contract vulnerabilities, exchange hacks, and consensus algorithm exploits have exposed significant weaknesses. Moreover, the surge in remote working arrangements and mobile connectivity has expanded the attack surface and exacerbated insider threats. Employees accessing corporate networks from unsecured devices or public Wi-Fi networks create security gaps that threat actors may exploit. To address these challenges, organizations must adopt a multi-layered defense strategy encompassing network segmentation, endpoint protection, encryption, and continuous monitoring. Additionally, proactive threat intelligence gathering and information sharing among industry peers are crucial in identifying emerging risks and swiftly implementing defensive measures.

Real-time threat detection and incident response capabilities are imperative in mitigating the impact of cyber intrusions. Security operations centers (SOCs) equipped with advanced analytics, machine learning algorithms, and behavior-based anomaly detection play a pivotal role in identifying and neutralizing threats. However, effective cybersecurity extends beyond technological measures; it demands a cultural shift towards robust cyber hygiene, awareness training, and a heightened sense of vigilance across all organizational levels. By fostering a cyber-aware workforce and maintaining close collaboration with industry partners, governments, and law enforcement agencies, institutions can collectively fortify global digital networks against persistent and evolving cyber threats.

STATE-SPONSORED CYBER ACTIVITIES: RISKS AND RESPONSES

State-sponsored cyber activities pose significant risks in the context of global cybersecurity. Nation-states increasingly leverage their cyber capabilities to conduct espionage, disrupt critical infrastructure, influence public opinion, and engage in offensive operations against other countries. These activities often have far-reaching consequences, impacting not only the targeted nation but also the international community at large. One of the primary challenges in addressing state-sponsored cyber activities is accurately attributing the attacks to specific actors. Sophisticated attack techniques and proxy entities make it difficult to identify the true source of cyber incursions, leading to complexities in formulating effective response strategies. The responses to state-sponsored cyber activities entail a multi-faceted approach that involves diplomatic, economic, legal, and technical measures. Diplomatic efforts focus on engaging in dialogue with the perpetrating state to communicate concerns, establish norms of behavior in cyberspace, and seek international cooperation in addressing cyber threats. Economic responses may include imposing sanctions or other financial repercussions to deter malicious cyber behavior. Legal mechanisms aim to enhance international cyber law frameworks, promote accountability for state-sponsored cyber attacks, and bolster cybercrime legislation at the national level. From a technical standpoint, defending against state-sponsored cyber activities involves enhancing network security, developing robust intrusion detection systems, and investing in advanced threat intelligence capabilities. Collaboration and information sharing among government agencies, private sector entities, and international partners are crucial in building collective resilience against state-sponsored cyber threats.

Moreover, fostering a culture of cybersecurity awareness and resilience at the societal level is essential in mitigating the impact of such activities. As the digital landscape continues to evolve, nations must adapt and enhance their cybersecurity posture to counter state-sponsored cyber activities effectively. Establishing clear deterrence measures, promoting responsible behavior in cyberspace, and strengthening global partnerships will be instrumental in safeguarding the integrity and security of digital networks in the face of state-sponsored cyber threats.

CORPORATE CYBER DEFENSE STRATEGIES

Corporations face ever-increasing cybersecurity threats in the digital age, with potential consequences ranging from financial loss and reputational damage to regulatory violations and legal liabilities. Therefore, robust corporate cyber defense strategies are imperative to safeguard sensitive data, protect intellectual property, and maintain operational continuity. The foundation of a comprehensive corporate cyber defense strategy lies in proactive risk assessment and threat intelligence. Organizations can implement preventive measures tailored to their specific risk profiles by identifying potential vulnerabilities and understanding prevailing cyber threats. This entails conducting regular security assessments, penetration testing, and vulnerability scanning to mitigate potential weaknesses proactively. Securing network architecture and access control is another crucial aspect of corporate cyber defense. Implementing robust firewalls, intrusion detection systems, and data encryption protocols can fortify the organization's digital perimeter, preventing unauthorized access and data exfiltration.

Moreover, adopting multi-factor authentication and strict access management policies can further bolster the defense against internal and external threats. Furthermore, employee training and awareness programs are pivotal in mitigating human-related cybersecurity risks. Educating employees about phishing scams, social engineering tactics, and best practices for handling sensitive information can significantly reduce the likelihood of insider threats and accidental data breaches. In addition to preventive measures, rapid incident response capabilities are essential components of corporate cyber defense. Establishing a well-defined incident response plan, including clear protocols for threat containment, evidence preservation, and stakeholder communication, ensures an organized and effective response to cyber incidents. This approach minimizes the impact of a breach and facilitates swift recovery. Collaboration with industry peers, information-sharing networks, and cybersecurity forums can provide valuable insights into emerging threats and effective defense measures. Continuous monitoring, threat hunting, and forensic analysis are indispensable in maintaining a resilient cyber defense posture. Leveraging advanced security information and event management (SIEM) tools, endpoint detection and response (EDR) solutions, and threat intelligence feeds enables organizations to detect and respond to threats in real-time, enhancing overall cybersecurity resilience. By integrating these multifaceted strategies, corporations can proactively defend against evolving cyber threats, preserving the integrity and trustworthiness of their operations in an increasingly digital world.

CYBERSECURITY PROTOCOLS AND STANDARDIZATIONS

As the digital landscape evolves, robust cybersecurity protocols and standardizations become increasingly critical. Cyber threats do not adhere to geographical boundaries, so global collaboration on cybersecurity measures is imperative.

Organizations and nations must align their cybersecurity efforts with internationally accepted standards to ensure a unified approach to combating cyber threats. Developing and implementing comprehensive protocols and standards can foster interoperability and information sharing between entities, enabling a more coordinated response to emerging cyber risks. Standardization also facilitates benchmarking and assessment of cybersecurity measures, allowing for continuous improvement in addressing vulnerabilities and mitigating potential attacks. Additionally, adherence to established protocols can enhance trust and confidence among stakeholders, such as businesses, governments, and individuals, in security measures. Moreover, harmonized cybersecurity standards reduce redundant processes and minimize the resources required to address cyber threats, thereby promoting efficiency and cost-effectiveness.

Furthermore, with the proliferation of connected devices and the Internet of Things (IoT), establishing standardized cybersecurity protocols is crucial in safeguarding interconnected systems and preventing widespread disruptions. Policymakers, regulatory bodies, and industry leaders must collaborate in developing and promoting internationally recognized cybersecurity standards adaptable to the evolving threat landscape. By fostering a culture of compliance with cybersecurity protocols and standardizations, organizations and nations can bolster their resilience against cyber threats while contributing to the overall stability of the digital ecosystem. In conclusion, the establishment of robust cybersecurity protocols and standardizations is fundamental in fortifying defenses against cyber threats in an interconnected world. Through collective adherence to established standards, entities can better protect their assets, promote trust, and mitigate the impacts of malicious activities, ultimately contributing to a more secure and resilient digital environment.

PUBLIC-PRIVATE PARTNERSHIPS IN CYBERSECURITY INITIATIVES

In cybersecurity, collaboration between the public and private sectors is essential for addressing the ever-evolving digital threats that permeate our interconnected world. Public-private partnerships (PPPs) are the cornerstone for developing effective and proactive strategies to safeguard critical infrastructure, sensitive information, and economies from cyber attacks. These partnerships bring together the resources, expertise, and capabilities of government entities, corporations, and civil society to collectively mitigate risks and respond to cyber incidents. One of the primary advantages of PPPs is their ability to foster information sharing and intelligence exchange, enabling a more comprehensive understanding of potential threats and vulnerabilities across different industries and national boundaries. Additionally, PPPs facilitate the development of innovative technologies and best practices, promoting an environment of continuous improvement in cybersecurity defense mechanisms. By pooling resources and knowledge, PPPs can significantly enhance incident response capabilities, enabling swifter and more coordinated actions in the face of cyber emergencies.

Furthermore, these collaborations promote the standardization of cybersecurity protocols and frameworks, ensuring a cohesive approach to risk management and resilience building. Moreover, PPPs contribute to the establishment of regulatory guidelines and compliance standards, aligning the efforts of both public and private entities with legal and ethical cybersecurity requirements. The symbiotic relationship between the public and private sectors also extends to capacity building and skill development initiatives, as PPPs support the training of cybersecurity professionals and disseminating best practices in threat detection and mitigation. Governments and industry stakeholders need to recognize the mutual benefits of effective PPPs, including improved threat intelligence, enhanced cybersecurity postures, and more robust defense against persistent and emerging cyber threats. As the digital landscape evolves, fostering and nurturing these collaborative relationships will be crucial in shaping a secure and resilient cyberspace for both present and future generations.

IMPACT OF ARTIFICIAL INTELLIGENCE ON CYBER THREATS AND SECURITY

Artificial intelligence (AI) has emerged as a transformative force in cybersecurity, revolutionizing how organizations defend against and respond to cyber threats. AI's impact on cybersecurity is multi-faceted, offering unprecedented opportunities and new challenges. At the core of AI's influence is its ability to analyze vast amounts of data at speeds unattainable by humans, enabling it to detect anomalies and identify potential threats more effectively than traditional approaches. This enhanced capability empowers cybersecurity professionals to mitigate risks and respond to attacks with greater agility proactively. Additionally, AI is crucial in automating routine security tasks, freeing human resources to focus on more complex and strategic issues.

Furthermore, AI-powered security solutions can evolve in real-time, continuously learning from new data and adapting to evolving threat landscapes. However, the proliferation of AI in cybersecurity also introduces complexities and ethical considerations. As AI becomes increasingly integrated into security infrastructure, concerns around potential vulnerabilities in AI models and the implications of adversarial attacks on AI systems have surfaced. The use of AI in cyber attacks, including automated malware and phishing campaigns, raises questions about the dual-edge nature of AI technology. Moreover, the ethical use and regulation of AI in cybersecurity demand careful consideration, particularly in defining guidelines for the appropriate application of AI-driven defense mechanisms and ensuring transparency in AI decision-making processes. Beyond these considerations, the reliance on AI also necessitates a concerted effort to address issues of bias and fairness in AI algorithms, ensuring that the benefits of AI in cybersecurity are equitably accessible and do not perpetuate existing disparities. As organizations navigate the intersection of AI and cybersecurity, comprehensive strategies must be formulated to harness the potential of AI while mitigating its inherent risks. This involves investing in robust AI-driven security solutions, nurturing a workforce skilled in AI-based defense mechanisms, and fostering global collaboration to establish ethical standards and regulatory frameworks. Ultimately, the effective integration of AI in cybersecurity hinges on a balanced approach that maximizes the advantages of AI while implementing safeguards against potential pitfalls.

LEGAL FRAMEWORKS AND INTERNATIONAL CYBER LAW

As the digital age continues to evolve, the significance of legal frameworks and international cyber law cannot be overstated. In a world where borders hold of minimal importance in the realm of cyberspace, it becomes imperative for nations to establish comprehensive legal structures that address the complexities of cyber activities. The primary objective of international cyber law is to define the rights and responsibilities of state actors, non-state entities, and individuals in the context of cyberspace. It encompasses a wide array of legal considerations, including privacy rights, intellectual property protection, data security, and the regulation of cyber warfare. Formulating effective legal frameworks at both national and international levels is crucial to fostering a secure and predictable environment in cyberspace. Global efforts have been made to establish treaties and agreements that outline norms of behavior, confidence-building measures, and cooperative mechanisms to address cyber threats. However, challenges arise due to the nations' diverse geopolitical priorities and varying levels of technological capabilities. Harmonizing these disparate interests poses a formidable task for policymakers and legal experts globally. An additional layer of complexity arises from the inherently borderless nature of cyber operations, making it difficult to enforce laws across jurisdictions. This underscores the need for enhanced cooperation and coordination among nations to develop universally applicable cyber laws and regulations. From a domestic perspective, nations must work toward enacting tailored legislation that addresses specific cyber-related concerns within their territories. This may include establishing regulatory bodies, data protection laws, and legal frameworks for incident response and digital forensics. Moreover, legal systems need to adapt to the rapidly evolving nature of cyber threats, requiring provisions for regular updates and amendments to statutes and regulations. Emphasizing the pivotal role of cooperation, states must engage in proactive information-sharing and capacity-building initiatives to strengthen legal responses to cyber incidents.

Furthermore, cultivating a cadre of legal professionals with specialized expertise in cyber law is indispensable. Legal education programs and professional development opportunities should be tailored to equip practitioners with the necessary skills to navigate the complex intersections of technology and law. As the digital landscape continues redefining global interactions, establishing clear legal frameworks and robust international cyber law is fundamental to ensuring the stability and security of the interconnected world.

CYBERSECURITY EDUCATION AND WORKFORCE DEVELOPMENT

As the landscape of cyber threats continues to evolve rapidly, the need for skilled cybersecurity professionals has become increasingly crucial. Cybersecurity education is vital in preparing individuals to navigate the complex challenges posed by malicious actors in the digital sphere. The demand for a well-educated workforce capable of deploying advanced security measures, conducting threat assessments, and implementing defensive strategies has never been greater.

In response to this demand, educational institutions and training programs worldwide have developed specialized curricula focusing on cybersecurity. These programs cover many topics, including network security, cryptography, ethical hacking, incident response, and risk management. By providing students with hands-on experience and theoretical knowledge, these programs aim to cultivate a new generation of cybersecurity experts equipped to tackle emerging threats.

Moreover, workforce development initiatives are being spearheaded by industry leaders, government agencies, and non-profit organizations. These initiatives seek to bridge the gap between traditional education and the practical skills demanded by the cybersecurity industry. Internship opportunities, mentorship programs, and apprenticeships are integral components in nurturing talent and providing aspiring professionals with the real-world exposure necessary to thrive in the field.

Recognizing the importance of continuous learning and professional development within the cybersecurity domain is imperative. Given the dynamic nature of cyber threats, practitioners must stay abreast of the latest developments in tactics and technologies. This ongoing education can take various forms, such as attending workshops, obtaining industry certifications, and engaging in community-driven knowledge sharing.

Furthermore, fostering diversity within the cybersecurity workforce is essential for promoting innovation and inclusivity. Encouraging participation from individuals of diverse backgrounds and perspectives not only enhances the talent pool but also brings forth a variety of strategic approaches to addressing cybersecurity challenges. Initiatives promoting gender equality and inclusivity in cybersecurity are gaining traction, aiming to create an environment where everyone has equal opportunities to contribute and excel.

Looking ahead, integrating cybersecurity education into mainstream academic curricula and professional training programs will be pivotal in cultivating a robust and resilient workforce. Additionally, collaborative efforts between academia, industry, and policymakers can lead to establishing standards and best practices that elevate the quality of cybersecurity education and promote continuous improvement. By investing in education and workforce development, societies can fortify their defenses against cyber threats and build sustainable resilience in an increasingly interconnected digital world.

FUTURE TRENDS AND PREDICTIVE ANALYSIS IN CYBERSECURITY

In the rapidly evolving cybersecurity landscape, staying ahead of emerging threats is paramount for organizations and governments worldwide. Predictive analysis is increasingly critical as technology advances in identifying potential cyber risks and developing proactive defense strategies. Looking ahead, several key trends are poised to shape the future of cybersecurity.

One notable trend is the rising prominence of machine learning and artificial intelligence (AI) in cybersecurity. These technologies offer the capability to analyze vast amounts of data in real-time, enabling more accurate threat detection and faster response times. As cyber threats become more sophisticated, AI-driven predictive analysis will be essential in identifying anomalous behavior and preempting potential attacks.

Additionally, the proliferation of Internet of Things (IoT) devices presents both opportunities and challenges for cybersecurity. With billions of interconnected devices, including smart home gadgets, industrial sensors, and medical equipment, the attack surface for cyber threats expands exponentially. Predictive analysis must adapt to the unique vulnerabilities posed by IoT, offering advanced monitoring and anomaly detection capabilities to safeguard interconnected systems.

Another crucial aspect of future cybersecurity trends is an increasing emphasis on behavioral analytics. By understanding typical user behaviors within digital environments, predictive analysis can identify deviations that may signal unauthorized access or malicious activities. Behavioral analytics combined with predictive modeling can enhance security postures by providing early warnings and reducing response times to potential threats.

Furthermore, the cybersecurity landscape will face unprecedented challenges as quantum computing technology progresses. Quantum computing has the potential to render many existing encryption methods obsolete, necessitating innovative approaches to secure data transmission and storage. Predictive analysis must anticipate the implications of quantum computing advancements and develop resilient cryptographic solutions to address these vulnerabilities.

Going forward, international cooperation and information sharing will be pivotal in predicting and mitigating global cyber threats. Collaborative efforts among nations and organizations enable the collection and analysis of threat intelligence worldwide. Predictive analysis can leverage this shared knowledge to forecast potential cyber incidents and bolster defensive measures across borders.

In conclusion, the future of cybersecurity will heavily rely on predictive analysis to anticipate, detect, and mitigate evolving threats. Embracing machine learning, AI, behavioral analytics, and quantum-resistant encryption will be instrumental in shaping effective cybersecurity strategies. By proactively adopting these future trends, organizations can fortify their defenses and protect against the ever-changing cyber threat landscape.

CHAPTER 16

Migration and Human Capital: Critical Factors in Global Success

MIGRATION TRENDS AND HUMAN CAPITAL

In the contemporary global landscape, migration trends and the strategic deployment of human capital have become pivotal factors driving economic growth and societal development. Understanding the intricate interplay between migration and human capital is essential for comprehending the shifting dynamics of labor markets, knowledge economies, and cross-cultural exchange. By delving into the multi-faceted dimensions of this phenomenon, we can glean valuable insights into how nations harness the potential of their diverse populations to fuel innovation, entrepreneurship, and sustainable progress. Moreover, the interconnectedness of migration trends and human capital underscores the need for comprehensive policies that address labor mobility, talent retention, and skills alignment on a global scale. This section will explore the complexities of international migration, the evolving nature of human capital, and their combined influence on the contemporary socio-economic fabric.

THEORETICAL FRAMEWORK: UNDERSTANDING THE MIGRATION-CAPITAL NEXUS

The movement of people across borders profoundly impacts the distribution and accumulation of human capital around the globe. In this theoretical framework, we delve into the intricate relationship between migration and capital, seeking to understand how human mobility influences economic development and prosperity. At its core, the migration-capital nexus encompasses various dimensions, including transferring knowledge, skills, and social capital across different regions and countries. This intellectual exchange can significantly enhance human capital in sending and receiving societies. From a theoretical standpoint, scholars have proposed several models to explain the dynamics of this interplay. The neoclassical economics perspective emphasizes the role of migration in optimizing the allocation of labor and capital, thereby bolstering overall productivity and economic growth.

Moreover, human capital theory posits that migrants bring valuable skills and expertise to their destination countries, positively impacting technological innovation and knowledge-based industries. Additionally, sociological frameworks highlight the social networks formed by migrants, which serve as conduits for transmitting cultural norms, business practices, and entrepreneurial acumen. Understanding these theoretical underpinnings is essential for crafting effective policies that leverage migration and capital formation synergies. By investigating how migrant communities foster innovation, entrepreneurship, and investment in host economies, policymakers can design initiatives to harness the full potential of human capital inflows. Furthermore, analyzing the impact of brain circulation and knowledge spillovers can provide insights into how migration fosters global interconnectedness and cross-border collaborations. Through a nuanced exploration of the migration-capital nexus, we can better appreciate the intricate web of relationships underpinning the contemporary global economy. This understanding will be instrumental in devising strategies that optimize the mutual benefits of migration and capital formation, ensuring sustainable development and inclusive growth for nations worldwide.

CASE STUDIES: MIGRATION AND ITS IMPACT ON NATIONAL ECONOMIES

Migration has been a significant force in shaping the economic landscapes of nations across the globe. In this section, we will delve into compelling case studies that reveal the multifaceted impact of migration on national economies. Each case study provides valuable insights into the complex dynamics, offering a nuanced understanding of the interplay between migration flows and economic outcomes. One such notable case study examines the migration trends in Canada, where skilled migrants have played a pivotal role in driving innovation and filling crucial skill gaps in various industries. By attracting and retaining top talent worldwide, Canada has bolstered its economic competitiveness and achieved remarkable growth in key sectors. Similarly, the case of Germany offers an intriguing perspective on the positive correlation between migration and economic revitalization. With its strategic immigration policies and initiatives to attract skilled workers, Germany has experienced a surge in productivity and innovation, leading to enhanced global prominence.

Conversely, we cannot overlook the challenges witnessed in certain regions, as exemplified by the complexities of migration in parts of sub-Saharan Africa. Here, the impact of brain drain due to the emigration of skilled professionals has posed formidable obstacles to sustainable economic development, highlighting the delicate balance between reaping the benefits of global talent mobility and safeguarding local human capital resources. Furthermore, examining the case of the United Arab Emirates unveils the integral role of migrant labor in fueling the nation's rapid infrastructural and economic expansion. The intricate interdependence between migration patterns and financial performance becomes evident through these diverse case studies, underscoring the critical importance of comprehensive immigration policies and inclusive economic frameworks. Through these real-world examples, we gain insight into how migration catalyzes economic growth yet necessitates astute governance and strategic planning to harness its full potential.

SKILL GAPS AND THE GLOBAL DEMAND FOR TALENT

In today's interconnected world, the demand for talent has transcended geographical boundaries. As economies evolve and integrate with the global marketplace, the need for individuals possessing specific skill sets has become increasingly paramount. However, this demand has highlighted a concerning issue—significant skill gaps in various sectors and regions. Understanding these skill gaps is crucial to addressing the global challenges of migration and human capital.

The global economy is characterized by a relentless pursuit of innovation and technological advancement. As a result, industries are constantly seeking individuals with specialized skills in artificial intelligence, data science, renewable energy, and cybersecurity. This heightened demand for niche expertise has created fierce competition for talent, compelling organizations to cast their recruitment nets wider, often beyond their national borders.

Moreover, demographic shifts and an aging workforce in many developed nations have exacerbated the shortage of skilled labor. The impending retirement of seasoned professionals in key industries and declining birth rates have underscored the urgency of replenishing the workforce with proficient individuals. This has increased reliance on migrant workers to fill essential roles and sustain economic growth.

However, the mismatch between the skills demanded, and those available within domestic labor pools have widened the global talent deficit. Developing countries often grapple with a brain drain as their brightest minds seek opportunities abroad, leaving behind skill shortages and hindering local development. Conversely, advanced economies require specialized skills that may not be readily accessible within their borders, prompting them to recruit talent from overseas actively.

The intersecting dynamics of skill shortages and surpluses across nations contribute to the complex landscape of contemporary migration patterns. To address this, policymakers and stakeholders must proactively identify skill deficits and surpluses at both national and international levels. Collaborative efforts to streamline educational pathways, vocational training programs, and talent exchange initiatives can play a pivotal role in mitigating skill gaps and fostering a more equitable distribution of human capital on a global scale.

Ultimately, enhancing the accessibility of cutting-edge knowledge and expertise will bolster individual career prospects and constitute a vital driver for sustainable economic development. As the global demand for talent continues to outpace localized supply, harnessing the potential of a diverse, skilled workforce through responsive policies will be fundamental in shaping the future of human capital and migration.

MIGRATION POLICIES: COMPARATIVE ANALYSIS OF G7 AND BRICS NATIONS

Migration policies play a pivotal role in shaping the socio-economic landscape of nations, especially in the context of talent retention and attraction. In this section, we will delve into a comparative analysis of migration policies adopted by the G7 and BRICS nations, examining their approaches to immigration, emigration, and the integration of migrants. The G7 countries, comprising the United States, Canada, United Kingdom, Germany, France, Italy, and Japan, have traditionally been sought-after destinations for skilled migrants due to their robust economies and employment opportunities. Conversely, the BRICS nations, including Brazil, Russia, India, China, and South Africa, are witnessing substantial inflows of highly skilled and low-skilled workers, reflecting diverse migration patterns within the bloc. One of the critical distinctions between the migration policies of G7 and BRICS nations is the emphasis on attracting high-skilled workers. While G7 nations typically implement selective immigration systems tailored to attract professionals and individuals with specialized expertise, the BRICS nations showcase a more varied approach, aiming to address labor shortages and knowledge transfer through educational exchange programs and technology partnerships.

Furthermore, the regulatory frameworks surrounding family reunification, asylum, and refugee resettlement differ significantly between the two groups. G7 countries often prioritize family reunification and offer robust mechanisms for refugee protection. In contrast, BRICS nations are increasingly grappling with complex geopolitical challenges influencing their stance on accommodating refugees and asylum seekers. Additionally, the ease of obtaining residency permits, citizenship, and pathways to permanent settlement varies considerably across the G7 and BRICS nations, impacting the overall effectiveness of their migration policies. It is essential to note that while G7 nations have historically established comprehensive immigration laws and administrative structures, some BRICS nations are undergoing reforms to modernize their immigration systems, addressing bureaucratic hurdles and transparency in visa processing. As globalization continues to drive interconnectedness among nations, analyzing and comparing the migration policies of G7 and BRICS nations becomes increasingly pertinent for policymakers, economists, and sociologists. By identifying best practices and areas for improvement, stakeholders can contribute to the development of balanced and inclusive migration policies that align with the evolving needs of societies and global labor markets.

CHALLENGES FACING MIGRANTS: SOCIAL INTEGRATION AND RIGHTS

Social integration and the protection of rights are crucial aspects that shape the experiences of migrants as they navigate the complexities of settling in a new country. One of the primary challenges facing migrants is the issue of social acceptance and integration into their host communities. Cultural differences, language barriers, and discrimination can hinder the smooth assimilation of migrants into local societies. Moreover, stereotypes and misconceptions about migrants often perpetuate social exclusion, making it difficult for them to feel a sense of belonging.

Social integration encompasses various facets, including access to education, healthcare, employment opportunities, and participation in community activities. Lack of adequate support mechanisms can result in marginalization, further exacerbating migrants' struggles. Additionally, the legal frameworks governing migrant rights vary across nations, posing significant challenges in ensuring equitable treatment and protection from exploitation.

Furthermore, the psychological impact of uprooting oneself from familiar surroundings and adapting to a new cultural milieu cannot be underestimated. Migrants often grapple with feelings of alienation, loneliness, and disorientation, which may affect their mental well-being. This emotional burden is compounded by the fear of being ostracized or facing hostility from the local populace.

Regarding rights protection, migrants frequently encounter barriers to justice, healthcare, and social services. They are particularly vulnerable to labor exploitation, human trafficking, and inadequate living conditions. The lack of legal awareness and language barriers adds another layer of complexity to the pursuit of recourse against injustices.

Moreover, family reunification and the preservation of familial ties pose critical challenges, especially when faced with stringent immigration policies and lengthy bureaucratic processes. Separation from loved ones and uncertainty about their welfare can impose immense emotional strain on migrants, affecting their ability to integrate fully into their newfound environments.

To address these multifaceted challenges, comprehensive policies and programs must be implemented to facilitate the social integration of migrants and uphold their fundamental rights. Initiatives that foster intercultural dialogue, promote diversity, and combat prejudices are essential in creating inclusive societies. Furthermore, legal reforms and support services should be tailored to address the specific needs of migrants, providing them with the tools to overcome obstacles and contribute meaningfully to their host countries.

Ultimately, embracing the richness of diverse perspectives and harnessing the potential of migrants fosters social cohesion and enhances the collective prosperity of nations. By championing the rights of migrants and fostering an environment of acceptance and understanding, societies can leverage the invaluable human capital brought forth by migration, paving the way for tremendous global success and unity.

ECONOMIC CONTRIBUTIONS OF IMMIGRANTS: A QUANTITATIVE ANALYSIS

Immigration has been a recurring theme in economic development and prosperity discourse. In this section, we will delve into a comprehensive quantitative analysis of the economic contributions made by immigrants to their host countries. As globalization continues to facilitate the movement of people across borders, understanding the impact of immigration on national economies has become increasingly vital. Through rigorous empirical research and data-driven approaches, we aim to provide an insightful examination of the multifaceted economic effects of immigrant populations.

The economic contributions of immigrants can be discerned across various sectors, including labor markets, entrepreneurship, and innovation. Studies have consistently demonstrated that immigrants play a significant role in driving economic growth by filling gaps in the labor force, particularly in industries that are facing shortages of skilled workers. Their willingness to undertake jobs that native-born citizens may not pursue has proven instrumental in sustaining key sectors such as agriculture, healthcare, and technology.

Moreover, immigrants have displayed remarkable entrepreneurial inclinations, establishing new businesses and contributing to job creation in their adopted homelands. Research indicates that immigrant entrepreneurs have introduced innovative products and services and enhanced competitiveness and productivity within local economies. These endeavors have yielded substantial social and economic benefits, illustrating the dynamism and resourcefulness brought by immigrant talents.

A critical aspect of the quantitative analysis involves examining the fiscal impact of immigrants. Contrary to misconceptions, studies have consistently shown that immigrants contribute positively to public finances through paying taxes and bolstering welfare systems. This empirical evidence dispels prevalent myths and underscores the vital role of immigrants in sustaining social programs and public services. Furthermore, the intergenerational economic mobility of immigrant families has been a subject of interest, shedding light on their long-term socioeconomic contributions.

It is imperative to consider the broader macroeconomic implications in truly comprehending the economic contributions of immigrants. Immigration drives consumption, investment, and demand for goods and services, fostering positive effects on overall economic performance. By harnessing diverse skillsets, immigrants enrich the knowledge base and promote technological diffusion, stimulating productivity gains and driving economic advancement.

As we navigate the landscape of global migration and human capital, this quantitative analysis is an indispensable tool for policymakers, businesses, and scholars to make informed decisions. The empirical insights garnered from this exploration can lead to the formulation of inclusive policies that leverage the potential of diverse workforces, creating prosperous societies that benefit from the manifold economic contributions made by immigrants.

BRAIN DRAIN VS. BRAIN GAIN: BALANCING NATIONAL INTERESTS

In today's globalized world, the movement of skilled workers across borders has sparked debates on the concept of brain drain and brain gain. Brain drain refers to the emigration of highly trained or educated individuals from their home country to seek better opportunities abroad. This phenomenon can have negative implications for the country of origin, as it may lose valuable human capital, leading to a shortage of skilled professionals in critical sectors such as healthcare, technology, and academia. Conversely, brain gain reflects the positive impact when skilled immigrants contribute to their host countries' economic and intellectual growth. It is essential to balance these two aspects to uphold national interests.

Governments often grapple with the dilemma of retaining talented individuals while also acknowledging their citizens' aspiration to explore opportunities beyond their borders. The challenge lies in formulating policies that harness human capital's potential without impeding skilled workers' mobility. One approach involves fostering an environment conducive to innovation and professional development, incentivizing skilled individuals to remain in or return to their home countries. Simultaneously, countries should strive to attract talent by offering competitive employment opportunities, research grants, and supportive immigration policies.

The impact of brain drain and brain gain extends beyond purely economic considerations. It also influences knowledge transfer, cultural diversity, and global interconnectedness. For instance, a diaspora of skilled professionals can serve as a bridge for international collaborations, fostering partnerships and exchanges that benefit both home and host countries. Moreover, dual citizenship and alumni networks facilitate ongoing engagement and skill exchange between nations, promoting a win-win scenario for all stakeholders.

Balancing national interests requires a comprehensive understanding of the socio-economic factors at play. Collaborative efforts among governments, international organizations, and private enterprises can mitigate the adverse effects of brain drain and amplify the benefits of brain gain. By integrating strategies for skills retention, reintegration, and transnational cooperation, countries can work towards maximizing their human capital's potential while respecting individuals' right to pursue global opportunities. Ultimately, embracing the concept of brain circulation – where skills flow freely across borders, contributing to both origin and destination societies – can lead to a more equitable and prosperous global community.

FUTURE TRENDS IN GLOBAL HUMAN CAPITAL

The evolving landscape of global human capital presents many emerging trends poised to shape the future of work, talent acquisition, and economic development. As we venture into the rapidly changing dynamics of the 21st century, several key trends stand out as influential factors in human capital. Firstly, digital transformation and technological advancements continue to redefine the skill sets demanded by industries worldwide. With automation, artificial intelligence, and data analytics becoming increasingly pivotal, the demand for workers proficient in these domains is expected to soar. Secondly, the ongoing demographic shifts, especially in developed economies, will have profound implications on labor forces, prompting organizations and governments to reassess their talent strategies. Many countries' aging population will necessitate innovative knowledge transfer and workforce sustainability approaches.

Similarly, the rising trend of remote and flexible work arrangements reshapes workplace and workforce management. The COVID-19 pandemic has accelerated this shift, reevaluating traditional employment structures and fostering an environment conducive to diverse talent pools. Furthermore, the heightened focus on diversity, equity, and inclusion within organizational settings reflects a cultural shift towards greater societal and environmental consciousness. Businesses that champion diversity not only foster more inclusive workplaces but also tend to yield better financial performance. Finally, the discourse around lifelong learning and upskilling has gained prominence as individuals and corporations recognize the imperative of adaptability and continuous education. Lifelong learning initiatives and investment in employee reskilling programs are becoming integral components of talent development strategies across various sectors. The convergence of these trends underscores the necessity for agile policies and proactive measures to harness the potential of global human capital. A forward-looking approach to talent acquisition, retention, and development will be indispensable in navigating the complexities and opportunities of the evolving human capital landscape.

CONCLUSIONS AND RECOMMENDATIONS FOR POLICY FRAMEWORKS

The future of global human capital is intricately intertwined with migration trends, making it imperative for policymakers to devise comprehensive frameworks that address the evolving needs of sending and receiving countries. The movement of people across borders will continue to shape the socio-economic landscape, creating opportunities and challenges that demand proactive policy responses.

To begin with, nations must adopt a holistic approach to immigration policies, one that prioritizes the attraction and retention of diverse talent while ensuring the socio-economic integration of migrants. This requires streamlining visa processes, leveraging technology to facilitate the recruitment of skilled workers, and promoting inclusive societal attitudes. Moreover, there is a pressing need for international cooperation in managing migration flows, emphasizing burden-sharing and responsibility allocation among nations.

As we look toward the future, it is evident that investing in education and skill development will be paramount for sustaining global competitiveness. Policies to nurture domestic talent and foster innovation must be complemented by initiatives to attract and retain foreign professionals, thereby bolstering the collective human capital base. Additionally, efforts to reduce brain drain from developing nations necessitate targeted strategies, such as knowledge transfer programs and collaborative research ventures.

Furthermore, the protection of migrant rights and the provision of support systems are indispensable components of sound policy frameworks. Access to healthcare, education, legal assistance, and social services should be guaranteed to all individuals, irrespective of their migration status. Comprehensive anti-discrimination laws and enforcement mechanisms are crucial in upholding the dignity and rights of migrants, contributing to societal harmony and shared prosperity.

In light of these considerations, it is recommended that governments engage in evidence-based policymaking, drawing on empirical insights and expert analysis to shape their national agendas. Moreover, establishing dialogue and knowledge exchange platforms between countries can foster best practices and innovative solutions in migration and human capital management. Collaborative initiatives at regional and global levels, guided by the principles of equity and justice, are integral to addressing the complexities of a rapidly changing world.

In conclusion, the convergence of migration and human capital represents an opportunity to cultivate diverse, dynamic societies and robust, innovative economies. As such, developing and implementing effective policy frameworks that harness the potential of global talent while safeguarding the welfare of migrants is not just a choice but a necessity for building a sustainable, interconnected future.

CHAPTER 17

Healthcare, Pandemics, and International Cooperation

GLOBAL HEALTH CHALLENGES

Global health challenges have brought to the forefront the interconnected vulnerabilities of our modern world, exposing the intricate web that binds nations and communities in the face of pandemics and health emergencies. The emergence of novel infectious diseases and the resurgence of known pathogens have underscored the global nature of these threats, transcending geographical boundaries and posing immediate risks to populations worldwide. Amidst this backdrop, it becomes imperative to delve into the implications of these challenges globally, examining the multifaceted impact on public health, socioeconomic stability, and international relations. The interplay between travel, trade, and technology has facilitated the rapid spread of diseases, amplifying the potential for a localized outbreak to escalate into a global crisis. Moreover, demographic shifts, urbanization, and environmental changes have contributed to the complex dynamics of health vulnerabilities, necessitating a reevaluation of existing frameworks for disease prevention, surveillance, and response. Countries find themselves intricately linked through shared risks, mandating collaborative efforts to mitigate the ripple effects of health crises effectively.

Furthermore, healthcare access and resource distribution disparities have emerged as central nodes of vulnerability, accentuating the need for comprehensive strategies that address the inequities driving global health disparities. In essence, understanding the interconnected vulnerabilities exposed by global health emergencies is a matter of public health concern and an indispensable aspect of international cooperation, resilience building, and sustainable development. By exploring the intricate tapestry of interconnected vulnerabilities, we can pave the way for proactive, cohesive approaches to confront and mitigate the far-reaching consequences of global health challenges.

HISTORICAL OVERVIEW OF PANDEMICS AND THEIR IMPACT

In examining the historical landscape of pandemics, it becomes evident that throughout the ages, humanity has been confronted with severe disease outbreaks that have left an indelible mark on societies and economies. From the Black Death in the 14th century to the Spanish flu in 1918, pandemics have reshaped the course of history, causing devastation and catalyzing significant societal changes. The relentless onslaught of pandemics has underscored the critical need for proactive measures to mitigate their impact and prevent catastrophic consequences. These global health crises have often laid bare the vulnerabilities within healthcare systems and revealed the world's interconnectedness in the face of infectious diseases. The narrative of pandemics serves as a stark reminder of the potential magnitude of the threat they pose to global stability and prosperity, transcending geographical, cultural, and socioeconomic boundaries.

Moreover, the historical review unveils the profound lessons learned from each pandemic, highlighting the necessity for robust, integrated global health strategies and collaborative efforts to combat and contain emerging infectious diseases effectively. Furthermore, examining past pandemics underscores the intrinsic link between public health and international cooperation, emphasizing the imperative for solidarity and coordinated action on a global scale. Understanding the historical context of pandemics allows us to glean valuable insights into the patterns and repercussions of these catastrophic events, informing our approach to current and future challenges in global health security.

HEALTH SYSTEMS PREPAREDNESS AND RESPONSE MECHANISMS

Amidst the interconnectedness of our modern world, health systems preparedness and response mechanisms have emerged as critical components in safeguarding global public health. The tumultuous landscape of pandemics and health crises necessitates a proactive stance towards mitigating their impact. Health systems preparedness encompasses a spectrum of measures, ranging from robust surveillance and early detection to efficient resource allocation and rapid response capabilities. Each nation's ability to anticipate, prevent, and effectively manage health emergencies reflects its internal resilience and commitment to international cooperation.

To address health crises effectively, health systems must have resilient infrastructure, cutting-edge technologies, and well-coordinated multisectoral collaborations. This involves bolstering healthcare facilities, ensuring an adequate supply of medical resources, and implementing comprehensive protocols for emergency response. Moreover, integrating digital health systems, real-time data analytics, and artificial intelligence offers promising avenues for enhancing early warning systems and decision-making processes during outbreaks.

The establishment of efficient response mechanisms is equally imperative in combating health crises. Prompt and transparent communication between local, national, and international health authorities is crucial for disseminating vital information, coordinating containment efforts, and facilitating the equitable distribution of medical supplies. Furthermore, adapting evidence-based strategies, dynamic risk assessments and simulation exercises enhances the readiness of health systems to tackle unforeseen challenges.

International collaboration is the cornerstone of effective health systems preparedness and response. Multilateral platforms and organizations play a pivotal role in fostering information sharing, harmonizing response efforts, and mobilizing financial and technical support for vulnerable regions. Through collaborative frameworks, such as the World Health Organization's International Health Regulations (IHR), nations can navigate intricate challenges by fortifying their public health capacities and solidarity in times of crisis.

Building resilient health systems and response mechanisms demands unwavering commitment, steadfast cooperation, and continual innovation. By investing in proactive preparedness, harnessing the power of emerging technologies, and nurturing a culture of international solidarity, nations can strive towards a future where the specter of pandemics is met with resolute unity and effective action.

ROLE OF INTERNATIONAL ORGANIZATIONS IN HEALTH CRISES

International organizations play a pivotal role in addressing and mitigating global health crises. With their broad mandates encompassing public health, emergency response, and humanitarian aid, these entities are at the forefront of coordinating international efforts to combat outbreaks, pandemics, and epidemics. As the leading global health authority, the World Health Organization (WHO) spearheads collaborative actions by providing technical guidance, mobilizing resources, and establishing protocols for disease surveillance and control. WHO's role in convening experts and member states to share information and strategies has been instrumental in shaping an effective global response to health emergencies. Additionally, organizations such as the Centers for

Disease Control and Prevention (CDC) and the European Centre for Disease Prevention and Control (ECDC) contribute expertise in disease surveillance, risk assessment, and capacity building, thus facilitating early detection and containment of potential health threats. Beyond these specialized agencies, multi-sectoral bodies like the United Nations (UN) and the International Red Cross and Red Crescent Movement play crucial roles in providing humanitarian aid, mobilizing resources, and advocating for equitable access to healthcare during crises. Their efforts often involve coordination with local governments, healthcare systems, and non-governmental organizations to ensure a cohesive and sustainable approach to health crisis management.

Furthermore, international financial institutions such as the World Bank and regional development banks have allocated significant funding to strengthen healthcare infrastructure and support health system resilience in vulnerable regions. Leveraging their extensive networks and expertise, these organizations foster partnerships, facilitate knowledge sharing, and provide technical assistance to bolster countries' preparedness and response capacities. Nevertheless, challenges persist in achieving seamless collaboration and coordination among diverse stakeholders, necessitating continued efforts to streamline communication, resource allocation, and decision-making processes in times of crisis. As the landscape of global health threats continues to evolve, the indispensable role of international organizations in fostering solidarity, innovation, and resilience remains paramount in safeguarding public health on a global scale.

TECHNOLOGICAL INNOVATIONS IN DISEASE SURVEILLANCE

In the modern era, technological advancements have dramatically transformed the landscape of disease surveillance, revolutionizing our ability to detect, track, and respond to health threats on a global scale. From traditional epidemiological methods to cutting-edge digital tools, the arsenal for monitoring and managing infectious diseases has expanded exponentially. This section delves into the myriad technological innovations in disease surveillance, examining their impact on public health and international cooperation. One of the most pivotal developments is the rise of digital surveillance systems that harness big data, artificial intelligence, and machine learning algorithms to identify patterns and anomalies in disease spread rapidly. These advanced analytics enable early detection of outbreaks, facilitating prompt intervention and containment efforts.

Furthermore, integrating geospatial mapping technologies has empowered health authorities to visualize and interpret epidemiological data in real time, enhancing situational awareness and strategic decision-making. Additionally, the utilization of mobile health applications and wearable devices has extended the reach of disease surveillance to the individual level, enabling real-time symptom reporting and geo-tagged tracking of potential exposure hotspots. This participatory approach empowers individuals to contribute to public health efforts and facilitates the timely identification of emerging clusters and trends. Moreover, the advent of genomics and molecular diagnostics has redefined pathogen characterization and surveillance, offering unprecedented insights into the genetic makeup and evolution of infectious agents. Whole genome sequencing and bioinformatics have revolutionized our understanding of disease transmission dynamics, facilitating the development of targeted interventions and personalized treatment modalities. Acknowledging the vital role of international collaboration in leveraging these technological innovations for effective disease surveillance is essential. Interconnected global health networks and information-sharing platforms enable rapid dissemination of critical data and best practices, fostering a collective response to emerging health threats. Integrating digital surveillance technologies with international reporting systems has fostered a more coordinated and transparent approach to global health security. However, alongside the opportunities presented by technological advancements, there are concurrent challenges such as ensuring data privacy, equity in access to technology, and building capacity in resource-constrained settings. As we navigate the evolving disease surveillance landscape, embracing ethical, inclusive, and sustainable technological solutions will be paramount in shaping a resilient global health architecture.

CASE STUDIES OF EFFECTIVE CROSS-BORDER HEALTH INTERVENTIONS

In today's interconnected world, global health challenges often require collaborative and cross-border interventions to address complex issues effectively. This section will delve into several compelling case studies that exemplify successful cross-border health initiatives. We will explore the coordinated efforts of countries, international organizations, and non-governmental entities in mitigating the impact of pandemics, improving healthcare delivery, and bolstering public health infrastructure across national boundaries.

One noteworthy case study revolves around the concerted response to the Ebola outbreak in West Africa. Amidst this unprecedented health crisis, numerous nations and humanitarian organizations joined forces to provide medical expertise, essential supplies, and logistical support to contain the spread of the virus. The collaboration encompassed immediate emergency aid and long-term capacity building, which proved pivotal in preventing future outbreaks.

Another compelling example pertains to the global initiative to combat HIV/AIDS. Through bilateral and multilateral partnerships, various countries have successfully pooled resources to enhance access to antiretroviral therapy, implement awareness programs, and support vulnerable populations. The sharing of best practices and innovations has been instrumental in reducing the prevalence of HIV and improving the quality of life for affected individuals worldwide.

Furthermore, the response to the COVID-19 pandemic has underscored the critical importance of cross-border collaboration in addressing emergent health crises. Multinational research consortia, rapid information sharing, and the equitable distribution of vaccines are indicative of the collective efforts aimed at curbing the pandemic's global impact. These collaborative endeavors have exemplified the significance of solidarity and mutual assistance in safeguarding public health.

The successful case studies presented in this chapter demonstrate that effective cross-border health interventions hinge upon shared goals, transparent communication, resource pooling, and mutual accountability among participating entities. By examining these examples, we gain valuable insights into the mechanisms that underpin successful global health cooperation, thereby paving the way for future strategies to confront health challenges collectively.

FUNDING AND RESOURCES ALLOCATION FOR GLOBAL HEALTH

The global community faces an ongoing challenge in allocating adequate funding and resources to address the myriad health needs across borders. During a pandemic, such as the recent COVID-19 crisis, the strain on healthcare systems underscores the crucial importance of robust funding and effective resource management. To strengthen global health security, nations and international organizations need to prioritize and allocate sufficient funding to build resilient healthcare infrastructure, strengthen disease surveillance, and improve emergency response capabilities.

In global health, financial resources are pivotal in bolstering public health interventions, research and development of vaccines and treatments, and ensuring universal access to essential healthcare services. Adequate funding enables countries to enhance their preparedness for health crises, establish rapid response mechanisms, and deploy critical medical supplies during emergencies. Moreover, sustained investments in bolstering healthcare systems in low- and middle-income countries can significantly impact population health outcomes globally.

However, while financial resources are crucial, these funds' equitable allocation and efficient utilization are equally significant. Nations must collaborate through intergovernmental initiatives to ensure that funding is channeled towards initiatives that yield the most significant impact. Additionally, transparency and accountability in resource allocation are paramount to maintaining trust and facilitating practical stakeholder cooperation.

Furthermore, it is essential to acknowledge the importance of long-term sustainable financing mechanisms for global health. Volatile funding streams can impede the continuity of vital health programs, disrupt disease control efforts, and limit the capacity for proactive health system strengthening. Therefore, fostering sustainable financial frameworks, such as innovative financing mechanisms and multilateral partnerships, can bolster long-term resilience in addressing global health challenges.

Another critical aspect of resource allocation pertains to human resources, technological advancements, and logistical support. Building and retaining a skilled workforce in the public health sector, harnessing technology for efficient healthcare delivery, and optimizing supply chain management play pivotal roles in maximizing the impact of allocated resources. Investment in research and development is also instrumental in driving progress toward novel solutions, advancing medical innovations, and ultimately mitigating the burden of diseases on a global scale.

Addressing the funding and resource allocation gaps in global health necessitates a collective effort from all stakeholders, including governments, philanthropic organizations, private sector entities, and civil society. By pooling resources, sharing best practices, and aligning strategies, the global community can work towards achieving health equity, promoting sustained investment in healthcare, and building a more resilient and responsive global health architecture for current and future generations.

LEGAL AND ETHICAL CONSIDERATIONS IN THE FACE OF PANDEMICS

In the face of pandemics, addressing legal and ethical considerations is paramount to ensure a coordinated and just response. The intersection of public health emergencies with legal and ethical frameworks presents complex challenges that require careful navigation. One of the fundamental ethical considerations during pandemics is the balance between protecting public health and respecting individual liberties and rights. Governments and health agencies must carefully weigh the implementation of public health interventions against potential infringements on civil liberties, privacy, and autonomy. Crises often prompt the need for temporary measures, but the oversight and transparency of such actions are crucial to maintaining trust and legitimacy.

Additionally, allocating scarce medical resources raises ethical dilemmas, as healthcare providers face difficult decisions regarding prioritizing care and distributing life-saving treatments. Transparency, equity, and accountability should underpin the decision-making process to uphold ethical principles in resource allocation. From a legal perspective, clarity in jurisdiction, authority, and responsibilities is essential to facilitate a cohesive pandemic response. Nations may encounter challenges in harmonizing legal frameworks across borders, particularly in quarantine, travel restrictions, and data sharing. Collaborative efforts to establish international legal standards and agreements can streamline pandemic response and enhance mutual support.

Furthermore, the ethical implications of research practices and experimentation amid outbreaks necessitate stringent ethical review processes and international cooperation to uphold research integrity and protect vulnerable populations. The moral dimension extends to issues of misinformation and disinformation, emphasizing the importance of truthful, transparent communication from authorities and credible sources. Awareness of cultural and social contexts is crucial in effectively shaping communication strategies to combat misinformation. Across these domains, respect for human rights and ethical norms remains imperative. Ultimately, balancing upholding public health imperatives and safeguarding individual liberties requires ongoing dialogue, engagement, and adaptability within a robust legal and ethical framework. By integrating these considerations into pandemic preparedness and response plans, nations can mitigate risks and demonstrate commitment to preserving human dignity and well-being amidst crises.

BUILDING RESILIENT HEALTHCARE INFRASTRUCTURE

Building resilient healthcare infrastructure is imperative for addressing the current global health challenges and preparing for future pandemics and health crises. The foundation of a robust healthcare infrastructure lies in establishing well-equipped medical facilities, a trained workforce, and effective supply chain management. Investing in state-of-the-art medical technologies, strengthening public health surveillance systems, and enhancing access to essential medicines and vaccines are vital to building resilience. Additionally, ensuring equitable distribution of healthcare resources and services across geographical regions is necessary to mitigate healthcare access and outcomes disparities. Integrating traditional and digital healthcare platforms to optimize patient care delivery and health information management is crucial. Collaborative efforts between public and private sectors and international partnerships play a pivotal role in bolstering healthcare infrastructure, particularly in resource-constrained settings. Moreover, advancing research and development in medical science and promoting interdisciplinary collaboration can lead to groundbreaking disease prevention, diagnostics, and treatment innovations. Sustainable funding mechanisms and innovative financing models are essential to support the maintenance and expansion of healthcare infrastructure.

Furthermore, emphasizing community engagement and health education programs can empower individuals to actively manage their health actively, thereby reducing the burden on healthcare systems. Embracing the concept of universal health coverage and prioritizing primary healthcare services are fundamental steps in building resilient healthcare infrastructure globally. By focusing on preventive measures, early detection, and timely interventions, healthcare systems can better withstand and respond to public health emergencies. In conclusion, building resilient healthcare infrastructure necessitates a multi-faceted approach encompassing investments in infrastructure, technology, human resources, and collaborative partnerships at local, national, and international levels, aiming to safeguard populations' health and well-being worldwide.

FUTURE DIRECTIONS FOR ENHANCED INTERNATIONAL COOPERATION

In the wake of the unprecedented global health crisis, it has become evident that enhanced international cooperation is imperative to build a more resilient and responsive healthcare ecosystem. Several key areas present opportunities for countries and international bodies to collaborate and strengthen their collective capacity to address future pandemics and health challenges.

First and foremost, there is a pressing need to establish a more robust framework for information sharing and data exchange among nations. Real-time access to accurate and comprehensive health data is crucial for early detection, rapid response, and effective containment of emerging threats. This involves ensuring the transparency and accuracy of reporting within individual countries and fostering a culture of open collaboration in sharing vital health information across borders.

Furthermore, developing coordinated global strategies for vaccine research, production, and distribution is essential for addressing future pandemics. This entails establishing mechanisms for equitable access to vaccines and therapeutics and promoting technology transfer and knowledge sharing to bolster vaccine manufacturing capabilities in developing regions. Collaborative efforts in research and development can lead to breakthroughs in novel vaccine technologies and broad-spectrum antiviral treatments, offering invaluable tools for combating a wide range of pathogens.

Another critical aspect of enhanced international cooperation lies in advancing the resilience of healthcare supply chains. Diversification of production facilities, stockpiling essential medical resources, and coordinated contingency planning are vital to building a more resilient and agile supply chain infrastructure. By working together to mitigate potential disruptions and shortages, countries can better ensure the continuous and equitable availability of medical supplies during health crises.

Moreover, it is paramount to implement unified preparedness and response frameworks at regional and global levels. This involves harmonizing surveillance systems, standardizing protocols for public health interventions, and conducting joint training exercises to enhance the collective readiness of healthcare personnel. Strengthening partnerships between public health agencies, emergency response organizations, and humanitarian aid providers can significantly improve the coordination and effectiveness of international responses to health emergencies.

In addition to these measures, financial commitments and resource mobilization are integral to bolstering global health security. Investment in pandemic preparedness, healthcare infrastructure, and capacity-building initiatives is crucial for fortifying national and international defenses against future health threats. Furthermore, streamlining funding mechanisms and fostering greater coherence in international aid efforts can maximize the impact of resource allocation and expedite targeted support to vulnerable populations and healthcare systems.

Ultimately, sustained political will and diplomatic collaboration are indispensable for driving these future directions for enhanced international cooperation in global health. Establishing platforms for high-level dialogue, forging new health security agreements, and elevating health diplomacy's role in international relations can facilitate inclusive and actionable strategies for collective action. By harnessing the strengths and expertise of diverse nations, the global community can build a more interconnected and resilient defense against the unpredictable landscape of infectious diseases and pandemics.

CHAPTER 18

Global Terrorism and Security Measures by G7 and BRICS

TERRORISM IN THE GLOBAL CONTEXT

Terrorism is a persistent global challenge that has thrived in the interconnected world shaped by globalization. The increased ease of communication, travel, and resource mobilization across international borders has significantly amplified the transnational nature of modern terrorism. This globalized environment has provided terrorist groups with unprecedented opportunities to organize, recruit, and carry out attacks with relative mobility and anonymity.

The impact of globalization on terrorism cannot be understated. The removal of traditional barriers to communication and movement has enabled extremist ideologies and strategies to transcend geographical boundaries, fostering a networked approach to perpetrating acts of terror. Moreover, the interconnectedness of financial systems and supply chains has facilitated the flow of resources essential for sustaining terrorist activities, further blurring the lines between domestic and international security concerns.

International boundaries have played a pivotal role in influencing the nature and scope of terrorist activities. The porosity of borders has allowed for the seamless movement of individuals, weaponry, and illicit funding, complicating the task of national law enforcement and security agencies in detecting and thwarting potential threats. Additionally, the availability of safe havens and cross-border sanctuary has afforded terrorist organizations the capacity to operate beyond the reach of singular jurisdictions, making coordinated international efforts imperative in combating terrorism.

Understanding the interplay between globalization, international borders, and the dynamics of terrorism is essential for devising effective counterterrorism measures that transcend conventional national security paradigms. By acknowledging the complexities of this multifaceted threat landscape, policymakers and security experts can better comprehend the strategic imperatives required to confront and mitigate the evolving challenges posed by transnational terrorism.

HISTORICAL OVERVIEW OF TERRORISM: G7 VS. BRICS

Terrorism has been a constant threat to global peace and security, with the G7 nations and BRICS countries experiencing distinct historical trajectories in dealing with this menace. The emergence of modern terrorism traces back to different events in the 20th century, shaping the response of these two influential groups of nations. The G7, comprising major industrialized democracies, faced significant challenges during the Cold War era due to the rise of state-sponsored terrorism and ideological conflicts. On the other hand, the BRICS countries, representing major emerging economies, encountered terrorism primarily in the form of non-state actors and separatist movements influenced by colonial legacies and internal power struggles. The divergent historical experiences have shaped the perceptions and approaches of both the G7 and BRICS towards fighting terrorism and promoting global security. Understanding their unique historical contexts is crucial for devising effective collaborative strategies against terrorism in the contemporary world.

EVOLVING THREATS AND SECURITY CONCERNS IN G7 NATIONS

Terrorism poses a significant and evolving threat to the G7 nations, which encompass Canada, France, Germany, Italy, Japan, the United Kingdom, and the United States. The multifaceted nature of modern terrorism presents complex security concerns that require comprehensive and adaptive strategies. In recent decades, the rise of non-state terrorist actors, such as Al-Qaeda and ISIS, has transformed the security landscape, prompting G7 nations to reassess their security measures continuously.

One of the primary security concerns facing G7 nations is the persistent threat of radicalization and homegrown terrorism. Radicalized individuals, often influenced by extremist ideologies disseminated through online platforms and social networks, pose a formidable challenge to law enforcement and intelligence agencies. Moreover, the interconnectedness of global finance and technology has facilitated the proliferation of cyberterrorism, which has the potential to disrupt critical infrastructure and destabilize national security.

In addition to traditional threats, G7 nations are also confronted with asymmetric warfare tactics employed by terrorist groups. These methods include the use of improvised explosive devices (IEDs), guerrilla warfare, and the exploitation of mass media for propaganda dissemination. Moreover, the proliferation of sophisticated weaponry and the illicit trade of arms further exacerbate security vulnerabilities within G7 nations.

The diversity of threats faced by G7 nations underscores the necessity for cross-border collaboration and information sharing among security agencies. The fluidity of transnational terrorism necessitates international cooperation in intelligence gathering, surveillance, and joint operations. Furthermore, as debates on privacy laws and government surveillance intensify, the G7 nations must navigate the delicate balance between protecting civil liberties and effectively countering terrorism.

As threats continue to evolve, G7 nations are compelled to adopt proactive and anticipatory security measures. This includes investments in advanced technologies for threat detection, enhancing border security protocols, and bolstering counter-radicalization initiatives. Moreover, fostering international partnerships with non-G7 countries and engaging in multilateral forums such as the United Nations Security Council are instrumental in addressing the global dimension of terrorism.

SECURITY AGENCIES AND THEIR ROLES WITHIN THE G7

Within the G7 nations, security agencies play a pivotal role in safeguarding their respective countries from the evolving threats of terrorism. These agencies are responsible for gathering intelligence, analyzing potential risks, and implementing strategies to mitigate security breaches. The Federal Bureau of Investigation (FBI) is a prominent agency focused on counterterrorism efforts in the United States. With a wide-reaching network and specialized task forces, the FBI operates both domestically and internationally to identify and neutralize terrorist threats.

The United Kingdom's security apparatus includes MI5 and MI6, which specialize in domestic security and foreign intelligence operations. These agencies coordinate to monitor and disrupt terrorist activities and share critical intelligence with international partners. France's Direction Générale de la Sécurité Intérieure (DGSI) and Germany's Bundesamt für Verfassungsschutz (BfV) are also instrumental in identifying and neutralizing threats within their borders.

In addition to specific national agencies, the G7 also leverages collaborative efforts through established international organizations such as INTERPOL and Europol. These organizations facilitate multilateral cooperation, information sharing, and joint operations to combat cross-border terrorism. Furthermore, the G7 nations have established joint task forces and intelligence-sharing agreements to enhance global security.

The roles of these security agencies extend beyond traditional intelligence gathering to encompass proactive measures such as cybersecurity initiatives, border security, and counter-radicalization programs. Integrating advanced technology and data analytics has further enabled these agencies to anticipate and prevent potential terrorist threats.

Effective communication and coordination among security agencies are crucial in addressing transnational security challenges. Regular joint exercises, simulated emergency responses, and real-time information sharing are fundamental to maintaining preparedness against evolving threats. Moreover, continuous adaptation to emerging trends and advancements in tactics employed by terrorist organizations is essential for ensuring effective response mechanisms.

As the landscape of terrorism evolves, the collaboration and synergy among G7 security agencies remain vital in confronting global security threats. By fostering partnerships, sharing best practices, and harnessing technological advancements, these agencies aim to uphold the safety of their citizens and contribute to a more secure international environment.

COUNTERTERRORISM STRATEGIES USED BY BRICS COUNTRIES

In the global fight against terrorism, BRICS countries have implemented diverse strategies to counter and prevent terrorist activities within their borders and beyond. Each member nation – Brazil, Russia, India, China, and South Africa – faces unique challenges and employs various measures to combat terrorism effectively. Brazil, for instance, has focused on strengthening its border security and enhancing intelligence-sharing capabilities among law enforcement agencies to thwart potential threats. Meanwhile, Russia has employed a blend of military and diplomatic approaches in addressing terrorism, especially in regions such as Chechnya. India, with its long-standing experience in dealing with cross-border terrorism, has emphasized international cooperation while maintaining a solid focus on intelligence gathering and technological advancements in surveillance and counterterrorism operations. China, amidst its domestic security concerns, has employed stringent measures and technological innovations to combat extremism and separatist movements in its volatile regions like Xinjiang.

Furthermore, South Africa has prioritized regional coordination and collaboration with neighboring nations to tackle terrorism and extremist ideologies. Notably, BRICS nations have also engaged in joint military exercises, intelligence-sharing initiatives, and capacity-building programs to bolster their collective counterterrorism efforts. While there may be disparities in the approaches adopted by each country, the collaboration and exchange of best practices within the BRICS framework have contributed to a more proactive and unified response to the global menace of terrorism. Understanding and analyzing these distinctive strategies makes it apparent that BRICS nations have invested significant resources and expertise into combating terrorism while navigating the complex geopolitical and ideological landscapes.

COLLABORATIVE EFFORTS AGAINST TERRORISM BETWEEN G7 AND BRICS

In the face of growing global terrorism threats, collaborative efforts between the G7 and BRICS countries have become imperative to ensure the safety and security of nations and their citizens. Despite geopolitical differences and varying ideologies, both groups recognize the need for unified action against terrorism, which transcends borders and impacts every corner of the globe.

Collaboration between the G7 and BRICS involves information sharing, joint training exercises, and intelligence cooperation to combat terrorist organizations. While the G7 nations possess advanced technology and extensive experience in counterterrorism measures, the

BRICS countries bring diverse perspectives and innovative strategies to the table.

One key collaboration area is the exchange of best practices in border security, cybersecurity, and financial monitoring to prevent illicit funding channels for terrorist activities. Both groups recognize the importance of addressing the root causes of radicalization and implementing proactive measures to disrupt terrorist networks before they can execute their plans.

Furthermore, collaborative efforts extend to diplomatic channels, where the G7 and BRICS engage in dialogues aimed at establishing a unified stance against state-sponsored terrorism and violent extremist ideologies. Through multilateral forums and international conventions, joint declarations are made to condemn acts of terror and strengthen legal frameworks for prosecuting terrorists and their supporters.

Mutual assistance in capacity-building programs, such as training local law enforcement and enhancing crisis response capabilities, is another pivotal aspect of collaboration between the G7 and BRICS. By leveraging each other's strengths and expertise, both groups aim to bolster global security infrastructure and resilience against evolving terrorist threats.

It is important to note that while cooperation is essential, challenges exist in aligning the diverse interests and priorities of G7 and BRICS members. These include differing regional priorities, historical alliances, and divergent foreign policy objectives. Overcoming these challenges requires sustained dialogue, mutual respect, and a shared commitment to advancing common security goals.

The evolving landscape of global terrorism demands a flexible and dynamic approach to collaboration between the G7 and BRICS. As new threats emerge and tactics evolve, both groups must adapt their cooperative strategies to address the ever-changing face of terrorism effectively. By fostering trust, transparent communication, and collective action, the G7 and BRICS can work towards a safer and more secure world for future generations.

IMPACT OF GLOBAL TERRORISM ON INTERNATIONAL TRADE AND POLITICS

Global terrorism has far-reaching implications on international trade and politics, creating a complex web of challenges that affect the global socio-economic landscape. The threat of terrorism has led to increased security measures at borders and strategic locations, disrupting trade flows and supply chains. This has caused delays in the movement of goods and services, impacting businesses and economies worldwide. Additionally, terrorist activities often lead to heightened geopolitical tensions, affecting diplomatic relations and foreign policies between nations. The perception of security risks can influence investment decisions and bilateral trade agreements, leading to shifts in global economic alliances and partnerships.

Furthermore, the impact of terrorism on international politics cannot be overstated. Terrorist incidents can spark political instability, social unrest, and internal conflicts within nations, which in turn may have regional and global repercussions. In response to terrorist threats, governments may introduce stringent security measures and policies, potentially infringing on civil liberties and human rights. This delicate balance between security and individual freedoms can create significant controversies in the political arena, shaping public discourse and influencing policy debates at both national and international levels.

Moreover, the global economy's interconnectedness means that acts of terrorism in one region can reverberate across the world, affecting financial markets, commodity prices, and investor confidence. The resultant economic volatility can undermine macroeconomic stability and impede sustainable growth and development efforts. Furthermore, the erosion of trust and confidence due to terrorism-related uncertainties can hinder cross-border investments and financial transactions, amplifying the economic fallout.

Counterterrorism efforts have become a focal point for multilateral cooperation and diplomacy in international politics. Countries must navigate the intricate dynamics of collective security while respecting the sovereignty of individual states. Collaboration in intelligence sharing, law enforcement, and legal frameworks is essential to effectively address transnational terrorist networks. However, differing ideological perspectives and divergent national interests within international bodies challenge cohesive and unified actions against terrorism.

Ultimately, the impact of global terrorism on international trade and politics underscores the critical need for comprehensive and coordinated responses from the global community. Balancing security imperatives with promoting open and free trade and navigating the intricate interplay between geopolitics and international economics remain formidable tasks for policymakers and leaders worldwide.

TECHNOLOGY'S ROLE IN MODERN SECURITY MEASURES

Technology's increasing sophistication and ubiquity have revolutionized the landscape of modern security measures in combating global terrorism. Technology is pivotal in identifying, preventing, and responding to security threats in today's interconnected world. The deployment of advanced surveillance systems, artificial intelligence, and big data analytics has significantly enhanced the capabilities of security agencies within the G7 and BRICS nations. These technologies enable early threat detection, real-time monitoring, and the analysis of large volumes of data to unveil patterns indicative of potential security risks. Moreover, advancements in biometric identification and facial recognition technologies have augmented border control and entry point security, effectively thwarting the movement of known terrorists or individuals of interest across international boundaries. Cybersecurity, another critical aspect, has seen substantial investment and innovation to defend against cyber-attacks that significantly threaten national security and critical infrastructure. The G7 and BRICS member states have initiated collaborative efforts to develop standardized cybersecurity protocols and frameworks to bolster their defenses against online threats. Unquestionably, unmanned aerial vehicles (UAVs) – commonly referred to as drones – have emerged as invaluable tools in surveilling and securing vast areas susceptible to terrorist activities. Leveraging these aerial platforms offers a cost-effective and efficient means of conducting surveillance, tracking suspects, and executing targeted strikes with minimal collateral damage. However, ethical and legal considerations must be carefully navigated to ensure the responsible and lawful use of drone technology in security operations. Alongside this, the growing influence of quantum computing and cryptography is reshaping the landscape of encryption methods, enabling more secure communication channels for intelligence agencies and government bodies. Cutting-edge technologies such as blockchain are increasingly being explored to fortify information sharing and storage while minimizing vulnerabilities to exploitation by malicious actors.

Nevertheless, the rapid pace of technological advancement also raises concerns about potential misuse or circumvention by adversaries seeking to undermine security measures. The proliferation of deepfakes, for instance, presents a formidable challenge, as it allows the manipulation of audiovisual content to deceive and propagate misinformation. Security agencies must stay ahead of such emerging technologies and constantly adapt their strategies to address new security risks. As technology continues to evolve, the collaboration between G7 and BRICS nations in harnessing its potential will be pivotal in shaping the future of modern security measures and ensuring a safer global environment.

CHALLENGES IN IMPLEMENTING INTERNATIONAL SECURITY LAWS

Implementing international security laws is inherently complex, as it requires coordination and cooperation among sovereign nations with divergent legal systems, priorities, and levels of resources. One of the primary challenges lies in achieving harmonization and mutual recognition of laws across different jurisdictions. The lack of uniformity in legal frameworks poses obstacles to effective collaboration and extradition processes when dealing with transnational terrorist activities. Moreover, the interpretation and enforcement of these laws vary widely, leading to potential discrepancies in addressing security threats. In addition, differing cultural and political contexts can shape the perception and application of security laws, posing challenges in achieving consensus on critical issues. Another significant obstacle is the balancing act between upholding civil liberties and safeguarding national security. Striking the right balance calls for a nuanced approach that respects human rights while ensuring robust measures to counter-terrorism.

Furthermore, the rapid evolution of technology presents a persistent challenge in enforcing security laws. Terrorist organizations adeptly leverage digital platforms and encryption techniques, complicating efforts to monitor, track, and intercept illicit activities. This dynamic landscape demands continuous adaptation of legal frameworks to address emerging technological threats effectively. Resource constraints and capacity gaps in many countries impede the effective implementation of international security laws. Disparities in financial capabilities, technological infrastructure, and law enforcement resources hinder comprehensive enforcement and compliance.

Moreover, sustained training and skill development among law enforcement and judicial personnel is crucial for successfully executing security laws. Finally, navigating the complexities of cross-border cooperation and information sharing poses inherent difficulties in the fight against global terrorism. Overcoming jurisdictional limitations, language barriers, and diplomatic sensitivities requires persistent multilateral efforts and diplomatic finesse. Achieving seamless collaboration while respecting sovereignty and data privacy remains a formidable challenge. Addressing these multifaceted challenges in implementing international security laws demands proactive engagement, mutual understanding, and continuous dialogue among nations. While daunting, overcoming these impediments is essential to establishing a practical global security framework capable of countering present and future terrorist threats.

FUTURE DIRECTIONS IN COUNTERTERRORISM

As we stand on the cusp of a new era filled with geopolitical uncertainties, the future directions in counterterrorism are critical components that require thorough analysis and strategic planning. The evolving nature of terrorism and rapid technological advancements demands a proactive approach to mitigate potential threats and address emerging challenges. Several key areas will shape the trajectory of counterterrorism efforts for the G7 and BRICS nations, each representing a unique set of challenges and opportunities. Firstly, the role of artificial intelligence and machine learning in identifying and thwarting terrorist activities cannot be overstated. Leveraging advanced algorithms and predictive analytics will enable security agencies to stay one step ahead of potential threats, allowing for more targeted and effective interventions.

Moreover, collaboration among nations in developing a unified framework for sharing intelligence and conducting joint operations will be pivotal in ensuring a cohesive global response to terrorism. By bolstering information-sharing mechanisms and promoting interoperability among security agencies, the international community can effectively combat transnational terrorist organizations that operate across borders. Furthermore, addressing the root causes of radicalization and extremism through comprehensive social and economic initiatives will be indispensable in preventing the proliferation of terrorism. Empowering disenfranchised communities, promoting education, and fostering intercultural dialogue are essential elements in countering the allure of extremist ideologies. Additionally, the role of cybersecurity in safeguarding critical infrastructure and communication networks from cyberterrorism cannot be overlooked. As interconnected systems become increasingly integral to modern societies, safeguarding these digital domains is imperative in upholding national and international security. Future advancements in biometric technologies and border security measures will be crucial in enhancing screening processes and preventing illicit movement of individuals involved in terrorist activities. This necessitates investment in cutting-edge detection systems and the establishment of robust protocols to fortify entry points and transit hubs. Finally, building resilience and preparedness at the societal level is paramount to mitigate the impact of terrorist attacks and minimize disruption. Public awareness campaigns, emergency response drills, and collaboration with private sector entities will be central in fortifying community resilience and enhancing the overall security posture. The way forward in counterterrorism demands a holistic and forward-looking approach that addresses multifaceted dimensions in an ever-evolving threat landscape. Embracing innovation, fostering collaboration, and prioritizing prevention will undoubtedly define the future of counterterrorism efforts for both the G7 and BRICS nations.

CHAPTER 19

Legal and Regulatory Frameworks: Ensuring Compliance across Borders

LEGAL AND REGULATORY FRAMEWORKS IN THE INTERNATIONAL CONTEXT

In a rapidly globalizing world, multinational corporations operate across multiple jurisdictions, each with legal and regulatory frameworks. Understanding the nuances and complexities of these global legal landscapes is imperative for these entities' sustainable growth and success. Navigating the intricacies of diverse legal systems, compliance requirements, and regulatory environments is essential to mitigate risks, ensure ethical business conduct, and foster positive relationships with host countries and international partners. Global corporations must proactively engage with legal experts, regulatory bodies, and industry associations to gain comprehensive insights into the legal frameworks that govern their operations. This understanding enables them to align their business strategies with the applicable laws and regulations, minimizing legal disputes, penalties, and reputational damage. By comprehensively assessing legal considerations before entering new markets or engaging in cross-border transactions, multinational corporations can demonstrate respect for local laws and cultural norms, contributing to sustainable partnerships and socio-economic development.

Moreover, an in-depth understanding of international legal frameworks empowers corporations to champion responsible corporate citizenship, uphold human rights standards, and promote environmental sustainability. This, in turn, enhances their reputation, strengthens stakeholder trust, and facilitates access to global markets. Recognizing the importance of legal and regulatory compliance as a fundamental aspect of corporate governance, forward-thinking organizations invest in robust internal compliance programs, transparent reporting mechanisms, and regular audits to ensure adherence to international legal standards. Such proactive measures safeguard the corporation from legal liabilities and contribute to shaping a conducive global business environment characterized by fair competition, transparency, and accountability. Therefore, it is evident that understanding and respecting the legal and regulatory frameworks in the international context is not just a legal obligation but a strategic imperative for multinational corporations seeking to thrive in the global marketplace.

COMPARATIVE ANALYSIS OF G7 AND BRICS REGULATORY ENVIRONMENTS

Regulatory environments play a pivotal role in shaping the economic landscape and business activities of countries worldwide. Comparing regulatory frameworks between the G7 and BRICS nations reveals distinct approaches and priorities guiding their legal and policy systems. Understanding these differences is crucial for multinational enterprises, investors, and policymakers seeking to navigate a complex and interconnected global market.

The G7 nations, comprising the United States, Canada, France, Germany, Italy, Japan, and the United Kingdom, have historically been characterized by a strong emphasis on regulatory transparency, adherence to international standards, and robust enforcement mechanisms.

Their legal frameworks often prioritize investor protection, intellectual property rights, and competition regulation. The regulatory environment in the G7 is influenced by established legal traditions and a commitment to upholding the rule of law, which fosters stability and confidence in economic activities.

In contrast, the BRICS nations—Brazil, Russia, India, China, and South Africa—exhibit diverse regulatory landscapes shaped by their unique developmental trajectories and geopolitical considerations. While these countries increasingly harmonize their regulatory frameworks, disparities persist in intellectual property protection, labor laws, and environmental regulations. BRICS economies emphasize sovereign control over strategic sectors, promoting domestic industries, and crafting rules that reflect their specific social and economic challenges.

Furthermore, the differing attitudes toward cross-border investment and trade governance between the two blocs contribute to variations in their regulatory approaches. The G7 favors open markets, free trade agreements, and regulatory convergence with partners, aiming for a level playing field for businesses across borders. On the other hand, BRICS nations often advocate for fairer representation within global governance institutions and seek to amplify their influence in shaping new norms and standards that align with their developmental aspirations.

A comprehensive comparative analysis also delves into regulatory oversight, compliance costs, and administrative burdens placed on businesses operating in these jurisdictions. The regulatory environment can significantly impact corporate entities' ease of doing business, innovation capabilities, and risk management. Understanding the nuances of regulatory environments in the G7 and BRICS countries assists stakeholders in devising tailored strategies for achieving operational efficiency while ensuring compliance with diverse legal requirements.

Studying G7 and BRICS regulatory frameworks offers valuable insights into the intersections of law, politics, and commerce as the global economy evolves and interdependence deepens. This comparative analysis is a foundation for fostering dialogue, identifying best practices, and encouraging convergence where mutual benefits can be realized. Recognizing the evolving nature of regulation and its impact on international business is imperative for building sustainable partnerships and fostering an environment conducive to inclusive growth and prosperity.

CROSS-BORDER COMPLIANCE CHALLENGES IN MULTINATIONAL OPERATIONS

As the global economy becomes increasingly interconnected, multinational corporations face many challenges in ensuring compliance with diverse legal and regulatory frameworks across different jurisdictions. One of the primary challenges in this context is navigating the complex landscape of laws and regulations that govern business operations in multiple countries. From varying taxation policies to diverse employment laws, companies operating across borders must adeptly maneuver through a web of rules to avoid non-compliance and mitigate associated risks.

Moreover, cultural and ethical differences pose significant challenges for multinational operations. What may be considered acceptable business practices in one country could be deemed unethical or even illegal in another. Navigating these cultural nuances while upholding a consistent standard of corporate governance requires a deep understanding of local customs and an unwavering commitment to ethical conduct.

Another critical aspect that adds complexity to cross-border compliance is data privacy and security. With the proliferation of digital technologies, the collection and transfer of personal data have become integral to business operations. However, differing data protection laws and regulations across jurisdictions necessitate careful consideration to ensure compliance while maintaining operational efficiency.

Furthermore, the geopolitical landscape introduces additional compliance challenges for multinational operations. Sanctions, embargoes, and export controls imposed by various nations can significantly impact companies' ability to conduct business across borders. Navigating these legal and political obstacles demands a nuanced understanding of international relations and an agile approach to compliance.

In addition to these challenges, multinational corporations face complexities related to contractual agreements and dispute resolution mechanisms when engaging in cross-border transactions. Navigating the intricacies of international contract law and resolving disputes in multiple jurisdictions require robust legal strategies and a proactive approach to risk management.

Achieving cross-border compliance in multinational operations requires a comprehensive understanding of the legal, regulatory, cultural, and geopolitical factors at play. It necessitates a proactive stance towards compliance, extensive due diligence, and the cultivation of strong relationships with legal experts and regulatory authorities in each jurisdiction where the company operates. By effectively addressing these challenges, multinational corporations can navigate cross-border complexities while upholding the highest standards of legal and ethical conduct.

INTELLECTUAL PROPERTY RIGHTS IN THE GLOBAL MARKET

In today's interconnected global economy, protecting intellectual property rights (IPR) has become crucial to international business and trade. Intellectual property encompasses many innovations, including patents, trademarks, copyrights, and trade secrets. As multinational corporations expand their operations across borders, they encounter diverse legal landscapes regarding IPR, necessitating a comprehensive understanding of global intellectual property frameworks.

One of the fundamental challenges in the global market is the differences in intellectual property regulations among G7 and BRICS nations. While G7 countries have well-established and robust IPR laws and enforcement mechanisms, BRICS nations are navigating the complex terrain of intellectual property protection amid rapid economic growth and technological advancement. The disparities in IPR standards and enforcement pose significant hurdles for multinational firms, requiring them to tailor their strategies according to the specific legal requirements in each jurisdiction.

Furthermore, the rise of digital technologies and e-commerce has brought about unique challenges related to intellectual property rights. Online piracy, counterfeiting, and copyright infringement have gained prominence, prompting international discussions on harmonizing digital IP regulations. The need to protect digital assets and online content has propelled initiatives to fortify the legal framework governing intellectual property in the digital age.

Effective IPR management fosters innovation and creativity in the global marketplace. Companies must navigate the complexities of licensing, technology transfer, and collaborative research while safeguarding their intellectual assets. Balancing the need for open innovation with the imperative of protecting proprietary knowledge presents a delicate but essential task for firms competing on the world stage.

In conclusion, the significance of intellectual property rights in the global market cannot be overstated. As the nexus of innovation, technology, and commerce continues to evolve, meticulous attention to intellectual property protection will remain pivotal for multinational enterprises. By addressing the intricacies of international IPR regimes and adapting to the evolving digital commerce landscape, businesses can effectively secure their innovative endeavors and contribute to advancing global economic prosperity.

DATA PROTECTION LAWS AND INTERNATIONAL BUSINESS

Data protection has become a paramount concern in today's interconnected global business landscape. As organizations engage in cross-border activities and leverage digital technologies, they must navigate a complex web of data protection laws and regulations varying across jurisdictions. These laws protect sensitive information, including personal data, trade secrets, and intellectual property, from unauthorized access, use, and disclosure. Compliance with data protection laws is a legal requirement and essential for maintaining trust and credibility in international business operations.

Data protection laws such as the European Union's General Data Protection Regulation (GDPR) and the California Consumer Privacy Act (CCPA) have significantly influenced the global regulatory framework. These laws impose strict requirements on how organizations collect, process, store, and transfer personal data to give individuals greater control over their information. For instance, the extraterritorial scope of GDPR applies to businesses operating outside the EU if they offer goods or services to EU residents or monitor their behavior. This has compelled many multinational corporations to reassess their data-handling practices and implement robust measures to ensure compliance.

The evolving nature of data protection laws presents challenges and opportunities for international businesses. Organizations must grapple with data localization requirements, cross-border data transfers, and privacy impact assessments to align with diverse regulatory mandates. Non-compliance can lead to severe penalties, reputational damage, and legal repercussions, making it imperative for businesses to integrate data protection considerations into their strategic planning and operations.

Amidst these complexities, there is a growing call for harmonization and standardization of data protection laws at an international level. This could streamline regulatory compliance for businesses, facilitate secure cross-border data flows, and enhance consumer trust. However, achieving consensus among nations with varying legal traditions and cultural values remains formidable, requiring concerted efforts from policymakers, industry stakeholders, and advocacy groups.

As international business transactions increasingly rely on digital information exchanges, data protection's role in shaping global commerce will continue to expand. Understanding and adhering to the intricate web of data protection laws is not merely a legal obligation but a strategic imperative for businesses seeking sustained success in the international arena.

ANTI-CORRUPTION MEASURES AND ENFORCEMENT MECHANISMS

Corruption is a pervasive global issue that undermines economic growth, distorts market competition, and erodes public trust in governance. In the international business landscape, enforcing anti-corruption measures is crucial to ensure fair and transparent practices. This section delves into the multifaceted approaches G7 and BRICS nations employ in combating corruption and the mechanisms for effective enforcement.

The legislative and regulatory initiatives designed to prevent, detect, and prosecute corrupt activities are at the core of any robust anti-corruption framework. G7 nations have often been at the forefront of shaping international standards through conventions such as the United Nations Convention against Corruption (UNCAC) and the OECD Anti-Bribery Convention. These treaties provide a common ground for signatory countries to align their laws and regulations, fostering cooperation in investigations and extradition procedures and promoting the recovery of stolen assets. On the other hand, within the BRICS bloc, efforts have been made to establish regional agreements and frameworks to address corruption, acknowledging the need for tailored approaches that consider the unique socio-economic contexts of member states.

In addition to legislation, the effective implementation and enforcement of anti-corruption measures require robust institutional structures and adequate resources. G7 countries often invest in specialized anti-corruption agencies and task forces equipped with extensive powers to investigate and prosecute corruption cases. Furthermore, the independence and integrity of the judiciary play a critical role in ensuring that perpetrators are held accountable without undue influence or bias. Conversely, BRICS nations have established oversight bodies and anti-corruption commissions, adapting their strategies to combat public and private sector corruption while promoting sound governance principles.

Furthermore, anti-corruption efforts are complemented by promoting ethical business conduct, transparency, and accountability. G7 nations have encouraged the adoption of compliance programs and integrity standards within corporate entities, emphasizing the role of due diligence and risk assessment in preventing corrupt practices. Similarly, BRICS countries have stressed the importance of corporate social responsibility and ethical behavior, seeking to integrate anti-corruption measures into business operations and supply chains.

International collaboration and mutual legal assistance are instrumental in addressing transnational corruption cases, often involving multiple jurisdictions. Establishing mutual evaluation processes and exchanging best practices between G7 and BRICS countries facilitate joint efforts to combat bribery, money laundering, and embezzlement. In this context, frameworks such as the Egmont Group, an international network of financial intelligence units, foster information-sharing and coordination to track illicit financial flows associated with corrupt activities.

In conclusion, the fight against corruption demands a comprehensive and concerted approach that brings together legal, institutional, and ethical dimensions. Both G7 and BRICS nations continue to refine their anti-corruption frameworks, recognizing the imperative of promoting integrity and accountability in the global marketplace.

TRADE REGULATIONS AND THEIR IMPACT ON INTERNATIONAL ECONOMICS

Trade regulations are crucial in shaping the global economic landscape, influencing the flow of goods, services, and investments across international borders. As nations seek to maximize their financial potential and protect domestic industries, trade regulations are critical in managing international trade relationships. This section will delve into the multifaceted impact of trade regulations on global economics, including their influence on market access, competitive advantage, and overall economic growth.

Trade regulations encompass a wide range of policies and measures governing cross-border trade. These include tariffs, quotas, subsidies, and non-tariff barriers such as sanitary and phytosanitary standards. The varying application of these regulations by different countries leads to complex trade dynamics that directly affect the patterns of global commerce. Moreover, trade agreements and organizations, such as the World Trade Organization (WTO) and regional trade blocs, further shape the regulatory environment, creating opportunities and challenges for businesses operating in multiple jurisdictions.

One of the primary impacts of trade regulations is their influence on market access. Tariffs and non-tariff barriers can significantly impact firms' ability to enter foreign markets and compete with domestic producers. By restricting market access, trade regulations shape the distribution of economic gains and losses, affecting businesses, consumers, and workers. Furthermore, trade regulations can protect strategic industries, promote national security interests, and address labor and environmental concerns.

In addition to market access, trade regulations profoundly affect competitive advantage and global supply chains. Companies must navigate the complexities of trade regulations to optimize their production processes and supply chain management. Regulation changes can disrupt established supply chains and necessitate sourcing, manufacturing, and distribution strategy adjustments. As a result, businesses continually assess the regulatory environment and its impact on their cost structures, operational efficiency, and overall competitiveness.

From a macroeconomic perspective, trade regulations directly influence economic growth and development. Regulatory changes can lead to comparative advantage and specialization shifts, affecting trade volumes, investment patterns, and overall welfare. Moreover, trade regulations intersect with other economic policies, such as monetary and fiscal measures, shaping the broader economic landscape of nations and regions. Understanding the intricacies of trade regulations is essential for policymakers, economists, and industry stakeholders to anticipate and respond to the evolving dynamics of international trade.

Fostering international trade while safeguarding national interests requires continual assessment and negotiation among nations. Achieving a harmonized, transparent, and equitable global trade framework remains challenging. Ultimately, the impact of trade regulations on international economics underscores the interdependence of nations and the imperative of cooperation to navigate the complexities of the modern global economy.

LABOR LAWS AND EMPLOYEE RIGHTS ACROSS DIFFERENT JURISDICTIONS

Labor laws and employee rights are crucial to the legal and regulatory frameworks governing international business operations. Labor law variations across different jurisdictions can significantly impact how employers manage their workforce and employee rights. Multinational corporations and organizations operating across borders must comprehend these differences and ensure compliance to maintain ethical employment practices. This section will explore the complexities of navigating labor laws and upholding employee rights in diverse global jurisdictions.

One of the fundamental aspects of labor laws pertains to regulating working hours and conditions. While some countries enforce strict limits on the number of hours an employee can work per week, others have more flexible regulations. Understanding these disparities is essential for organizations overseeing operations in multiple countries to prevent exploitation and ensure fair treatment of employees.

Furthermore, employee rights regarding wages, benefits, and leaves vary significantly across jurisdictions. For instance, certain countries mandate a minimum wage, while others may not have such regulations.

Additionally, parental leave policies, healthcare benefits, and retirement plans are subject to variance, necessitating careful consideration by multinational companies to provide equitable treatment to their employees worldwide.

Another critical area of divergence is worker safety and health regulations. The enforcement of occupational safety standards varies across jurisdictions, impacting workplace environments and employers' obligation to safeguard their employees from hazards and occupational risks. Organizations must strategically assess and implement measures to ensure stringent compliance with occupational health and safety laws to protect the well-being of their employees globally.

Moreover, termination procedures and severance regulations also differ significantly across jurisdictions. While some countries prioritize stringent job security measures and compensation packages for terminated employees, others have comparatively lenient rules. Multinational corporations must understand and adhere to each region's severance laws and procedures to ethically and legally manage their workforce reductions.

The intricate landscape of labor laws and employee rights across various jurisdictions demands meticulous attention from global businesses. To foster a harmonious and equitable work environment, organizations must navigate these complexities responsibly, protecting and promoting the well-being and rights of their diverse workforce. By comprehensively understanding and adhering to labor laws and employee rights across different jurisdictions, businesses can cultivate a positive corporate image, secure employee loyalty, and contribute to sustainable economic development.

ENVIRONMENTAL STANDARDS AND SUSTAINABILITY PRACTICES

As the global economy becomes increasingly interconnected, the need for environmental standards and sustainability practices has garnered significant attention in both G7 and BRICS nations. Environmental degradation, climate change, and resource depletion have posed critical challenges that require concerted multinational efforts to address. This section delves into the diverse approaches different jurisdictions adopt to mitigate environmental impact and promote sustainable practices, acknowledging the varied cultural, economic, and political contexts in which these efforts operate.

One of the fundamental aspects of environmental standards is the establishment of regulatory frameworks that outline permissible levels of pollution, guidelines for resource conservation, and laws governing waste disposal. While G7 countries tend to have more stringent regulations, often with comprehensive enforcement mechanisms, BRICS nations increasingly recognize the imperative of strengthening their environmental governance structures to balance economic growth with ecological stewardship.

Sustainability practices encompass many initiatives, including investments in renewable energy, sustainable agriculture, and green infrastructure development. The divergent levels of economic growth within the BRICS bloc influence the prioritization and implementation of sustainability measures, with some members focusing on modernizing industrial processes. In contrast, others concentrate on rural development and biodiversity conservation.

Furthermore, the international community has witnessed growing collaboration between governmental bodies, NGOs, and corporate stakeholders to bolster sustainability efforts. Initiatives such as public-private partnerships, eco-certifications, and carbon offset programs are noteworthy examples of collective action to minimize environmental harm while fostering innovative solutions for long-term sustainability.

It is evident that achieving harmonization and transparency in environmental standards and sustainability practices across borders remains a complex endeavor. Striking a balance between economic aspirations and environmental preservation requires continuous dialogue, knowledge sharing, and capacity building. As the international community navigates through this intricate landscape, the importance of mutual respect for sovereignty, cultural nuances, and developmental disparities cannot be overstated. Moving forward, policymakers, industry leaders, and civil society must collaborate in developing cohesive strategies that uphold environmental integrity while promoting inclusive and equitable prosperity for current and future generations.

CONCLUSION: MOVING TOWARD HARMONIZATION AND TRANSPARENCY

In the fast-evolving global landscape, fostering harmonization and transparency within legal and regulatory frameworks is imperative for sustainable development and international cooperation. As explored in this book, environmental standards and sustainability practices are integral to this broader effort, reflecting the growing recognition of the interconnectedness between economic activities and ecological well-being. However, achieving a comprehensive framework for harmonization and transparency involves multiple dimensions that extend beyond environmental considerations. It necessitates alignment across diverse legal systems, regulatory bodies, and industry practices underpinned by a commitment to ethical governance and accountability. One crucial aspect of moving toward harmonization and transparency is promoting consistency in regulatory approaches and standards, ensuring a level playing field for businesses operating across borders. This entails harmonizing laws and regulations concerning intellectual property rights, data protection, anti-corruption measures, and trade rules to mitigate discrepancies and facilitate equitable competition.

Moreover, efforts to enhance transparency must address the complexities of multinational corporations' cross-border compliance challenges. By fostering greater collaboration among nations, sharing best practices, and leveraging emerging technologies, it becomes feasible to streamline compliance processes while upholding the highest ethical and legal standards. The journey toward harmonization and transparency also demands a focus on enhancing corporate social responsibility and sustainable business practices. By integrating labor laws and employee rights across different jurisdictions, businesses can contribute to societal welfare and uphold human dignity, fostering a more equitable and inclusive global economy. Furthermore, an integral element of this transition involves reinforcing environmental standards and sustainability practices and employing innovative solutions to diminish the ecological footprint of industrial operations. Striving for harmonization and transparency within legal and regulatory frameworks embodies a proactive response to the evolving needs of the globalized world, emphasizing the pivotal role of international collaboration and adaptive governance. As we look toward the future, we must recognize that this endeavor requires ongoing dialogue, diplomacy, and a willingness to embrace change. By aligning our aspirations for harmonization and transparency, we can bridge legal divides, cultivate trust, and pave the way for a more equitable, sustainable, and prosperous global community.

CHAPTER 20

Gender Equality and Inclusivity in Global Governance

CONTEXTUALIZING GENDER EQUALITY IN GLOBAL GOVERNANCE

Gender equality is a fundamental human rights issue and a foundation for a peaceful, prosperous, and sustainable world. Integrating gender equality principles in high-level decision-making processes is not just a matter of morality but also of practicality and economic imperatives. Historically, political systems have been plagued by gender inequity, with women being systematically excluded from positions of power and influence. This exclusion has had far-reaching implications, leading to skewed policy priorities, limited perspectives, and missed opportunities for addressing critical global challenges. To ensure that global governance is truly representative and responsive to the needs of all individuals, irrespective of gender, it is imperative to examine and address the historical factors that have perpetuated gender inequality in political systems. By doing so, we can better comprehend the current landscape and identify strategies to mitigate the effects of these historical injustices.

Moreover, exploring the importance and benefits of integrating gender equality principles in high-level decision-making processes goes beyond simply rectifying past wrongs; it is an essential step toward harnessing the full potential of diverse perspectives and talents. Research consistently demonstrates that diverse leadership teams, including equitable gender representation, are associated with enhanced creativity, innovation, and problem-solving, yielding better outcomes for organizations and societies. Therefore, understanding the historical context of gender inequality in global governance is crucial for building a compelling case for inclusive decision-making and fostering environments where all voices are heard and respected. This section seeks to delve deeply into this vital topic, shedding light on both the challenges and opportunities that arise from embracing gender equality in the realm of global governance.

HISTORICAL OVERVIEW OF GENDER INEQUITY IN POLITICAL SYSTEMS

Gender inequity in political systems has been a pervasive issue throughout history, with women often marginalized and excluded from participating in governance structures. Women have faced significant barriers from ancient civilizations to modern nation-states when seeking political representation. In many early societies, the political sphere was predominantly male-dominated, with power dynamics favoring men and relegating women to subordinate roles. The exclusion of women from political decision-making processes created a historical pattern of gender inequity that has persisted over centuries. Throughout the ages, various social and cultural norms reinforced the idea that women were unsuited for leadership, perpetuating a systematic disenfranchisement of half the population. The suffrage movement of the late 19th and early 20th centuries marked a pivotal turning point in the fight for gender equality in politics. Women activists and allies campaigned tirelessly for the right to vote and hold public office, challenging deeply ingrained societal beliefs about women's capabilities in governance. Despite these efforts, progress towards gender parity in political systems has been slow and uneven. Even after gaining the right to vote, women continued encountering formidable obstacles in pursuing political careers. Discriminatory laws, social biases, and institutionalized sexism have all contributed to the historical marginalization of women in politics. A complex interplay of legal, cultural, and structural challenges marks the struggle for gender equity in political systems. Many pioneering women have defied societal norms and paved the way for future generations of female leaders, yet systemic barriers persisted. It was not until the latter half of the 20th century that significant strides were made towards addressing gender inequity in political systems. International initiatives and advocacy efforts propelled the issue of women's representation onto the global stage, leading to the adoption of landmark declarations and conventions aimed at promoting gender equality in governance. Despite these advancements, persistent gaps remain in achieving full and equal participation for women in political decision-making processes worldwide. Understanding the historical context of gender inequity in political systems is crucial in comprehending today's challenges and charting a course toward a more inclusive and equitable future.

ANALYZING CURRENT GENDER REPRESENTATION IN G7 AND BRICS NATIONS

Gender representation in global governance has emerged as a critical measure of progress towards inclusivity and equality. Within the G7 and BRICS nations, gender representation in political leadership positions is a compelling gauge of societal attitudes towards gender equity and the extent to which women are empowered to participate in decision-making. Analyzing the current state of gender representation in these influential groups reveals both disparities and everyday challenges. Across the G7 nations, notably Canada and Germany, they have demonstrated commendable efforts in promoting gender diversity in political roles, with women holding significant cabinet positions and making marked impacts on policy formulation. However, despite progress, gender parity remains a persistent challenge, particularly in key areas such as executive leadership and ministerial portfolios that traditionally shape national policy agendas.

Conversely, within the BRICS nations, Brazil and South Africa have showcased encouraging trends in the participation of women in political spheres. These countries have implemented affirmative action policies and legal frameworks to enhance gender representation in governmental structures. Nevertheless, challenges persist, and gender imbalance hinders comprehensive and equitable governance. Identifying the factors influencing gender representation in these influential blocs requires an examination of cultural norms, historical contexts, and institutional barriers that perpetuate male dominance in political leadership. The interplay between political will, societal attitudes, and legislative mechanisms shapes the landscape of gender inclusion in global governance. As the world grapples with complex geopolitical and socioeconomic issues, it is imperative to critically assess and address the underlying impediments that impede women's full and meaningful participation in decision-making processes. By fostering environments conducive to equal representation, both the G7 and BRICS nations can harness their populations' diverse perspectives and talents, leading to more robust, inclusive, and effective governance. The analysis of current gender representation in these influential global networks unveils multifaceted challenges and opportunities for progress, underlining the significance of advancing gender equality as an integral component of sustainable and impactful global governance.

BARRIERS TO FEMALE LEADERSHIP IN POLITICS AND GOVERNANCE

The underrepresentation of women in political leadership roles and governance is a pervasive issue that persists across the G7 and BRICS nations despite advances in gender equality. Numerous barriers impede female leadership in these crucial sectors, inhibiting the realization of diverse and inclusive decision-making bodies. One prominent barrier is entrenched gender bias and stereotypes, which often shape societal perceptions of women's leadership abilities. Preconceived notions regarding traditional gender roles may influence the electorate and internal party dynamics, creating challenges for women seeking political office. Additionally, systemic obstacles such as unequal access to resources, limited networking opportunities, and discriminatory practices within political institutions further hinder women's progression into leadership positions. These inequities contribute to a significant disparity between the number of men and women holding influential political and governance roles. Cultural and social norms also play a substantial role in perpetuating gender-based barriers to leadership. Deep-seated beliefs about gender roles and responsibilities can present formidable challenges for women aspiring to pursue careers in politics and governance. Moreover, the lack of supportive policies and frameworks tailored to address women's unique obstacles in these fields exacerbates the problem. Inadequate family support, unequal parental leave policies, and the absence of affordable childcare options are additional factors that limit women's participation in political leadership and governance.

Furthermore, the prevalence of harassment and gender-based discrimination in political environments can create a hostile climate that dissuades women from pursuing leadership roles. The insidious nature of these barriers reinforces the need for concerted efforts to address and dismantle the obstacles preventing female representation in political and governance spheres. Recognizing and understanding these impediments is critical in devising effective strategies to promote gender parity and inclusivity at all levels of leadership.

CASE STUDIES OF SUCCESSFUL GENDER-INCLUSIVE POLICIES

This section delves into case studies of successful gender-inclusive policies that have impacted women's representation and participation in global governance. Rwanda is an exemplary model, where proactive measures have resulted in a remarkable increase in female political representation. Through legislative quotas, Rwanda achieved a record-breaking 61% female representation in its lower house of parliament. This deliberate effort demonstrates the effectiveness of affirmative action and showcases the transformative power of policy interventions.

Furthermore, the Nordic countries provide compelling case studies of successful gender-inclusive policies. Countries like Iceland, Norway, and Sweden have implemented comprehensive strategies to address gender disparities in governance, increasing female participation in decision-making processes. These nations have enacted family-friendly policies, including generous parental leave and affordable childcare, which have facilitated more excellent female representation at all levels of government.

Turning to corporate governance, Norway's quota legislation mandating at least 40% female representation on corporate boards has demonstrated substantive progress. Studies have shown that companies with diverse boards are more financially successful, emphasizing the economic benefits of gender-inclusive policies. Moreover, Norway's success has influenced other European countries to adopt similar measures, contributing to a broader movement towards gender diversity in corporate leadership.

In addition, the case of Canada underlines the importance of strategic initiatives to support the advancement of women in governance. Implementing gender-based analysis frameworks across government policies and budgeting has led to more gender-responsive policy outcomes. Canada's commitment to mainstreaming gender perspectives throughout policymaking has proven integral in fostering inclusivity and addressing gender-related inequities.

These case studies demonstrate that gender-inclusive policies yield substantial benefits, enhancing women's representation in governance, fueling economic growth, and optimizing decision-making processes.

By examining successful models from different parts of the world, it becomes apparent that proactive and targeted interventions can drive meaningful change and create more inclusive and effective governance structures.

ECONOMIC OUTCOMES OF INCREASED FEMALE PARTICIPATION

Increased female participation in governance and decision-making processes yields significant economic outcomes essential to advancing global societies. As historical gender disparities gradually diminish, a more diverse and inclusive representation in leadership roles has positively affected economic performance, innovation, and sustainable development. Research indicates that companies with higher gender diversity on their boards demonstrate more robust financial performance. This is attributed to the broader range of perspectives and skills brought about by female board members, leading to improved decision-making and risk management. Moreover, increased female labor force participation contributes to higher productivity and greater GDP growth, fostering economic resilience and competitiveness within nations. When women are empowered to enter and remain in the workforce, the potential for economic expansion and prosperity experiences a considerable upsurge. Addressing gender-based pay gaps and promoting equal access to economic opportunities further bolsters overall productivity and fosters a more equitable distribution of wealth.

Furthermore, empowering women in leadership positions has proven to enhance corporate social responsibility initiatives, driving positive societal impacts through philanthropy, community engagement, and ethical business practices. In addition, increased investment in female entrepreneurship and SMEs can lead to job creation, stimulate local economies, and drive innovation. The economic outcomes of increased female participation extend beyond traditional metrics, encompassing a wider spectrum of macro and microeconomic indicators that collectively contribute to comprehensive and sustainable growth. Therefore, prioritizing gender equality and inclusivity in global governance remains imperative for harnessing the full economic potential of nations and advancing the well-being of societies.

IMPACT OF SOCIAL MOVEMENTS ON POLICY CHANGES

Social movements advocating for gender equality have played a pivotal role in driving policy changes and reshaping the landscape of global governance. These movements encompass diverse initiatives and campaigns that seek to address systemic gender inequality and promote inclusivity within government structures. From grassroots activism to large-scale demonstrations, these movements have made significant strides in raising awareness and garnering support for gender parity in political decision-making processes. These movements have effectively influenced policymakers and catalyzed meaningful reforms by utilizing various advocacy strategies, including public protests, media campaigns, and coalition building. One notable example is the #MeToo movement, which exposed widespread sexual harassment and misconduct, prompting legislative action and corporate policy changes worldwide.

Moreover, social movements have been instrumental in elevating underrepresented voices, amplifying the call for equal representation in leadership positions, and dismantling entrenched barriers that impede women's political participation. Through persistent advocacy and mobilization, these movements have compelled governments and international organizations to prioritize gender-sensitive policy formulation and implementation, leading to tangible improvements in addressing gender disparities at the decision-making level. Additionally, these movements have fostered an environment conducive to open dialogue and collaboration between stakeholders, fostering a sense of urgency and collective responsibility in mainstreaming gender considerations within policy agendas. As a result, policy changes informed by the demands of social movements have contributed to reshaping institutional norms, challenging discriminatory practices, and establishing frameworks that actively promote gender diversity and inclusivity. The intersectionality of these movements with broader social justice causes has further enriched the discourse on governance and precipitated comprehensive changes that transcend traditional political boundaries. In essence, the impact of social movements on policy changes has been transformational, heralding a new era of progressive governance that prioritizes equity and representation. Their influence reverberates across global platforms, signaling a paradigm shift towards more inclusive and responsive decision-making processes.

STRATEGIES FOR CULTIVATING GENDER PARITY IN GOVERNMENT ROLES

Gender parity in government roles is crucial for creating inclusive and effective governance systems. Several key strategies can be implemented to cultivate gender parity. First, it is essential to promote mentorship and leadership development programs tailored to women in politics and public administration. These programs should provide guidance, support, and skills training to empower women to pursue leadership roles confidently. Additionally, targeted recruitment efforts to identify and encourage qualified female candidates can help increase their representation in government positions.

Moreover, implementing gender quotas or targets within political parties or government agencies can serve as a proactive measure to ensure the inclusion of diverse perspectives and experiences. Such mechanisms have been successfully utilized in several countries to elevate the participation of women in decision-making bodies. Furthermore, investing in policies that support work-life balance, such as parental leave, flexible working arrangements, and childcare provisions, is instrumental in enabling women to engage in politics while managing family responsibilities actively. Effective advocacy and public awareness campaigns are also vital for challenging gender biases and stereotypes and fostering a supportive environment that values and promotes women's leadership in governance. Beyond these internal measures, collaboration with civil society organizations and academia can facilitate knowledge exchange and initiatives to advance gender equality in government. By harnessing the expertise and experience of various stakeholders, governments can develop comprehensive strategies for cultivating gender parity. Policymakers, political leaders, and international organizations must recognize the importance of gender diversity in governance and commit to implementing these strategies to ensure women's meaningful participation and representation in decision-making processes.

ROLE OF INTERNATIONAL ORGANIZATIONS IN ADVOCATING GENDER EQUALITY

The role of international organizations in advocating for gender equality within the sphere of global governance cannot be overstated. These organizations serve as crucial platforms for promoting policy dialogue, knowledge sharing, and capacity building to address gender disparities at the global level. Furthermore, they are pivotal in fostering collaboration among nations to implement initiatives that advance gender equality and inclusivity in decision-making processes. International organizations provide a forum for member states to exchange best practices, strategies, and resources to overcome systemic barriers to women's full participation in governance. Whether through the United Nations, regional organizations, or specialized agencies, these bodies exert influence on shaping policies and norms that aim to elevate the status of women in leadership positions across diverse sectors. By leveraging their convening power, international organizations broker partnerships between governments, civil society, and the private sector to drive collective action towards achieving gender parity and empowering women in political roles. Through research, advocacy, and monitoring mechanisms, these entities generate valuable data and insights that substantiate the case for gender-responsive governance, helping to hold governments accountable for their commitments to closing the gender gap. Significantly, international organizations leverage their influence to mobilize financial support and technical assistance to implement gender mainstreaming initiatives that seek to embed gender perspectives in all policies and programs. This comprehensive approach addresses systemic inequalities and promotes gender-sensitive policymaking, ensuring that women are represented and have a meaningful voice in shaping the decisions that affect their lives and communities.

Moreover, international organizations act as catalysts for normative change, setting global standards and benchmarks for gender equality that guide national efforts toward achieving substantive gender representation and equal leadership opportunities. As custodians of international law and human rights frameworks, these organizations are vital in advancing gender-responsive legal and institutional reforms, reinforcing the essential principles of non-discrimination and equality. Their advocacy also encompasses raising awareness about the impact of gender disparities on sustainable development and peace-building, urging stakeholders to integrate a gender perspective into conflict resolution, post-conflict reconstruction, and humanitarian actions. In summary, international organizations are crucial champions in advocating for gender equality in global governance by driving policy coherence, fostering partnerships, and mobilizing resources to transform rhetoric into tangible actions that promote an inclusive and equitable world.

CONCLUSION: THE PATH FORWARD FOR EQUITABLE GOVERNANCE

In concluding our discussion on the path forward for equitable governance, it is essential to emphasize that achieving gender equality and inclusivity in global governance is not merely a matter of social justice but also a critical factor for sustainable economic growth, effective decision-making, and creating a more stable and peaceful world.

As we have witnessed throughout this book, the underrepresentation of women in leadership positions within political systems and international organizations has significant implications for the quality and legitimacy of governance. Therefore, addressing the barriers that hinder women's full participation in governance is crucial for ensuring progress and prosperity for all. It is evident that while some progress has been made in promoting gender equality in governance, significant challenges still exist. These challenges range from social and cultural norms to institutional biases and structural impediments. To pave the way for equitable governance, concerted efforts are required at multiple levels – from national policies to global initiatives. The first step towards achieving equitable governance involves instituting proactive measures to remove systemic barriers to women's participation in decision-making processes. This requires fostering an environment that encourages and supports the advancement of women into leadership roles.

Furthermore, enhancing the representation of women in governance demands a commitment to address underlying socio-economic disparities, promote inclusive education, and challenge discriminatory attitudes. Such efforts are indispensable for breaking the vicious cycle of inequality and empowering women to contribute fully to governance and policy-making. Moreover, fostering institutional mechanisms to elevate and amplify women's voices in global governance is essential for driving sustainable change. This can be achieved through empowering existing international bodies, such as the United Nations and regional organizations, to spearhead initiatives that advocate and enforce gender-inclusive governance frameworks. Additionally, developing mentorship programs, leadership training, and capacity-building initiatives targeted at aspiring female leaders will be pivotal in nurturing a pipeline of capable women leaders. Collaboration between governments, non-governmental organizations, and private sectors is imperative to drive changes. By forging partnerships and alliances, stakeholders can collectively work towards eliminating the discrepancies in gender representation and influence within governance structures. Ultimately, the realization of equitable governance hinges on the willingness of societies and nations to embrace diversity and harness the collective talent and perspectives of all individuals, regardless of gender. As we aspire towards the future, it is paramount to recognize that achieving equitable governance is an ongoing endeavor that demands unwavering commitment and continuous evaluation of progress. By persistently championing the cause of gender equality and inclusivity, we can construct a more just and prosperous global governance landscape.

CHAPTER 21

The Future of Education and Research Collaboration

THE IMPERATIVE FOR ENHANCED EDUCATIONAL AND RESEARCH COLLABORATION

The imperative for enhanced educational and research collaboration among countries has never been more pressing in today's interconnected world. As nations grapple with complex and interdependent global challenges, from climate change and public health crises to technological advancements and socioeconomic disparities, the need for concerted efforts in advancing education and research programs is paramount. Countries can leverage their expertise, resources, and perspectives by working together globally to tackle these pressing issues effectively. Collaborative initiatives in education and research not only foster knowledge exchange but also facilitate the development of innovative solutions that transcend geographical boundaries. Moreover, they promote cultural understanding and mutual respect, paving the way for a more harmonious and cohesive global community. As the world becomes increasingly interconnected, the value of educational and research networks cannot be overstated. These networks are pivotal in bridging diverse academic communities, fostering cross-cultural collaborations, and nurturing the next generation of pioneering thinkers and leaders.

Furthermore, in an era marked by rapid technological advancements and evolving geopolitical landscapes, shared educational and research endeavors enable countries to stay at the forefront of innovation and maintain their competitiveness in the global arena. They serve as incubators for breakthrough discoveries and transformative insights that drive progress and prosperity. The imperative for enhancing collaboration in education and research goes beyond individual interests; it represents a collective commitment to addressing shared global challenges and shaping a sustainable future for future generations. Therefore, exploring this imperative's multifaceted dimensions is intellectually stimulating and crucial for navigating the complexities of our rapidly changing world.

HISTORICAL OVERVIEW OF GLOBAL EDUCATION AND RESEARCH NETWORKS

The evolution of global education and research networks has been a testament to humanity's pursuit of knowledge and intellectual progress. From the ancient centers of learning in civilizations such as Mesopotamia, Egypt, Greece, and India to the medieval universities of Europe, the development of educational networks has been intertwined with the advancement of human civilization. The circulation of ideas, philosophies, and scientific knowledge through these early networks laid the foundation for the interconnected world of learning that we witness today—the Renaissance period further catalyzed the formation of international scholarly communities, fostering collaborations across borders and bringing diverse perspectives into a shared academic arena. During this era, the concept of research collaboration started gaining momentum, establishing formal channels for scholarly exchange. The 19th and 20th centuries brought about significant advancements in educational and research networks fueled by industrialization, technological innovation, and globalization. The founding of prestigious universities, the proliferation of scientific journals, and the creation of international associations marked a pivotal shift towards a more unified global academic landscape. The post-World War II era saw the emergence of international organizations promoting educational cooperation and research synergies among nations. Initiatives like the Fulbright Program and UNESCO have played instrumental roles in fostering cross-border partnerships and facilitating the exchange of scholars, scientists, and researchers. With the advent of the internet and digital communication, the late 20th and early 21st centuries witnessed a paradigm shift in global educational and research networks. The connectivity the World Wide Web provided revolutionized how knowledge is shared, opening up new avenues for collaboration and creating virtual spaces for intellectual discourse. Massive open online courses (MOOCs), collaborative research platforms, and virtual academic conferences have further democratized access to education and expanded the scope of research collaboration globally. The historical trajectory of global education and research networks reflects an ongoing quest for synergy, inclusivity, and the pursuit of knowledge without boundaries.

CURRENT LANDSCAPE: MAJOR COLLABORATIVE INITIATIVES AND THEIR IMPACT

In today's interconnected world, collaborative initiatives in education and research are rapidly evolving to meet the challenges of globalization and technological advancement. Major collaborative initiatives spanning continents and disciplines are playing a pivotal role in shaping the future of academia. These initiatives encompass a wide array of partnerships between institutions, governments, and industry players, all aimed at fostering knowledge exchange and driving impactful research outcomes. The impact of these collaborations is felt not only within the academic community but also in society at large.

One of the most significant impacts of these initiatives is the breaking down traditional barriers to knowledge dissemination and acquisition.

By transcending geographical boundaries and fostering cross-cultural collaboration, these initiatives are instrumental in creating a truly global pool of knowledge, expertise, and innovation. Moreover, the democratization of educational resources through online platforms and open-access journals has allowed for unparalleled dissemination of scholarly work, thereby enriching the academic community worldwide.

Furthermore, major collaborative initiatives have led to groundbreaking discoveries and innovations by leveraging diverse perspectives and expertise. Interdisciplinary research endeavors facilitated through international cooperation have resulted in novel approaches to complex societal challenges in healthcare, sustainability, or technology. The synergistic effect of pooling together resources and intellectual capital from multiple sources has accelerated the pace of scientific progress and technological breakthroughs, leading to transformative changes in various domains.

The ongoing impact of these initiatives extends beyond mere knowledge creation and dissemination. These collaborations have proven instrumental in nurturing the next generation of global leaders and thinkers, fostering a culture of academic excellence, and promoting the spirit of inquiry and innovation in young minds. Moreover, such initiatives have played a crucial role in addressing global challenges such as climate change, public health crises, and economic disparities by promoting a unified, cooperative approach to problem-solving that transcends borders.

As we navigate this ever-dynamic landscape, it becomes evident that major collaborative initiatives are not merely advancing the frontiers of knowledge but redefining the essence of global education and research. The interplay of diverse perspectives, cutting-edge technologies, and shared goals lays the groundwork for a more integrated, inclusive, and impactful academic ecosystem that holds immense promise for the future.

TECHNOLOGICAL INNOVATIONS SHAPING THE FUTURE OF ACADEMIA

In shaping the future of academia, technological innovations are proving to be transformative forces that redefine traditional educational paradigms. The integration of technology into education has the potential to enhance learning experiences, increase access to academic resources, and facilitate research collaboration on a global scale. One of the key technological innovations shaping the future of academia is the proliferation of online learning platforms and virtual classrooms. These platforms offer unprecedented opportunities for students and researchers to engage in meaningful academic pursuits regardless of geographical boundaries. Through interactive lectures, virtual laboratories, and collaborative projects, these platforms democratize education and foster a culture of inclusivity.

Additionally, using artificial intelligence (AI) and machine learning algorithms is revolutionizing teaching and learning methodologies. AI-powered adaptive learning systems are tailored to individual learner needs, providing personalized feedback and educational content that caters to diverse learning styles. Furthermore, virtual reality (VR) and augmented reality (AR) technologies are creating immersive learning environments that transcend the limitations of physical classrooms. Students can explore historical sites, conduct scientific experiments, or engage in simulated professional scenarios, expanding their educational horizons. The advancement of big data analytics and predictive modeling is also instrumental in shaping the future of academia. Institutions are harnessing the power of data to track educational outcomes, identify areas for improvement, and tailor curricula to meet evolving societal needs. This data-driven approach enables educators and policymakers to make informed decisions that optimize the learning environment and promote student success.

Moreover, the rise of blockchain technology offers secure and transparent mechanisms for credential verification, academic accreditation, and intellectual property protection. By leveraging blockchain, educational institutions can streamline administrative processes, mitigate fraud, and establish trusted networks for research collaboration. As technological innovations evolve, academia must adapt to embrace these advancements to improve education and research.

POLICY FRAMEWORKS FACILITATING INTERNATIONAL COOPERATION

The drive for international cooperation in education and research has propelled the necessity of developing comprehensive policy frameworks that can effectively facilitate and regulate collaborative efforts across borders. These policy frameworks are pivotal in aligning diverse national interests, fostering mutual trust, and orchestrating collective action toward common academic and research objectives.

At the heart of these frameworks is recognizing the immense value in harmonizing standards, promoting reciprocity, and enhancing the mobility of students, scholars, and researchers. This involves the establishment of clear guidelines for credit transfers, mutual recognition of qualifications, and facilitation of cultural and intellectual exchange. By incorporating principles of transparency and accountability, these policies aim to ensure fairness and equal opportunities for participation, thereby nurturing an inclusive environment for international collaboration.

Moreover, policy frameworks are instrumental in addressing regulatory challenges inherent in multinational partnerships. They provide a roadmap for navigating legal, ethical, and operational differences, offering mechanisms for dispute resolution and establishing codes of conduct. Through strategic alignment with global treaties and agreements, these frameworks create a conducive environment for sustainable cross-border initiatives, fostering a culture of respect for intellectual property rights and ethical research practices.

Furthermore, these policies acknowledge the critical role of funding and resource allocation in promoting international collaboration. They outline strategies for leveraging public and private investments, encouraging joint ventures, and incentivizing cross-national cooperative projects. By bridging financial disparities and providing mechanisms for equitable resource distribution, these frameworks enable the pursuit of ambitious interdisciplinary research and educational undertakings, transcending geographical constraints.

In addition, policy interventions are vital for addressing geopolitical and diplomatic hurdles that may hinder smooth cooperation between nations. They aim to streamline visa and immigration processes, mitigate administrative barriers, and establish platforms for dialogue, cultivating an atmosphere of goodwill and trust among participating countries. Moreover, by integrating cultural respect and diversity appreciation principles, these policies strive to foster a spirit of interconnectedness and shared purpose, transcending political narratives and regional tensions.

Ultimately, these policy frameworks act as catalysts for building resilient and dynamic global networks that aid in disseminating knowledge, preserving academic freedom, and fulfilling intellectual curiosity. They underscore the principle that collaboration knows no boundaries, embodying the spirit of collective progress and human advancement through unified educational and research endeavors, reflecting the aspirations of an interconnected global community.

BARRIERS TO COLLABORATION AND STRATEGIES FOR OVERCOMING THEM

Numerous challenges in global education and research collaboration hinder seamless cooperation among institutions, nations, and stakeholders. One of the primary barriers is the diversity of academic systems and regulatory frameworks across different countries. This disparity often complicates harmonizing curriculum standards, accreditation processes, and research funding mechanisms. Additionally, language barriers pose a significant obstacle, impeding effective communication and knowledge sharing between international partners. Cultural differences and varying academic traditions also contribute to the difficulty in aligning objectives and methodologies, thus impacting the efficiency of collaborative efforts.

Moreover, logistical constraints such as visa regulations, travel costs, and time zone disparities can impede regular interactions and hinder the progression of joint projects. Furthermore, intellectual property rights and data-sharing protocols present legal and ethical dilemmas, making it challenging to foster open collaboration without compromising individual interests and security. To surmount these barriers, proactive strategies must be implemented. First and foremost, establishing standardized frameworks and mutual recognition agreements can streamline academic equivalencies and facilitate credit transfers, thereby promoting international mobility and interdisciplinary research. Embracing multilingualism and cultural competency within educational settings can also enhance cross-border communication and cultivate a more inclusive collaborative environment. Leveraging digital platforms and virtual collaboration tools can mitigate the constraints of physical distance and time disparities, fostering continuous engagement and real-time information exchange.

Additionally, developing clear guidelines for intellectual property rights, data ownership, and publication privileges is pivotal in building trust and ensuring equitable contributions from all collaborators. Strengthening diplomatic ties and advocating for streamlined visa procedures and research grants can alleviate administrative hurdles, enabling scholars and students to engage in cross-border exchanges more easily. Furthermore, cultivating a culture of transparency, respect for diverse perspectives, and conflict resolution mechanisms is essential for sustaining harmonious partnerships. By addressing these barriers through strategic initiatives and concerted efforts, the global education and research landscape can evolve into a more interconnected and collaborative ecosystem, driving innovation and advancement truly internationally.

CASE STUDIES: SUCCESSFUL PARTNERSHIPS AND THEIR OUTCOMES

In examining successful partnerships between educational and research institutions, it becomes evident that collaborative efforts have resulted in significant advancements across various domains. Case study 1: The partnership between Harvard University and Cambridge University in biomedical research is a testament to the power of international collaboration. By pooling resources, expertise, and infrastructure, these institutions made groundbreaking discoveries in treating rare diseases, illustrating the potential of cross-border research synergies in addressing global health challenges. Case study 2: The joint initiative between the National University of Singapore and Stanford University led to the development of innovative sustainable energy solutions by leveraging each institution's unique capabilities and knowledge base. This partnership yielded technological breakthroughs and fostered cultural exchange and cross-disciplinary learning, enriching the academic experience for students and researchers involved.

Furthermore, case study 3: The strategic alliance between Oxford University and the University of Tokyo in artificial intelligence led to the creation of cutting-edge algorithms with various applications, from autonomous vehicles to predictive analytics in healthcare. Through this collaborative endeavor, both institutions have capitalized on their strengths to address societal needs and drive progress in the field. Each of these case studies underscores the transformative impact of global research partnerships, demonstrating how shared knowledge and diverse perspectives can lead to pioneering outcomes that benefit humanity.

THE ROLE OF PRIVATE SECTOR AND NGOS IN PROMOTING RESEARCH SYNERGIES

The collaboration between private sector entities, non-governmental organizations (NGOs), and academic institutions has become increasingly pivotal in shaping the landscape of global research synergies. As the traditional boundaries between these sectors blur, new opportunities and challenges emerge, necessitating a deeper exploration of their roles in advancing collaborative research endeavors. The private sector, driven by a profit-oriented ethos, brings unique resources, including funding, technological expertise, and industry-specific knowledge. This makes them critical in steering research agendas toward addressing real-world challenges and fostering innovation. Moreover, the influence of multinational corporations in both developed and emerging economies underscores their potential impact on shaping global research priorities. Concurrently, NGOs, driven by social and humanitarian objectives, possess a distinct ability to advocate for research initiatives that address pressing global issues such as public health, environmental sustainability, and social equity. Their grassroots connections, advocacy efforts, and mobilization of diverse stakeholders offer a valuable avenue for amplifying the societal impact of collaborative research projects.

Furthermore, NGOs often operate in regions or domains where traditional academic institutions may have limited reach, thereby enabling the expansion of cross-cultural and interdisciplinary research collaborations. However, while these partnerships hold great promise, they are not without complexities. Balancing corporate interests with academic freedom and safeguarding against conflicts of interest is a perennial challenge. Likewise, aligning the advocacy-driven nature of NGOs with the rigorous methodologies of academic research requires careful navigation. Addressing these concerns demands clear ethical guidelines, transparent governance structures, and moral decision-making processes. Looking ahead, the coalescence of these diverse stakeholders presents an unprecedented opportunity to forge a holistic approach to global research synergies. Embracing a shared vision, where private sector entities, NGOs, and academic institutions collaborate based on mutual respect, transparency, and social responsibility, can yield transformative outcomes. Leveraging their collective strengths, these partnerships have the potential to drive breakthrough innovations, cultivate sustainable solutions, and amplify the societal relevance of research findings. As we venture into an era of interconnectedness and interdependence, nurturing these partnerships will be integral to realizing a truly inclusive and impactful global research ecosystem.

FUTURE TRENDS: PREDICTIONS FOR THE NEXT DECADE OF COLLABORATION

As we look ahead to the next decade, it is clear that collaboration in education and research will continue to evolve in response to global challenges and technological advancements. One significant trend that is expected to shape future cooperation is the increasing use of virtual reality (VR) and augmented reality (AR) technologies in educational settings. These immersive technologies have the potential to revolutionize the way students learn, offering realistic simulations and interactive experiences that transcend traditional classroom boundaries.

Furthermore, the rise of artificial intelligence (AI) and machine learning is anticipated to impact research collaboration significantly. AI-powered tools could streamline data analysis, automate routine tasks, and even contribute to discoveries in various fields. This will enhance the efficiency of collaborative research projects and pave the way for unprecedented breakthroughs.

Another crucial trend on the horizon is the growing emphasis on cross-disciplinary collaboration. In an increasingly interconnected world, the intersection of diverse fields such as science, technology, engineering, arts, and mathematics (STEAM) will foster innovation and address complex societal issues. Multidisciplinary approaches will become the norm, cultivating a culture of knowledge exchange and creativity that transcends traditional academic silos.

Moreover, the global demand for lifelong learning and continuous skill development will likely drive a surge in international educational partnerships. Collaborative initiatives aimed at providing accessible, high-quality education to learners of all ages and backgrounds will gain momentum, addressing the evolving needs of the workforce and society at large.

In addition, the research funding and investment landscape is expected to witness significant shifts over the next decade. With the rise of public-private partnerships and impact-driven philanthropy, funding mechanisms will become more diversified and interconnected. This diversification holds the potential to fuel ambitious collaborative research endeavors and catalyze transformative solutions to pressing global challenges.

On the international stage, geopolitical dynamics and policies will also play a pivotal role in shaping future collaboration. Strategic alliances and diplomatic initiatives will influence the flow of knowledge, talent, and resources across borders, presenting opportunities and challenges for global educational and research networks.

Adopting open access principles and transparency protocols is poised to redefine scholarly communication and foster greater international engagement. Open access publishing, data sharing, and collaborative intellectual property frameworks will democratize knowledge dissemination, facilitating equitable participation in the global educational and research landscape.

As we navigate the complex terrain of the next decade, adaptability and resilience will be essential attributes for successful collaboration. The ability to leverage emerging technologies, facilitate interdisciplinary dialogues, and navigate regulatory complexities will define the trajectory of global educational and research partnerships. By embracing these key trends and proactively addressing the associated opportunities and obstacles, we can collectively steer toward a future characterized by inclusive, sustainable, and impactful collaboration.

CONCLUSION: ENVISIONING A UNIFIED GLOBAL EDUCATIONAL ECOSYSTEM

In conclusion, the vision of a unified global educational ecosystem is nothing short of ambitious yet entirely indispensable. As we scrutinize the trends and potential trajectories for collaboration in education and research over the next decade, it becomes apparent that interconnectedness will be the key theme driving progress. This unified ecosystem hinges on bridging geographical, cultural, and institutional divides to create a borderless realm of learning and knowledge creation. Such a paradigm calls for concerted efforts from policymakers, educators, researchers, and the private sector to recalibrate their strategies and embrace a holistic approach toward fostering collaboration. The challenge lies in breaking down silos and cultivating an environment where intellectual exchange knows no bounds.

A foremost element in envisioning this unified global education structure is the infusion of digital technologies and innovative pedagogical approaches. By leveraging advanced digital tools, augmented reality, virtual classrooms, and adaptive learning systems, educational establishments can transcend physical limitations and offer immersive, tailored experiences to learners worldwide. Moreover, open-access platforms and repositories can democratize knowledge dissemination while nurturing cross-border academic partnerships. Similarly, research collaboration can harness big data analytics, AI-driven simulations, and collaborative workspaces to drive breakthrough discoveries while fostering interdisciplinary exchanges that defy national frontiers.

From a policy standpoint, envisioning a unified educational ecosystem necessitates harmonizing regulations, accreditation standards, and quality assurance mechanisms across nations. A conducive regulatory environment empowers equitable access to academic resources, facilitates staff and student mobility, and ensures mutual recognition of qualifications. Intergovernmental agreements and initiatives are instrumental in fostering research networks, joint funding schemes, and collaborative scientific ventures that transcend geopolitical rivalries while addressing shared global challenges.

An essential facet of this vision involves recognizing and mitigating the disparities between regions and institutions. Creating an inclusive ecosystem demands concerted efforts to narrow the gap in educational infrastructure, resource allocation, and faculty expertise among diverse ecosystems. Established institutions can support emerging educational hubs through strategic capacity-building programs, mentorship networks, and twinning arrangements while promoting knowledge transfer and skill development. Simultaneously, fostering a culture of inclusivity entails integrating indigenous knowledge systems, languages, and epistemologies into the global academic discourse, thereby enriching the tapestry of human understanding.

In conclusion, envisioning a unified global educational ecosystem necessitates embracing a mindset shift that underscores collaboration over competition, solidarity over isolation, and diversity as a source of strength. It is imperative to realize that the quest for a unified educational landscape transcends territorial aims; it embodies a collective pursuit of humanity's intellectual advancement and societal betterment. We sow the seeds of future prosperity, innovation, and global understanding by laying the foundations for a connected educational framework.

CHAPTER 22

Global Leadership: Who Will Guide Tomorrow's World?

GLOBAL LEADERSHIP

The concept of global leadership has evolved significantly in response to the complex dynamics of an interconnected world. As the global landscape continues to undergo profound shifts, the traditional leadership models are challenged by new paradigms that demand a more nuanced understanding of international relations. In this era of globalization, leaders are required to navigate diverse cultural, economic, and political terrains, emphasizing the need for a multifaceted approach to leadership. The interconnectedness of economies, technological advancements, and geopolitical complexities has redefined the scope and expectations of global leaders. Moreover, the emergence of non-traditional power centers and the growing influence of regional players have further complicated the dynamics of global leadership. In light of these developments, it is crucial to scrutinize the evolution of leadership models and assess their effectiveness in addressing contemporary challenges. This section will delve into an in-depth analysis of current and past leadership models, aiming to examine the shifting paradigms in global leadership comprehensively.

ASSESSING CURRENT AND PAST LEADERSHIP MODELS

Throughout history, various leadership models have emerged and evolved, shaping the course of nations and societies. As we stand on the precipice of a new era, it is imperative to critically assess these models to glean insights into effective global leadership for the 21st century. Autocratic leadership was prevalent in ancient civilizations, with rulers wielding absolute power over their domains. While this centralized authority allowed for swift decision-making, it often resulted in authoritarian rule and limited individual freedoms. Moving forward, the feudal system introduced hierarchical structures where allegiance to a lord was paramount, setting the stage for centuries of dynastic reigns and class-based societies. The Industrial Revolution ushered in a new paradigm as bureaucratic leadership emerged within large-scale organizations, emphasizing hierarchies and standardized processes. This model revolutionized manufacturing and commerce, giving rise to inflexible bureaucracies and stifling innovation. Concurrently, transformational leadership began to gain prominence, focusing on inspiring and empowering followers to achieve exceptional outcomes. Despite its positive impact on motivation and productivity, the reliance on charismatic leaders posed challenges in sustaining long-term success. Servant leadership has recently garnered attention for its emphasis on serving others and fostering a sense of community. This model strives to transcend self-interest and prioritize the well-being of all stakeholders. However, critics argue that it may not always align with the demands of complex geopolitical landscapes. Today, a nuanced approach to leadership is indispensable as we navigate an interconnected world facing multifaceted challenges. It calls for integrating diverse models to cultivate adaptive leaders capable of navigating ambiguity and driving meaningful change. By drawing on the lessons of history and the advancements of contemporary thought, we can forge a path toward holistic and inclusive global leadership.

CRITERIA FOR EFFECTIVE GLOBAL LEADERSHIP IN THE 21ST CENTURY

In the rapidly evolving landscape of the 21st century, effective global leadership demands a nuanced understanding of the complex interplay between diverse cultures, shifting geopolitical dynamics, and technological advancements. The criteria for effective global leadership in this era go beyond traditional notions of authority and command, encompassing a broad spectrum of competencies. Firstly, global leaders must demonstrate adaptability and resilience in uncertainty. The ability to navigate volatile geopolitical environments and swiftly respond to rapidly changing circumstances is integral to effective leadership. Moreover, a deep understanding of cultural diversity and an inclusive mindset are critical attributes for leaders seeking to build cohesive, global consensus. A leader's capacity to foster collaboration and communication across divergent cultural contexts is pivotal in the 21st-century global arena. Beyond this, ethical acumen and integrity constitute dynamic global leadership's cornerstone. Leaders must uphold transparency and ethical conduct, guided by a strong moral compass that transcends geographical boundaries. They should be exemplary in promoting accountability and fairness, thereby earning the trust and respect of diverse stakeholder groups. Another key criterion for effective global leadership lies in the aptitude for leveraging technology as an enabler of progress. Leaders in today's interconnected world must harness the power of digital platforms and emerging technologies to facilitate innovation, connectivity, and sustainable development. This necessitates a continuous pursuit of technological literacy and strategic foresight to steer organizations and nations toward prosperity amidst the digital revolution. Furthermore, the ability to inspire and empower a diverse workforce and populace is a defining characteristic of impactful global leaders. By championing inclusivity and empowering talents from all walks of life, leaders can harness the collective potential of a diverse talent pool, driving innovation and progress. Lastly, forward-thinking leaders prioritize environmental sustainability and social responsibility, recognizing the interconnectedness of global challenges and the imperative to address them collaboratively. These criteria collectively delineate the essence of effective global leadership in the 21st century – a multifaceted paradigm requiring versatility, ethical fortitude, technological adeptness, and a vision for a better tomorrow.

INFLUENCE OF TECHNOLOGY ON LEADERSHIP DYNAMICS

In today's rapidly evolving global landscape, technology has redefined leadership's nature and influence dynamics. The proliferation of digital platforms, the advent of artificial intelligence, and the unprecedented interconnectedness facilitated by the internet have altered traditional leadership paradigms. These technological advancements have not only accelerated the pace of decision-making but have also expanded the reach and impact of leaders across the globe.

Communication is one of the primary ways technology influences leadership dynamics. Leaders can now engage with diverse stakeholders instantaneously, transcending geographical barriers and time zones. Platforms such as video conferencing, collaborative software, and social media enable leaders to maintain direct lines of communication with their teams and constituents, fostering transparency and accessibility. Additionally, the digital age has amplified the significance of effective and strategic communication, as leaders must navigate the complexities of conveying their vision and policies amidst the deluge of information and diverse perspectives available online.

Moreover, the strategic use of data and analytics has revolutionized leadership practices. With vast amounts of real-time data, leaders can make informed decisions, predict trends, and identify potential challenges more accurately. This quantitative approach to leadership empowers decision-makers to formulate evidence-based strategies, optimize resource allocation, and mitigate risks. However, it also demands a deeper understanding of data interpretation and ethical considerations to ensure responsible and moral leadership.

Furthermore, technology has reshaped organizational structures and operational frameworks, presenting leaders with new opportunities and challenges. The rise of remote work facilitated by virtual collaboration tools has prompted leaders to reimagine workforce management, performance evaluation, and the cultivation of organizational culture. Adaptive leaders leverage technology to foster a cohesive and motivated workforce while navigating the complexities of a decentralized and diverse workplace.

The emergence of disruptive technologies such as blockchain, robotics, and the Internet of Things (IoT) has also heightened the imperative for leaders to embrace innovation and adaptability. Leaders must navigate the ethical dimensions of emerging technologies, address concerns about automation's impact on employment, and harness the transformative potential of these innovations to drive sustainable growth and societal progress.

In conclusion, the influence of technology on leadership dynamics is undeniable, necessitating a paradigm shift in leadership competencies and strategies. As the Fourth Industrial Revolution unfolds, leaders must cultivate digital fluency, embrace rapid change, and champion ethical, human-centered leadership in the face of technological disruption.

REGIONAL PLAYERS WITH GLOBAL AMBITIONS

In today's rapidly evolving geopolitical landscape, numerous regional players seek to elevate their influence and global standing. These emerging powers, often characterized by a unique combination of economic prowess, political stability, and strategic geographical positioning, increasingly assert their ambitions on the world stage. Their aspirations to become prominent global actors pose significant challenges to the existing leadership dynamics dominated by traditional power centers such as the G7 and BRICS nations. Regional players like India, Brazil, South Korea, and Nigeria have demonstrated remarkable economic growth and development, leading them to pursue more assertive roles in shaping global agendas. India, for instance, has emerged as a key player, leveraging its demographic dividend and technological innovation to expand its sphere of influence across South Asia, the Indian Ocean region, and beyond.

Similarly, Brazil, with its abundant natural resources and growing industrial capability, envisions a leadership role in Latin America and within broader international forums. South Korea, propelled by its advancements in technology and trade, aims to exert more significant influence in East Asia and the wider Pacific region. Meanwhile, Nigeria, as the most populous country in Africa and a major oil producer, seeks to leverage its economic potential to enhance its position as a pivotal player on the African continent and in global energy markets. The rise of these regional players with global ambitions introduces a new dimension to the worldwide leadership landscape, challenging established power structures and necessitating a reevaluation of traditional alliances and diplomatic strategies. As they expand their reach and influence, these emerging powers will likely significantly impact the formulation and implementation of international policies, trade agreements, and security arrangements. Understanding their motivations, capabilities, and aspirations is paramount for envisioning a future world order reflecting contemporary geopolitics' multifaceted nature.

IMPACT OF ECONOMIC SHIFTS ON LEADERSHIP ROLES

Economic shifts play a pivotal role in shaping the landscape of global leadership. As the world undergoes profound changes in financial structures and patterns, leaders are compelled to adapt and recalibrate their approaches to navigate the complexities of international relations and governance. The emergence of new economic powers, such as those within the BRICS bloc, has challenged the traditional dominance of G7 nations, leading to a reconfiguration of global leadership roles. These shifts have created a multi-polar world where collaboration and strategic alliances have become increasingly crucial for effective leadership. Leaders must grapple with the evolving dynamics of trade, investment, and technological innovation, as these factors influence power distribution across the global stage.

Furthermore, the interconnectedness of modern economies has elevated the significance of cross-border cooperation and diplomacy, prompting leaders to actively engage in economic forums and summits to advocate for their respective nations' interests. At the same time, economic disparities within and between countries pose pressing challenges for leaders, requiring them to address inequality, poverty, and sustainable development. Effective leadership calls for a deep understanding of economic interdependencies and the ability to formulate inclusive policies that promote prosperity while mitigating adverse impacts. Moreover, the advent of digital economies and disruptive technologies introduces new dimensions to leadership roles, necessitating leaders to foster an environment conducive to innovation and adaptation. They must harness the potential of emerging sectors and ensure that their countries remain competitive in an ever-evolving economic landscape. Economic shifts profoundly influence global leadership, compelling leaders to comprehend and respond adeptly to the intricacies of a rapidly changing global economy.

CULTURAL AND ETHICAL CONSIDERATIONS IN LEADERSHIP

Leadership, especially globally, demands a deep understanding and appreciation of diverse cultural backgrounds and ethical frameworks. In an increasingly interconnected world, influential leaders must navigate complex cultural landscapes with sensitivity and insight. Leaders must recognize the impact of cultural differences on communication styles, decision-making processes, and overall organizational dynamics. Furthermore, ethical considerations play a pivotal role in shaping leaders' behavior and decision-making. Upholding ethical standards and promoting integrity, transparency, and fairness are essential for maintaining trust and credibility in leadership roles.

Additionally, leaders must be aware of the ethical implications of their actions on various stakeholders, including employees, customers, and the broader society. Cultural intelligence, or the ability to understand and adapt to different cultural contexts, is a must-have skill for global leaders. This involves recognizing and respecting cultural diversity and leveraging it as a source of strength and innovation. Leaders who embrace cultural diversity and foster an inclusive environment are better equipped to drive collaboration and creativity within their organizations. Moreover, they are positioned to make more informed and culturally sensitive decisions that resonate across diverse audiences. Ethical leadership requires a commitment to doing what is morally right, even when faced with difficult choices. It involves setting clear ethical standards, leading by example, and holding oneself and others accountable for ethical conduct. Leaders who exhibit ethical behavior earn the respect and loyalty of their teams, inspiring greater dedication and productivity. By integrating cultural awareness and ethical considerations into their leadership approach, global leaders can foster an environment of mutual respect, understanding, and ethical excellence. Such leadership qualities are integral to building sustainable relationships, driving positive change, and navigating the complexities of a rapidly evolving global landscape.

CASE STUDIES: SUCCESSES AND FAILURES IN GLOBAL LEADERSHIP

In global leadership, case studies serve as invaluable tools for understanding the complex interplay of factors that contribute to the success or failure of leaders on the world stage. By scrutinizing both positive and negative examples, we can derive critical insights into the multifaceted nature of global leadership. One compelling case study is the successful leadership of Nelson Mandela in South Africa. Mandela's unwavering commitment to reconciliation and unity in the aftermath of apartheid showcased the transformative power of compassionate and inclusive leadership. Through strategic negotiations and a vision of justice, Mandela not only united a fractured nation but also garnered international respect and admiration.

Conversely, the leadership failure exemplified by the Rwandan genocide serves as a harrowing reminder of the catastrophic consequences of leadership devoid of ethical considerations. The failure of global leadership to intervene and prevent the mass atrocities highlighted the dire need for moral courage and robust international cooperation. This case study underscores the profound impact of leadership choices on global stability and human welfare. Shifting the focus to business leadership, the Apple Inc. case under Steve Jobs's stewardship provides insight into visionary leadership and its impact on global markets. Jobs' innovation and risk-taking propelled Apple to the forefront of the technological revolution, fundamentally reshaping entire industries.

Conversely, Enron's downfall is a stark lesson in the repercussions of unethical and shortsighted leadership. Enron's fraudulent practices and lack of corporate governance led to one of the most notorious corporate collapses in history, underscoring the importance of integrity and ethical conduct in global business leadership. These case studies illustrate the intricate interplay of cultural, ethical, and strategic elements in shaping global leadership outcomes. They emphasize the enduring relevance of moral considerations, proactive decision-making, and long-term vision in the leadership landscape. As we navigate a rapidly changing world, these case studies serve as poignant reminders of the immense responsibility carried by global leaders and the far-reaching consequences of their actions.

FUTURE TRENDS IN POLITICAL AND BUSINESS LEADERSHIP

The global leadership landscape is continually evolving, shaped by many factors such as technological advancements, changing geopolitical dynamics, and economic developments. As we navigate the complexities of the 21st century, it becomes imperative to anticipate the future trends that will redefine political and business leadership on a global scale. One of the prominent future trends in political and business leadership pertains to the increasing emphasis on ethical and sustainable practices. Leaders are expected to not only drive profitability and growth but also uphold ethical standards and prioritize sustainability initiatives. This shift reflects a growing awareness of corporate social responsibility and the demand for leaders who can align business objectives with societal and environmental well-being.

Additionally, the rise of digital transformation is set to revolutionize leadership paradigms. Technology will continue to disrupt traditional business models, requiring leaders to adapt and embrace innovation to stay competitive. Furthermore, decentralizing power structures and democratizing information through digital platforms will necessitate a more inclusive and transparent approach to leadership. Another crucial trend is the globalization of leadership talent. With increased interconnectedness across borders, diverse perspectives and cross-cultural competencies are becoming essential for effective leadership. Leaders must possess the intercultural fluency to navigate global markets and foster collaboration among geographically dispersed teams.

Moreover, servant leadership is gaining traction as a transformative approach to governance and management. Empathy, humility, and a dedication to serving others lie at the core of this model, challenging traditional hierarchical leadership styles. As the demand for purpose-driven leadership intensifies, individuals who embody these qualities will likely shape the future landscape of global leadership. The convergence of political and business leadership is another notable trend, blurring the lines between public and private sector influences. Collaborative efforts between governmental bodies and corporations are increasingly required to address complex issues such as climate change, economic inequality, and global health crises. This convergence presents an opportunity for leaders to leverage collective resources and expertise for the betterment of society. Finally, the resurgence of moral leadership, characterized by integrity, transparency, and a commitment to the greater good, is poised to redefine the expectations placed on leaders. In an era of skepticism and disillusionment, leaders who uphold unwavering principles and demonstrate authentic leadership will garner trust and inspire positive change. Embracing these future trends will be instrumental in shaping a new breed of politically and economically astute leaders primed to navigate the challenges and opportunities that lie ahead.

STRATEGIES FOR DEVELOPING NEXT-GENERATION GLOBAL LEADERS

As we look to the future of global leadership, it becomes increasingly important to focus on developing the next generation of leaders who can navigate the complexities of an interconnected world. To achieve this, organizations and educational institutions must implement strategic initiatives that foster the growth and development of aspiring leaders. One key strategy is providing comprehensive leadership training programs incorporating interdisciplinary knowledge and skills. This approach ensures that future leaders are equipped to understand and address multifaceted global challenges with astuteness and innovation. Additionally, mentorship and coaching relationships are pivotal in nurturing leadership potential. Establishing mentorship programs that pair emerging leaders with seasoned professionals allows for the transfer of invaluable experience, wisdom, and networks.

Furthermore, exposure to diverse cultural experiences and perspectives is instrumental in shaping well-rounded global leaders. Encouraging international exchanges, study abroad programs, and multicultural interactions cultivates empathy, adaptability, and a nuanced understanding of global issues. In cultivating the next generation of global leaders, emphasis should be placed on cultivating ethical leadership values and behaviors. Integrating ethical frameworks into leadership development fosters a sense of responsibility, integrity, and accountability among aspiring leaders. Moreover, leveraging technology for leadership development can enhance accessibility and scalability. Virtual learning platforms, online resources, and digital collaboration tools offer flexible avenues for leadership skill enhancement and knowledge acquisition. Another critical strategy is to create opportunities for hands-on leadership experiences. Internships, project management roles, and community engagement initiatives enable aspiring leaders to apply theoretical knowledge to real-world scenarios, fostering confidence, decision-making prowess, and resilience. Lastly, instilling a continuous learning and adaptation mindset is vital for grooming future-ready global leaders. Encouraging a thirst for knowledge, a willingness to embrace change, and an openness to feedback empowers emerging leaders to evolve and thrive in dynamic global environments. By proactively implementing these strategies, stakeholders can contribute to the development of a robust pipeline of next-generation global leaders who are primed to steer the world towards greater prosperity, collaboration, and sustainable progress.

CHAPTER 23

Conclusion: Building a More Cooperative Peaceful World

REFLECTIONS ON PAST GOVERNANCE MODELS

Throughout history, the world has witnessed diverse governance systems, each leaving a distinct imprint on global cooperation. The ancient civilizations of Mesopotamia and Egypt laid the foundation for early forms of governance, characterized by monarchies and dynastic rule, which dominated the political landscape for centuries. This system fostered relative stability within the respective empires but was often marked by authoritarian practices that hindered broader international cooperation. As societies evolved, feudalism emerged in medieval Europe, entrenching a hierarchical social structure and decentralizing power among local lords, leading to fragmented political authority and limited cross-border collaboration. Moreover, the colonial era perpetuated exploitative governance models as imperial powers subjugated territories and established mercantilist economic structures, disrupting traditional social orders and impeding inclusive global partnerships. Over time, the rise of nation-states and the Westphalian system introduced modern diplomatic protocols, enshrining the principle of national sovereignty and promoting interstate relations based on mutual recognition. However, this system also sowed the seeds of geopolitical rivalries and conflicts, hindering multilateral peace efforts. The aftermath of World War II gave birth to the United Nations and ushered in an era of collective security and diplomacy, heralding aspirations for enhanced international collaboration. Despite these milestones, Cold War dynamics led to the polarization of the global order, exacerbating tensions and impeding cooperative endeavors. With the dawn of the 21st century, globalization underscored the interdependence of nations, underscoring the need for more inclusive and participatory governance paradigms. The emergence of regional blocs, such as the European Union and ASEAN, sought to navigate beyond traditional nation-state frameworks, striving for deeper integration and consensus-based decision-making. Furthermore, supranational organizations like the World Bank and the International Monetary Fund aimed to address economic disparities and promote development, reflecting the quest for cohesive global governance. Reflecting on these historical governance models is a critical juncture to appraise their impact on contemporary global cooperation, offering valuable insights to chart a more cooperative and peaceful future.

CURRENT TRENDS AND INNOVATIONS IN INTERNATIONAL DIPLOMACY

The landscape of international diplomacy is continually evolving, marked by shifting power dynamics, the emergence of non-state actors, and the increasing interconnectedness of global affairs. In an era characterized by rapid technological advancements and unprecedented access to information, traditional modes of diplomacy have been complemented – and at times challenged – by innovative approaches that transcend geographical boundaries. The digital age has not only redefined communication channels but has also revolutionized the practice of diplomacy, enabling real-time interactions, virtual summits, and instant dissemination of policy decisions.

Moreover, the proliferation of multilateral organizations and forums has expanded the scope of diplomatic relations, offering platforms for dialogue, negotiation, and consensus-building on various issues. From the United Nations to regional blocs such as the European Union and ASEAN, diplomats must navigate complex networks and engage with stakeholders from diverse backgrounds. This trend underscores the need for diplomats to possess astute negotiation skills, profound cultural understanding, and linguistic mastery.

Simultaneously, citizen diplomacy and public engagement have transformed the nature of diplomatic activities. With the advent of social media and online advocacy, diplomats are compelled to engage with global audiences, disseminate their nation's policies, and respond to public inquiries openly and transparently. This shift towards greater transparency and inclusivity signifies a departure from traditional closed-door negotiations and signals the impact of public opinion on diplomatic decision-making.

As diplomacy extends beyond the purview of state actors, there has been a notable surge in track-two diplomacy initiatives involving private enterprises, academic institutions, and civil society organizations. These collaborative efforts address global challenges, foster mutual understanding, and bridge cultural divides through dialogue and cooperation. The agility and flexibility inherent in these informal channels of diplomacy enable quick responses to emerging crises and allow for innovative problem-solving mechanisms.

Furthermore, the growing emphasis on 'network diplomacy' underscores the interconnectedness of contemporary diplomatic strategies. Diplomatic missions now extend beyond embassies and consulates, encompassing a web of partnerships, coalitions, and alliances that span regions and sectors. This trend is exemplified by the expanding roles of countries in conflict mediation, humanitarian assistance, and peacebuilding, reinforcing the value of collective action and shared responsibility in addressing world issues.

In light of these current trends and innovations, international diplomacy is transforming, guided by the imperatives of connectivity, inclusivity, and adaptability. As we strive towards constructing a more cooperative and peaceful world, these developments underscore the necessity for diplomats to willingly embrace change, harness technology judiciously, and prioritize sustainable, mutually beneficial solutions. The evolving dynamics of international relations demand an agile, forward-thinking approach with innovative strategies to navigate the complex challenges and opportunities that define our globalized era.

EVALUATING THE ROLE OF ECONOMIC INTERDEPENDENCY

Economic interdependency has become increasingly crucial in the contemporary global landscape, substantially impacting international relations and diplomacy. As nations continue to engage in trade, investment, and economic cooperation, the intricate web of emerging interdependencies often shapes their relationships' dynamics. Evaluating the role of economic interdependency involves a comprehensive analysis of its impact on geopolitical strategies, conflict resolution, and the establishment of mutual interests among nations. At the heart of this assessment lies the recognition that no single nation exists in isolation – instead, they are interconnected through complex networks of economic ties, influencing both their domestic policies and their interactions with other countries.

Furthermore, economic interdependency fosters more significant interconnectedness and interrelated interests among nations, creating a shared stake in each other's prosperity and stability. By closely examining the implications of economic interdependence, we can gain insights into how it both constrains and enables the behavior of states in the international arena. Moreover, understanding the intricacies of economic interdependency allows for a more informed approach to navigating the complexities of global governance and addressing the challenges associated with economic disparities and imbalances.

In addition, the evaluation of economic interdependency necessitates exploring how shifting economic landscapes and evolving trade patterns influence power dynamics and the distribution of resources at regional and global levels. The rise of emerging economies and the reconfiguration of traditional economic powerhouses have significantly reshaped the dynamics of economic interdependence, prompting a re-evaluation of established norms and practices. This re-evaluation also requires a deep understanding of the evolving roles of multinational corporations, financial institutions, and global supply chains, all of which play integral parts in shaping the contours of economic interdependency on the world stage.

Moreover, as we evaluate the role of economic interdependency, we must consider the implications of unforeseen events and disruptions, such as economic crises, natural disasters, or global pandemics, which can test the resilience of interdependent systems and require coordinated responses from the international community. Addressing these challenges demands a proactive and adaptive approach to managing economic interdependencies, emphasizing the importance of building robust mechanisms for cooperation, risk mitigation, and recovery. Through this evaluation, we can explore pathways to foster sustainable and equitable economic interdependencies that contribute to nations' stability, prosperity, and peace worldwide.

TECHNOLOGICAL ADVANCEMENTS: BRIDGING OR DIVIDING THE WORLD?

The rapid advancement of technology in today's interconnected world has presented unprecedented opportunities and challenges on a global scale. The proliferation of digital communication tools, artificial intelligence, and automation has significantly reshaped economies, societies, and international relations. While these technological advancements hold the potential to bridge gaps and facilitate more excellent global connectivity, they also can deepen existing divisions and exacerbate disparities. At the heart of this dichotomy lies how nations and societies harness and adapt to these innovations. The impact of technological advancements on global governance structures and power dynamics cannot be understated. Adopting emerging technologies has led to a new dimension of competition among nations, where those at the forefront of innovation seek to consolidate their influence and competitive edge. This pursuit of technological superiority can lead to a more divided world, with disparities in access to resources, opportunities, and influence.

Moreover, the rapid pace of technological change raises concerns about the destabilizing effects on traditional employment sectors, potential mass displacement of workers, and widening socioeconomic inequalities. These challenges demand profound policy responses at both national and international levels to ensure inclusive and sustainable development. However, despite the risks, technology also offers immense promise in bridging the world through enhanced communication, collaboration, and knowledge-sharing. Digital platforms and networks provide avenues for cross-cultural exchange, educational opportunities, and global solidarity. The democratization of information and access to digital resources can empower marginalized communities and amplify diverse voices on the global stage. In addition, technological solutions are instrumental in addressing pressing international issues, including climate change, public health, and humanitarian crises. Harnessing the potential of technological advancements for the collective betterment of humanity requires deliberate efforts to mitigate the associated risks, promote ethical and responsible innovation, and foster international cooperation. Striking a balance between competition and collaboration in the technological landscape is pivotal in building a more equitable and united world. Governments, businesses, civil society, and individuals must work towards leveraging technology as a unifying force, ensuring that its benefits are equitably distributed and shared. As we navigate the complexities of an increasingly digitized world, it becomes imperative to establish robust regulatory frameworks, ethical standards, and mechanisms for global tech governance. Embracing a collective vision for the responsible and inclusive use of technology is fundamental in shaping a future where technological advancements serve as bridges, rather than barriers, in our collective pursuit of peace and prosperity.

THE ENVIRONMENTAL IMPERATIVE: SUSTAINABILITY AS A UNIFYING GOAL

As our world grapples with the pressing challenges of environmental degradation and climate change, it has become increasingly clear that sustainability is a crucial unifying goal for all nations. The indiscriminate exploitation of natural resources and the unchecked emissions of greenhouse gases have imperiled the delicate balance of our planet's ecosystems, leading to ecological crises with far-reaching implications. In this context, embracing sustainable practices is not just an ethical choice but a necessity for safeguarding the future of humanity. Nations must recognize that a shared commitment to sustainability offers a pathway towards common ground, transcending geopolitical differences. Adopting sustainable development goals can serve as a blueprint for cooperative efforts, ensuring that economic progress is harmonized with environmental stewardship. This entails integrating renewable energy sources, advocating for biodiversity conservation, and prioritizing responsible consumption and production patterns.

Furthermore, sustainable urban planning and infrastructure development can ease the strain on natural resources while enhancing citizens' quality of life. Collaborative initiatives to combat deforestation, mitigate pollution, and preserve vital ecosystems are pivotal in collectively addressing global environmental challenges. International cooperation on climate action, driven by evidence-based policies and transparent accountability mechanisms, can propel us towards a greener, more sustainable future. Moreover, leveraging technological innovations and scientific advancements can substantially mitigate environmental risks and foster sustainable practices. Encouraging knowledge exchange and capacity-building among nations can facilitate the diffusion of best practices and solutions for environmental sustainability. Embracing a circular economy model, whereby resources are utilized efficiently, and waste is minimized, can further cement the foundation for a collaborative and sustainable global ecosystem. As we navigate the complexities of the modern world, it is essential to recognize that the environmental imperative transcends national boundaries and necessitates concerted international collaboration. By striving towards sustainability as a shared goal, nations can pave the way for a collective legacy of responsible stewardship and a more harmonious coexistence with nature.

CULTURAL UNDERSTANDINGS AND MISUNDERSTANDINGS

In the context of a rapidly globalizing world, the intricate tapestry of cultural diversity has emerged as a central theme in international relations. Understanding the nuances of different cultures and their impact on diplomatic interactions is essential for fostering cooperative and peaceful relationships among nations. Cultural understandings and misunderstandings play a significant role in shaping perceptions, attitudes, and, ultimately, the course of global affairs. Various cultural dynamics can drive collaboration and mutual respect or contribute to miscommunication and conflict. The need for cross-cultural competence and sensitivity is at the heart of this complex landscape. Cultural understanding encompasses more than mere tolerance; it requires a deep appreciation and awareness of diverse ideologies, beliefs, traditions, and practices. Misunderstandings often stem from the inability to navigate cultural differences effectively. This leads to misconceptions, prejudices, and even geopolitical tensions. Bridging these divides demands proactive measures such as promoting intercultural dialogue, education, and exchange programs. Realizing the potential of cultural diversity as a source of strength can lead to enhanced cooperation and innovative global problem-solving.

Moreover, addressing cultural misunderstandings involves acknowledging historical contexts, socioeconomic disparities, and power differentials that shape perceptions and interactions. Achieving a more culturally literate and empathetic global community necessitates initiatives to foster cultural intelligence and promote intercultural collaboration. Such efforts are crucial for building trust, fostering empathy, and mitigating conflicts that arise from cultural tensions. By recognizing and embracing the richness of global cultural heritages, nations can forge enduring relationships based on mutual respect and understanding. Cultivating a culture of inclusivity and mutual learning will undoubtedly contribute to constructing a more cooperative and peaceful world.

THE FUTURE OF GLOBAL SECURITY FRAMEWORKS

Amidst geopolitical tensions and rapid technological advancements, the future of global security frameworks stands at a critical juncture. Traditional notions of security have evolved beyond military capabilities to encompass a wide spectrum of non-traditional threats, including cyber warfare, terrorism, and pandemics. As such, security is no longer confined to physical borders but extends to the digital realm and public health landscapes. The proliferation of WMDs, asymmetric warfare, and state-sponsored cyber-attacks necessitates a paradigm shift in global security strategies. To address these challenges effectively, the international community must embrace a holistic approach that integrates hard and soft power initiatives. Establishing collaborative defense mechanisms, intelligence sharing, and joint counter-terrorism efforts are imperative in safeguarding nations against modern threats.

Furthermore, addressing the root causes of conflicts, promoting human rights, and strengthening international law enforcement are fundamental pillars of comprehensive security architecture. In addition to state-centric security measures, the role of international organizations such as the United Nations, NATO, and regional blocs cannot be overstated. As we look towards the future, the reformation and adaptation of these institutions to current geopolitical realities will be vital for maintaining global peace and stability. Moreover, security frameworks should also account for economic interdependencies, environmental sustainability, and social cohesion as integral components of a secure world. To mitigate emerging security risks, collaborative research and development, information sharing, and capacity building must be prioritized. Leveraging advanced technologies for threat detection, mitigation, and response is pivotal in staying ahead of evolving security challenges. However, ethical considerations surrounding AI, biotechnology, and autonomous weapons demand a coordinated global approach to prevent misuse and ensure accountability. Coordinated efforts in disarmament, non-proliferation, and arms control are essential for reducing the risks associated with conventional and unconventional weapons. Ultimately, the future of global security frameworks lies in fostering cooperative partnerships, transparent dialogue, and inclusive decision-making processes. By cultivating a shared understanding of security challenges and collective commitment to peace, the international community can pave the way for a more secure and prosperous future for future generations.

TOWARDS MORE INCLUSIVE GLOBAL INSTITUTIONS

The evolution of global governance has witnessed a gradual shift towards inclusivity, recognizing the need to incorporate diverse voices and perspectives in decision-making processes. This paradigmatic transformation underscores the imperative of empowering previously marginalized nations and communities worldwide, fostering a more equitable and just international order. Central to this endeavor is reforming existing multilateral institutions to represent the evolving geopolitical landscape better. By recalibrating the power dynamics within these institutions, a more inclusive approach can be achieved, ensuring that the concerns and aspirations of all stakeholders are given due consideration.

In parallel, forming new global forums and platforms has enhanced inclusivity in international affairs. These novel arenas allow emerging economies, regional groupings, and civil society organizations to dialogue with established powers, promoting mutual understanding and collaborative problem-solving. The democratization of global decision-making processes through such mechanisms can mitigate the risks of marginalization and exclusion, fostering a sense of shared ownership and responsibility for addressing transnational challenges.

Moreover, fostering inclusive global institutions requires earnest efforts to address systemic inequalities and architectural biases embedded within the existing frameworks. This necessitates proactive measures to enhance the representation of underrepresented regions and demographics in leadership positions, amplifying their influence in shaping international agendas. Embracing diversity at the highest decision-making echelons fosters a culture of empathy, understanding, and collective problem-solving, enriching the quality and effectiveness of global governance mechanisms.

Furthermore, greater inclusivity in global institutions entails reimagining the processes of norm-creation and standard-setting to accommodate the nuanced perspectives and priorities of a multipolar world. This demands an open-minded and adaptive approach to policy formulation that embraces the plurality of values, traditions, and developmental trajectories across different regions. By accommodating diverse viewpoints within the institutional architecture, a more robust and legitimate framework for global cooperation can be nurtured, reinforcing the credibility and relevance of international governance structures.

Ultimately, the pursuit of more inclusive global institutions serves not only as an ethical imperative but also as a pragmatic strategy for advancing peace, prosperity, and sustainable development on a global scale. By cultivating a culture of dialogue, reciprocity, and mutual respect, the international community can harness its collective wisdom and resources to confront shared challenges and seize common opportunities, thereby paving the way for a more harmonious and cooperative world order.

HARNESSING GLOBAL MEDIA FOR PEACE ADVOCACY

In today's interconnected world, the global media has emerged as a powerful force in shaping public opinion and influencing international affairs. The pervasiveness of digital communication platforms, from social media to online news portals, has exponentially increased the reach and impact of media on societies worldwide. This section explores the pivotal role of global media in advocating for peace and fostering understanding among nations.

Global media can be harnessed as a potent tool for peace advocacy by promoting dialogue, empathy, and mutual respect across diverse cultures and geographies. Through compelling storytelling, investigative reporting, and nuanced analysis, media professionals can play a critical role in humanizing global conflicts, shedding light on humanitarian crises, and elevating voices of reconciliation. Moreover, multimedia formats allow for impactful storytelling that can resonate with audiences on a visceral level, transcending linguistic and cultural barriers in the pursuit of peace.

Furthermore, responsible journalism and ethical media practices are essential pillars in leveraging the global media for peace advocacy. By adhering to accuracy, fairness, and impartiality principles, media practitioners can build trust with their audiences, dispel misinformation, and counter divisive narratives that fuel discord. Additionally, collaborative initiatives between media outlets, civil society organizations, and governmental agencies can amplify the reach and effectiveness of peace advocacy efforts, creating a unified front in advancing shared goals of harmony and understanding.

Strategic partnerships with influential figures in the entertainment industry, public intellectuals, and grassroots activists can also enhance the impact of media-driven peace advocacy. Artistic expressions, such as films, music, and visual arts, can evoke emotions and convey universal hope and solidarity, transcending geopolitical differences and stimulating collective action toward peaceful coexistence. By harnessing the power of celebrity endorsements and public campaigns, the global media can elevate the prominence of peacebuilding initiatives, garnering widespread attention and fostering a culture of global citizenship.

Moreover, with citizen journalism and user-generated content proliferation, individuals have unprecedented opportunities to contribute to peace advocacy through their narratives and experiences. Social media platforms serve as virtual town squares where grassroots movements and community-based peacebuilding efforts can mobilize support and galvanize public demand for diplomatic solutions to conflicts. This democratization of media empowerment creates a bottom-up approach to peace advocacy, amplifying diverse voices and perspectives that might otherwise remain marginalized in traditional media channels.

By harnessing the global media for peace advocacy, societies can bridge divides, cultivate empathy, and construct a narrative of interconnectedness and shared humanity. The ethical and strategic deployment of media resources, combined with collaborative partnerships and grassroots engagement, holds the potential to catalyze societal shifts toward a more peaceful and harmonious world.

STEPS FORWARD IN CONSTRUCTING A COOPERATIVE FUTURE

As we navigate the complex web of global challenges, it is evident that constructing a cooperative future requires concerted efforts across multiple facets of society. The intertwining forces of economics, politics, technology, and culture dictate the need for a new paradigm in global governance. Building a more cooperative and peaceful world hinges on several key steps forward. Firstly, fostering an environment that encourages open dialogue and understanding across diverse cultures and belief systems is essential. Embracing cultural diversity as a source of strength rather than division can lay the groundwork for mutual respect and collaboration.

In addition, cultivating economic interconnectedness and interdependency among nations offers a pathway toward shared prosperity and stability. It is imperative to reevaluate trade policies and global financial architecture to ensure inclusive growth and equitable resource distribution. Moreover, investing in technological advancements that bridge divides and enhance connectivity is vital in overcoming barriers and promoting cooperation in education, research, and communication endeavors.

Recognizing the global environmental imperative is an integral aspect of constructing a cooperative future. Sustainability must be championed as a unifying goal, transcending geopolitical boundaries. A commitment to addressing climate change, conservation, and sustainable development is crucial in nurturing a shared planet for present and future generations. Similarly, enhancing global security frameworks through cooperation, trust-building, and diplomacy is fundamental in mitigating conflict and fostering peace.

Looking ahead, it is essential to reform and revitalize existing global institutions to reflect the contemporary geopolitical landscape. This includes revisiting the roles and responsibilities of international organizations to ensure they are equipped to respond effectively to emerging challenges while upholding principles of accountability and transparency. Furthermore, leveraging the power of media for peace advocacy and ethical communication can shape public discourse and promote understanding, empathy, and unity.

In conclusion, the journey towards a more cooperative and peaceful world necessitates a collective endeavor encompassing diplomacy, economic collaboration, technological innovation, environmental stewardship, and cultural exchange. By embracing inclusivity, sustainability, and shared responsibility, we can strive towards a future where global cooperation supersedes division, and peace becomes a universal aspiration.

Bibliography

Abbondanza, G., & Wilkins, T. (2021). The Case for Awkward Powers. Awkward Powers: Escaping Traditional Great and Middle Power Theory.

Abdullateef, S. T. (2021). Remote Learning: Fostering Learning of 21st Century Skills through Digital Learning Tools. Arab World English Journal.

Abuhammad, S. (2022). Preparing for Future Pandemics: Challenges for Healthcare Leadership. Journal of Healthcare Leadership, 14, 131–136.

Acemoglu, D., & Robinson, J. A. (2012). "Why Nations Fail: The Origins of Power, Prosperity, and Poverty." Crown Business.

Acharya, T. (2022). ANALYSING THE CONNECTIVITY AND SECURITY PARTNERSHIP BETWEEN CENTRAL ASIA AND INDIA.

Aimar, Ventsel. (2022). Nicholas Mulder, The Economic Weapon: The Rise of Sanctions as a Tool of Modern War New Haven: Yale University Press, 2022.. World Trade Review, doi: 10.1017/s1474745622000489

Al-Harran. (1999). New Strategic Alliances Between Islamic Financial Institutions, International University Students and Entrepreneurs to Implement Musharakah Financing to Meet the Challenges of the 21st Century. Arab Law Quarterly, 14, 268–281.

Alatas, S. (2021). A Malaysian Perspective on Foreign Policy and Geopolitics: Rethinking West-Centric International Relations Theory. Global Studies Quarterly.

Alekseev, M. Y., Kolyandra, P. A., & Cheskidov, B. M. (2021). Military and Political Influence on the Portfolio of Global Reserve Currencies. Finance: Theory and Practice.

Alexander, K. (2009). Extending Economic Sanctions: the Financial War on Terror. 278–301.

AlKnawy, B., Kozlakidis, Z., Tarkoma, S., Bates, D., Honkela, A., Crooks, G., Rhee, K.-S., & McKillop, M. M. (2023). Digital public health leadership in the global fight for health security. BMJ Global Health, 8.

Armijo, L. E., & Roberts, C. (2014). The Emerging Powers and Global Governance: Why the BRICS Matter. In R. Looney (Ed.), Handbook of Emerging Economies (pp.

503-524). Routledge.

Armijo, L. E., Tirone, D. C., & Chey, H. (2017). Global Finance Meets Neorealism: Concepts and a Dataset (SWP 59).

Artamonova, U. (2022). "Popcorn Diplomacy": American Blockbusters and World Order. Russia in Global Affairs.

Asish, D., & Swarupa, C. K. (2022). De-centralized cross-border payments for global economic status quo. I-Manager's Journal on Management.

Avendano, L. (2017). Becoming a world power: The role of infrastructure alliances. Journal of Economics and Political Economy, 4, 318–328.

Bahgat, G. (2004). Oil, Terrorism, and Weapons of Mass Destruction: The Libyan Diplomatic Coup. Journal of Social, Political, and Economic Studies, 29, 373.

Bai, S., Dyeyeva, N., Melnyk, T., & Puhachevska, K. (2021). Ukrainian Business Under the Conditions of World Trade Wars: Observer, Participant or Victim?

Bai, S., Dyeyeva, N., Melnyk, T., & Puhachevska, K. (2021). UKRAINIAN BUSINESS UNDER THE CONDITIONS OF WORLD TRADE WARS: OBSERVER, PARTICIPANT OR VICTIM? 1, 504–514.

Baker, A. (2006). The Group of Seven: Finance ministries, central banks, and global financial governance. Routledge.

This work focuses on the financial aspects of the G7 and its historical role in global economic governance.

Bandono, A., Bastari, A., & Suharyo, O. S. (2021). The Education Perspective of Indonesia Maritime Geopolitics In the Indian Ocean. 27, 167–179.

Bass, H. (2017). New developments in world trade in the first quarter of the 21st century. International Business and Global Economy, 36, 105–113.

Basterrechea, S., Frich, J. C., & Garman, A. N. (2024). Future-ready healthcare leadership: the revised International Hospital Federation competency model. BMJ Leader.

Bayne, N. (2005). Staying together: The G8 summit confronts the 21st century. Routledge.

Bayne offers an in-depth analysis of the G7/G8 summits and their historical significance.

Bayne, N., & Woolcock, S. (2016). The New Economic Diplomacy: Decision-Making and Negotiation in International Economic Relations. Routledge.

Beeson, M., & Li, F. (2015). What Consensus? Geopolitics and Policy Paradigms in China and the United States. International Affairs, 91(1), 93-109.

Ben-Naceur, K. (2022). Sustainable Recovery: New Risks for Global Recovery. Journal of Petroleum Technology.

Benade, L., Gardner, M., Teschers, C., & Gibbons, A. (2014). 21st-century learning in New Zealand: Leadership insights and perspectives. Journal of Educational Leadership, Policy and Practice, 29, 47.

Bendin, A. Y., Isaev, A. V., Filatov, A. S., Kharitonov-Tanevsky, A. D., & Barakhvostov, P. (2023). Religious Institutions as Regulators of the Moral Principles in Geopolitics. Russia & World: Sc. Dialogue.

Bergsten, C. F., & Henning, C. R. (1996). Global economic leadership and the Group of Seven. Peterson Institute.

Berisha, F., Dema, A., Ademi, M., & Qerimi, I. (2023). Human Trafficking in Western Balkan: Case Study of Kosovo. Access to Justice in Eastern Europe.

Bernazzoli, R. (2010). "The End of Autocracy": Analysing Representations of the Austro-Hungarian Dissolution as the Foundation of US Hegemonic Discourse. Geopolitics, 15, 643–666.

Billionniere, E., & Rahman, F. (2020). Redesigning Learning Spaces and Credentials for 21st-Century Emerging Tech Careers. 985–990.

Binder, Martin, and Autumn Lockwood Payton. "With Frenemies Like These: Rising Power Voting Behavior in the UN General Assembly." British Journal of Political Science, vol. 52, 2021, pp. 381-398.(Sreejith et al., 2014)

Biscop, S. (2012). The European Union and Emerging Powers in the 21st Century: How Europe Can Shape a New Global Order.

Bland, J. (2019). What is Evidence-Based Functional Medicine in the 21st Century? Integrative Medicine, 18 3, 14–18.

Boholano, H., Balo, V. T. M., Pogoy, A. M., & Alda, R. C. (2020). Technology-Enriched Teaching in Support of Quality Education in the 21st Century Skills. Solid State Technology, 63, 6795–6804.

Boozeer, J. C. (2000). Unilateral Economic Sanctions: A Policy Assessment.

Bowen, T. (2017). Work Integrated Learning in the 21st Century. 32.

Bowers, I. (2018). Small State Deterrence in the Contemporary World by Ian Bowers.

Boyer, W., & Crippen, C. (2014). Learning and Teaching in the 21st Century: An Education Plan for the New Millennium Developed in British Columbia, Canada. Childhood Education, 90, 343–353.

Brichta, M., & Sagath, D. (2023). Building Sector Development Infrastructure for 21st-Century Space Economy: Reflections on Slovak Experience. New Space.

Brigden, C., & Kaine, S. (2015). Rethinking factional alliances and union renewal: Inter-union collaboration in the 21st century. Economic and Industrial Democracy, 36, 239–257.

Brown, S. S., & Hermann, M. (2020). Geopolitics and Transnational Crime. 15–31.

Burnham, K., & Anderson, D. R. (2014). P values are only an index to evidence: 20th- vs. 21st-century statistical science. Ecology, 95 3, 627–630.

Butt, K. M., & Butt, A. A. (2014). UN Sanctions Against Iraq: From Ailment to Chronic. Journal of Political Studies, 21, 271.

Butts, K., & Bradshaw, A. (1999). Caspian Sea International Environmental Security Game. Held at Carlisle Barracks, Pennsylvania on 16-17 November 1998.

Cai, C. (2013). New Great Powers and International Law in the 21st Century. European Journal of International Law, 24, 755-795.

Caldwell, Z. (2022). International Sanctions. In International Law.

Carvalho, H. R. (2017). O Brasil no Centro: Meridionalismo e Geopolítica da Integração Sul-Americana. 14, 20–30.

Çepel, Z. Ü. (2023). EUROPEAN UNION GLOBAL STRATEGY AND TURKEY: AN ANALYSIS OF THE TERM 2016-2021. Tesam Akademi Dergisi.

Cheng, E., & Tong, S. (2012). Speeches at the Seventh Forum of the World Association for Political Economy. World Review of Political Economy, 3, 269.

Cheru, F., & Modi, R. (Eds.). (2013). Agricultural Development and Food Security in Africa: The Impact of Chinese, Indian and Brazilian Investments. Zed Books.

Cid, A. (2017). Las claves del conflicto entre Rusia y Occidente después de Crimea y el conflicto con Ucrania. 57, 356–388.

Clawson, P. (2012). How Has Saddam Hussein Survived?: Economic Sanctions, 1990-93.

Cleveland, H. (2014). The twilight of hierarchy: speculations on the global information society. International Journal of Technology Management.

Codeço, R. R. (2021). WTO Crisis through the Lens of Hegemony Theories: When International Trade Law and Geopolitics Collide. New Global Studies, 16, 251–274.

Colatrella, S. (2015). THE CAUSES OF WORLD WAR 3: CLASS, GEOPOLITICS AND HEGEMONY IN THE 21ST CENTURY – A RE-READING OF ARRIGHI, THROUGH MCDERMOTT, SCHUMPETER AND VEBLEN. Austral: Brazilian Journal of Strategy and International Relations, 4.

Colin, Krainin., Robert, Schub. (2021). Alliance Dynamics in the Shadow of Shifting Power. International Studies Quarterly, doi: 10.1093/ISQ/SQAB049

Cooper, A. F., & Farooq, A. B. (2015). Testing the Club Dynamics of the BRICS: The New Development Bank from Conception to Establishment. International Organisations Research Journal, 10(2), 32-44.

Cooper, A. F., & Farooq, A. B. (2016). The Role of China and India in the G20 and BRICS: Commonalities or Competitive Behaviour? Journal of Current Chinese Affairs, 45(3), 73-106.

Cornelissen, S. (2009). Awkward Embraces: Emerging and Established Powers and the Shifting Fortunes of Africa's International Relations in the Twenty-First Century. Politikon, 36, 5-26.

Corrales-Suastegui, A., Fuentes-Franco, R., & Pavia, E. (2019). The mid-summer drought over Mexico and Central America in the 21st century. International Journal of Climatology, 40, 1703–1715.

Costello, A., Peterson, S., Rasanathan, K., Daelmans, B., & Bahl, R. (2018). Where's the leadership? Future commitments of Unicef and WHO for global child health. British Medical Journal, 362.

Craven, M. (2002). Humanitarianism and the Quest for Smarter Sanctions. European Journal of International Law, 13, 43-61.

Crawford, B. (1993). Economic Containment: CoCom and the Politics of East-West Trade. By Michael Mastanduno. Ithaca: Cornell University Press, 1992. 353p. 46.50 cloth, 18.95 paper. American Political Science Review, 87, 1057–1059.

Cruz, T. (2015). The Obama Administration's Unprecedented Lawlessness. Harvard Journal of Law and Public Policy, 38, 63.

Dailami, Mansoor and Paul R. Masson. "The New Multi-Polar International Monetary System." International Finance eJournal, 2009.(Thorstensen, 2015)

Daly, P., Reid, K., Buckley, P., & Doyle, E. (2016). Innovative business education design for 21st-century learning.

David, Petrasek. (2013). New Powers, New Approaches? Human Rights Diplomacy in the 21st Century. Social Science Research Network.

Degenhardt, L., & Duignan, P. (2010). Dancing on a Shifting Carpet: Reinventing Traditional Schooling for the 21st Century.

Delpech, T. (2012). Nuclear Deterrence in the 21st Century: Lessons from the Cold War for a New Era of Strategic Piracy.

DeSoucey, M., & Demetry, D. (2016). The dynamics of dining out in the 21st century: Insights from organizational theory. Sociology Compass, 10, 1014–1027.

Dixit, A. (2023). AN EXPLORATORY STUDY ON THE IMPORTANCE OF INTERNATIONAL RELATIONS IN SOLVING COMPLEX ISSUES OF CONFLICT THROUGH COOPERATION IN THE WORLD. Indian Journal Of Applied Research.

Dobson, H. (2007). The Group of 7/8. Routledge.

Dobson, H. (2020). The G7, Anti-Globalism and the Governance of Globalization. Routledge.

Doxey, M. (1981). Oil and Food as International Sanctions. International Journal, 36, 311–334.

Drezner, D. W. (2019). Toddler in Chief: What Donald Trump Teaches Us about the Modern Presidency. University of Chicago Press.

Duggan, N. (2015). BRICS and the Evolution of a New Agenda Within Global Governance. In M. Rewizorski (Ed.), The European Union and the BRICS (pp. 11-25). Springer.

Dyudikova, E. (2023). THE ASYMMETRIC PERCEPTION OF THE MODERNIZATION OF MONEY TURNOVER IN THE VECTOR OF CHANGING THE ECONOMIC STRUCTURE. Intellect. Innovations. Investments.

Elbeshbishi, A. N. (2019). Power, Character, and Leadership. Economic Dynamics of Global Energy Geopolitics.

Elliott, K. (2010). Assessing UN Sanctions after the Cold War. International Journal, 65, 85-97.

Emerson, M. (2014). Trade Policy Issues in the Wider Europe – That Led to War and Not Yet to Peace. Law & Society: International & Comparative Law eJournal.

Esty, D. (2017). Red Lights to Green Lights: From 20th Century Environmental Regulation to 21st Century Sustainability. Environmental Law, 47, 1.

Fabio, Ashtar, Telarico. (2023). Are sanctions for losers? A network study of trade sanctions. doi: 10.7251/noeen2333004t

Falk, R. (2014). Nonviolent Geopolitics: Law, Politics, and 21st Century Security.

Fedotova, I. V. (2022). «Future War»: the experience of analytical foresight of military conflict by Red Army intelligence practitioners. Omsk Scientific Bulletin Series Society History Modernity.

Ferguson, R. J. (2018). Preface: China, Eurasia and global order.

Fields, A. (2016). Partnerships and New Roles in the 21st-Century Academic Library: Collaborating, Embedding, and Cross-Training for the Future. Journal of Library & Information Services in Distance Learning, 10, 56–56.

Filipenko, A., Bazhenova, O., & Stakanov, R. (2020). ECONOMIC SANCTIONS: THEORY, POLICY, MECHANISMS. Baltic Journal of Economic Studies.

Finin, G. (2021). Associations Freely Chosen: New Geopolitics in the North Pacific. The China Alternative: Changing Regional Order in the Pacific Islands.

Firzli, M. N. J. (2018). The New Geopolitics of Globalization: Bulls, Pandas and the Road to Charlevoix. International Political Economy: Globalization eJournal.

Fitzgerald, P. L. (2008). Managing Smart Sanctions Against Terrorism Wisely.

Fontanel, J. (2016). La sécurité économique et sociétale. Paix et Sécurité Européenne et Internationale.

Foulkrod, M., & Lin, P. L. (2024). Global Leadership Adaptability Through Servant Leadership and Cultural Humility. Areté.

Franch, S. (2020). Global citizenship education: A new 'moral pedagogy' for the 21st century? European Educational Research Journal, 19, 506–524.

Fruyt, F. D., Wille, B., & John, O. (2015). Employability in the 21st Century: Complex (Interactive) Problem Solving and Other Essential Skills. Industrial and Organizational Psychology, 8, 276–281.

Funk, V. (2018). Collections-based science in the 21st Century. Journal of Systematics and Evolution, 56.

Garavoglia, M. (2016). The G7 and Global Governance. In The European Union and the G7 (pp. 11-29). Routledge.

Garba, S., Yusuf, B., & Busthami, A. H. (2015). Toward the Use of Technology and 21st Century Teaching-learning Approaches: The Trend of Development in Malaysian Schools within the Context of Asia Pacific. International Journal of Emerging Technologies in Learning (iJET), 10, 72–79.

Garfield, R. (1999). The Silent, Deadly Remedy: In the New World Order, Economic Sanctions May Leave No Dead Soldiers, Just Civilian Casualties. 14, 52.

Garfield, R. (2002). Economic Sanctions, Humanitarianism, and Conflict After the Cold War. Social Justice, 29, 94.

Geopolitical Struggles over and in the Central Asia. (2022).

George, I., & Kuruvilla, M. (2020). Conceptualizing Gender Mainstreaming and Women Empowerment in the 21st Century. Handbook of Research on New Dimensions of Gender Mainstreaming and Women Empowerment.

Ghaleb, A. (2012). An Anthropological Comparative Study Of The European Oil Sanctions Against Iran.

Glosny, M. A. (2010). China and the BRICs: A Real (but Limited) Partnership in a Unipolar World. Polity, 42(1), 100-129.

Goldstein, J. S. (1989). The impact of ideas on trade policy: the origins of U.S. agricultural and manufacturing policies. International Organization, 43, 31–71.

Goldthau, A., Keim, M., & Westphal, K. (2018). The geopolitics of energy transformation: governing the shift: transformation dividends, systemic risks and new uncertainties. 4.

Goodman, M. P., & Reinsch, W. A. (2021). Filling In the Indo-Pacific Economic Framework. Center for Strategic and International Studies (CSIS).

Graesser, A. (2013). Evolution of Advanced Learning Technologies in the 21st Century. Theory Into Practice, 52, 101–193.

Grochmalski, P. (2020). US-China rivalry for strategic domination in the area of artificial intelligence and the new AI geopolitics. 701, 5–25.

Guiora, A. (2013). Modern Geopolitics and Security: Strategies for Unwinnable Conflicts.

Gustavo, de, Souza., Naiyuan, Hu., Haishi, Li., Yuan, Mei. (2022). (Trade) War and Peace: How to Impose International Trade Sanctions. Social Science Research Network, doi: 10.2139/ssrn.4153921

Hage, J., & Powers, C. (1992). Post-Industrial Lives: Roles and Relationships in the 21st Century.

Hajnal, P. I. (2007). The G8 system and the G20: Evolution, role and documentation. Ashgate Publishing.

Haq, B. (2020). Scenario Planning - Russia The New Amendment 2020 – Putin the Iron Man Reforms Constitution. Social Science Research Network.

Harrel, E., Berland, L., Jacobson, J., & Addiss, D. (2021). Compassionate Leadership: Essential for the Future of Tropical Medicine and Global Health. American Journal of Tropical Medicine and Hygiene, 105, 1450–1452.

Harrison, M., & Joubert, A. (2018). French Language Policies and the Revitalisation of Regional Languages in the 21st Century.

Heffron, R., & Talus, K. (2016). The development of energy law in the 21st century: a paradigm shift? The Journal of World Energy Law & Business, 9, 189–202.

Hlobenko, I. (2022). On the way to the struggle of the Ukrainian people against Russian aggression. Analytical and Comparative Jurisprudence.

Hooijmaaijers, B., & Keukeleire, S. (2016). Voting Cohesion of the BRICS Countries in the UN General Assembly, 2006–2014: A BRICS Too Far? Global Governance, 22(3), 389-407.

Horner, R., & Hulme, D. (2017). Converging Divergence? Unpacking the New Geography of 21st Century Global Development. PSN: International Development Institutions (Topic).

Horner, R., & Hulme, D. (2019). From International to Global Development: New Geographies of 21st Century Development. Development and Change, 50, 347-378.

Hufbauer, G., & Oegg, B. (2000). Targeted Sanctions: A Policy Alternative? Law and Policy in International Business, 32, 11.

Hufbauer, G., & Oegg, B. (2003). Economic Sanctions: Public Goals and Private Compensation. Chicago Journal of International Law, 4, 6.

Hufbauer, G., Elliott, K., Cyrus, T. L., & Winston, E. (1997). US Economic Sanctions: Their Impact on Trade, Jobs, and Wages.

Huotaria, M., & Jeanb, S. (2022). Bolstering Europe's Economic Strategy vis-à-vis China.

Ibonye, V. (2017). Strategic Wisdom in the New Greater Middle Eastern Game? A De-escalatory Rethinking of the Syrian Conflict. Journal of Balkan and Near Eastern Studies, 20, 251–272.

Ienca, M., & Vayena, E. (2018). Dual use in the 21st century: emerging risks and global governance: Swiss Medical Weekly, 148, w14688.

Ikenberry, G. J. (2020). A World Safe for Democracy: Liberal Internationalism and the Crises of Global Order. Yale University Press.

Inglesby, T., & Cicero, A. (2017). Protecting the Nation from Health Security Threats. Health Security, 15, 1–5.

International Monetary Fund. (2023). "World Economic Outlook: Shifting Economic Dynamics between Advanced and Emerging Economies." IMF Publications.

Ion, Ignat., Gimia, Virginia, Bujancă. (2014). Power shifts in the global economy. transition towards a multipolar world order. USV Annals of Economics and Public Administration.

Ischinger, W., Smyser, W. R., Sandschneider, E., & Weisser, U. (2012). Whose century? The US and China compete for supremacy in the Asia-Pacific Sea.

Ivo, Daalder. (2010). A new alliance for a new century. RUSI Journal, doi: 10.1080/03071847.2010.530494

Jáuregui, C. Z. (2013). El multilateralismo actual: crisis y desafíos. 8, 45–60.

Javed, S., & Chattu, V. K. (2020a). Ineffective COVID-19 Pandemic Response due to Failed Global Leadership and International Cooperation: Reimagining the post-pandemic future through Global Health Diplomacy. Health Promotion Perspectives.

Javed, S., & Chattu, V. K. (2020b). Strengthening the COVID-19 pandemic response, global leadership, and international cooperation through global health diplomacy. Health Promotion Perspectives, 10, 300–305.

Jenkins, H. (2006). Confronting the Challenges of Participatory Culture: Media Education for the 21st Century.

Jessica, Tuchman, Mathews. (2022). Power shift. doi: 10.2307/20047909

Jolls, T., & Johnsen, M. (2018). Media Literacy: A Foundational Skill for Democracy in the 21st Century. Hastings Law Journal, 69, 1379.

Jong, S.D. et al. "New players, new game? The impact of emerging economics on global governance." 2013. (Moore, 2011)

Joyner, C. (2003). United Nations Sanctions after Iraq: Looking Back to See Ahead. Chicago Journal of International Law, 4, 7.

Joyner, C. (2003). United Nations Sanctions after Iraq: Looking Back to See Ahead. Chicago Journal of International Law, 4, 7.

Khan, H., Jumani, N. B., & Gul, N. (2019). Implementation of 21st Century Skills in Higher Education of Pakistan. Global Regional Review.

Kim, E. (2015). Korea's Middle-Power Diplomacy in the 21st Century. Pacific Focus, 30, 1-9.

Kim, S., & Martin-Hermosillo, M. (2013). The Effectiveness of Economic Sanctions Against a Nuclear North Korea. North Korean Review, 9, 99–110.

Kingah, S., & Quiliconi, C. (Eds.). (2016). Global and Regional Leadership of BRICS Countries. Springer.

Kirton, J. J. (2016). G20 governance for a globalized world. Routledge.

Kirton, J. J. (2019). G7 Summit Governance: Performance, Leadership, and Significance. Routledge.

Kivunja, C. (2014a). Do You Want Your Students to Be Job-Ready with 21st Century Skills? Change Pedagogies: A Pedagogical Paradigm Shift from Vygotskyian Social Constructivism to Critical Thinking, Problem Solving and Siemens' Digital Connectivism. The International Journal of Higher Education, 3, 81–91.

Kivunja, C. (2014b). Teaching Students to Learn and to Work Well with 21st Century Skills: Unpacking the Career and Life Skills Domain of the New Learning Paradigm. The International Journal of Higher Education, 4, 1–11.

Knawy, B. (2021). Global Data and Digital Public Health Leadership for Current and Future Pandemic Responses. Frontiers in Digital Health, 3.

Kose, M. A., & Prasad, E. S. (2010). "Emerging Markets: Resilience and Growth Amid Global Turmoil." Brookings Institution Press.

Kroenig, M. (2020). The Return of Great Power Rivalry. (Kühnhardt, 2017)

Krotz, U., & Schild, J. (2018). Shaping Europe: France, Germany, and Embedded Bilateralism from the Elysée Treaty to Twenty-First Century Politics. Oxford University Press.

Krupenya, I. (2023). POLICY OF NEW HORIZONS OF UKRAINE IN THE

ASIAN DIRECTION. ACTUAL PROBLEMS OF INTERNATIONAL RELATIONS.

Kühnhardt, L. (2017). A New World Order: The Global Society and Its Friends. 215–258.

Kupchan, C. A. (2012). No One's World: The West, the Rising Rest, and the Coming Global Turn. Oxford University Press.

Lakishyk, D. (2016). Evolution of US foreign policy: from George Bush to Barack Obama. 14–22.

Land, P. S. (2012). Negating the Threat of Libyan Weapons of Mass Destruction.

Layers, T. (2001). Law as a smart bomb or just a limited tool of coercion: Considering extra-territorial economic sanctions. The RUSI Journal, 146, 17–23.

Lee, H. (2017). Power Politics Behind the Transforming Geopolitics in East Asia. East Asia, 34, 307–320.

Lee, J. (2014). Not So Peaceful: China's Rise and Geopolitics in Asia.

Lee, K. J., & Choi, J. (2008). U.S. Sanctions and Treasury Department Actions against North Korea from 1955 to October 2007. North Korean Review, 4, 7–25.

Lee, W. et al. "KOREAN FOREIGN POLICY AND THE RISE OF THE BRICS COUNTRIES." Asian Perspective, vol. 31, 2007, p. 205.(Jong et al., 2013)

Lennon, A. T. J., & Kozłowski, A. (2008). Global Powers in the 21st Century: Strategies and Relations.

Li, X. (2019). The BRICS and Beyond: The International Political Economy of the Emergence of a New World Order. Routledge.

Lim, H. S. (2023). Research on U.S. Economic Sanctions on North Korea and the lifting process: Focusing on the lifting of Vietnam and Iran. Unification and North Korean Law Studies.

Lin, H. (2023). Spillover Effects of China-US Trade War on Southeast Asia. BCP Business & Management.

Lin, J. Y., & Wang, Y. (2020). "New Structural Economics: A Framework for Rethinking Development and Policy." The World Bank Economic Review, 34(3), 551-574.

Lin, T. C. W. (2016). Financial Weapons of War.

Lopez, G. A. (2007). Effective Sanctions: Incentives and UN-US Dynamics. Harvard International Review, 29, 50.

M., Moran, S., Guillermo, E., Ponce, Campos, Huete, A., Mitchel, P., Mcclaran, Zhang, Y., Erik, Hamerlynck, David, J., Augustine, Stacey, A., Gunter, ... Hernandez, M. (2014). Functional response of U.S. grasslands to the early 21st-century drought. Ecology, 95 8, 2121-2133.

Maass, M. M. (2011). Beyond economic sanctions: Rethinking the North Korean sanctions regime.

Magid, S., Cohen, K., & Katzovitz, L. S. (2021). 21st Century Cures Act, an Information Technology-Led Organizational Initiative. HSS Journal ®, 18, 42–47.

Magnus, Petersson. (2022). Military Alliances in the Twenty-First Century. Diplomacy & Statecraft, doi: 10.1080/09592296.2022.2143128

Mahbubani, K. (2022). What Biden Will Mean for the Rest of the World. China and Globalization.

Maisaia, V., & Kobaladze, K. (2019). Eurasian Geopolitics Importance to World Politics and China's Geostrategy. Ante Portas.

Malešević, S. (2017). The organization of military violence in the 21st century. Organization, 24, 456–474.

Manov, B. (2019). „THE SILK ROAD", "TTHEEURASIAN PROJECT AND „GREAT EURASIA" (GEOPOLITICAL READING). 17, 170–181.

Mansbach, R., & Ferguson, Y. H. (2021). The Return of Geopolitics and Declining U.S. Hegemony. 89–140.

Mathe, H. (2015). Living Innovation: Competing in the 21st Century Access Economy.

Mathews, J. (2015). Energizing Industrial Development: The Role of the State in 21st Century Greening Strategies. RSP, 66, 29–54.

McKimm, J., & McLean, M. (2020). Rethinking health professions' education leadership: Developing 'eco-ethical' leaders for a more sustainable world and future. Medical Teacher, 42, 855–860.

Mcluhan, M., & Powers, B. (1989). The Global Village: Transformations in World Life and Media in the 21st Century.

Mcnally, C. A. (2013). How emerging forms of capitalism are changing the global economic order. Asia Pacific Issues, 1.

Michalski, A., & Parker, C. F. (2024). The EU's evolving leadership role in an age of geopolitics: Beyond normative and market power in the Indo-Pacific. European Journal of International Security, 9, 263-280.(Javed & Chattu, 2020)

Miller, A., & Illipinar, G. (2022). "The Acronyms Club" Has the Ukraine Conflict Exposed the West and its History? The Most Comprehensive Study into How U.S. Hegemony Denies Sovereignties of Nations. International Journal of Scientific Research and Management.

Miller, R. K. (2017). Building on Math and Science: The New Essential Skills for the 21st-Century Engineer. Research-Technology Management, 60, 53–56.

Minde, N. (2018). The fabric of peace in Africa: looking beyond the state. Journal of Contemporary African Studies, 36, 416–418.

Mitterlechner, M. (2019). Leadership in Integrated Care Networks: A Literature Review and Opportunities for Future Research. International Journal of Integrated Care, 20.

Mohan, R., & Kapur, M. (2022). "Emerging Powers and Global Governance: Whither the IMF?" Princeton University Press.

Mondal, K. (2019). A Synergy of Artificial Intelligence and Education in the 21st Century Classrooms. IEEE International Conference on Dielectrics, 68–70.

Monteiro, L. V. (2018). Os Neogolpes e as Interrupções de Mandatos Presidenciais na América Latina: os casos de Honduras, Paraguai e Brasil. 49, 55–97.

Mustafa, S., Zafar, A., & Akhter, S. (2017). BRICS: Is the Group Really Creating Impact? Advanced Risk & Portfolio Management® Research Paper Series.

Muzaffar, M., Shah, S., & Yaseen, Z. (2018). PAX SINICA IN ASIA: CHINA EMERGENT GEOPOLITICS OF ECONOMIC CORRIDORS AND DREAM OF LEADERSHIP. Global Political Review.(Bendin et al., 2023)

Muzaffar, M., Shah, S., & Yaseen, Z. (2018). PAX SINICA IN ASIA: CHINA EMERGENT GEOPOLITICS OF ECONOMIC CORRIDORS AND DREAM OF LEADERSHIP. Global Political Review.

Naji, S., & Jawan, J. (2013). Geopolitics of the Islam World and world leadership in the post-Cold War geopolitical developments *.

Nam, P. S. (2010). China's Emergence as a Key Player in the Global Order and its Impacts on Geopolitics in Central Asia*. International Area Studies Review, 13, 155–165.

Navarro, P. (2006). The Coming China Wars: Where They Will Be Fought and How They Can Be Won.

Naylor, R. T. (2001). Economic Warfare: Sanctions, Embargo Busting, and Their Human Cost.

Nayyar, D. (2016). BRICS, Developing Countries and Global Governance. Third World Quarterly, 37(4), 575-591.

Nelson-Brantley, H. V., Bailey, K. D., Batcheller, J., Bernard, N., Caramanica, L., & Snow, F. (2019). Grassroots to Global: The Future of Nursing Leadership. Journal of Nursing Administration.

New, R. (2015). 21st Century Early Childhood Teacher Education: New Frames for a Shifting Landscape. 21–37.

Nti, K. (2023). National Identity and State Formation in Africa ed. by Manuel Castells and Bernard Lategan (review). African Studies Review, 66, 821–822.

Nuruzzaman, M. (2023). US-China Competition for Global Leadership - An Alternative Perspective. North South Journal of Peace and Global Studies.(Rokem & Boano, 2023)

Nye, J. S. (2020). Do Morals Matter?: Presidents and Foreign Policy from FDR to Trump. Oxford University Press.

O'Neill, J. (2021). "The New Economic Order: Comparing G7 and BRICS in the Global Economy." Journal of International Economics, 112, 103-121.

O'Loughlin, J. (1988). Political geography. Progress in Human Geography, 12, 121–137.

O'Sullivan, B., Zhong, A., Yin, L., Dogra, S., Chadop, M. T., Choonara, S., & Wong, B. L. H. (2023). The future of global health: restructuring governance through inclusive youth leadership. BMJ Global Health, 8.

Obalade, T. A. F. (2014). Analysis of Dumping as a Major Cause of Import and Export Crises.

OECD. (2022). "OECD Economic Outlook: The Shifting Balance of Global Economic Power." OECD Publishing.

Öge, K. (2015). Geopolitics and revenue transparency in Turkmenistan and Azerbaijan. Eurasian Geography and Economics, 56, 110–189.

Okoli, J., Arroteia, N., & Ogunsade, A. (2022). Failure of crisis leadership in a global pandemic: some reflections on COVID-19 and future recommendations. Leadership in Health Services, ahead-of-print ahead-of-print.

Oleksiyenko, A. (2019). "Academic Heartland": Epistemic Constraints, Ontological Forces. Knowledge Studies in Higher Education.

Omar, N. A. M., & Habil, H. (2023). Constructions of Solidarity and Leadership of Powerful Global Leaders in Post-Pandemic Recovery Speeches. International Journal of English Linguistics.

Pant, H. V. (2013). China's Naval Expansion in the Indian Ocean and India-China Rivalry. The Asia-Pacific Journal, 11(18), 1-22.

Passaris, C. (2015). Internetization and the New Global Economy of the 21st Century. 3197–3205.

Pavlov, N. (2021). Russia and Germany: Back to the Future? World Economy and International Relations.

Payne, A. (2008). The G8 in a changing global economic order. International Affairs, 84(3), 519-533.

Payne, E., Hodges, R., & Hernandez, E. P. (2017). Changing Demographics and Needs Assessment for Learning Centers in the 21st Century. The Learning Assistance Review, 22, 21–36.

Pertusot, V. (2012). THE EUROPEAN UNION AND EMERGING POWERS IN THE 21st CENTURY: HOW EUROPE CAN SHAPE A NEW GLOBAL ORDER, Thomas Renard et Sven Biscop (dir.), Burlington, VT, Ashgate, 2012, 208 pages. Politique Étrangère.

Peterson, E. W. (2023). Can Sanctions End Wars? Yeutter Institute International Trade Policy Review.

Petrasek, D. (2013). New Powers, New Approaches? Human Rights Diplomacy in the 21st Century.

Phongsirikul, M. (2017). A Learner of the 20th Century.

Picco, G. (2003). New Entente after September 11? the United States, Russia, China, and India. (Global Insights). Global Governance, 9, 15.

Pilvere-Javorska, A., Pilvere, I., & Rivza, B. (2020). Company capital structure's theoretical framework: historical assessment and trends in the 21st century.

Polonchuk, R. A. (2024). CHINESE MILITARY POLICY: HOW IS BEIJING PREPARING FOR AN ESCALATION OF CONFRONTATION? REVIEW OF THE MONOGRAPH AND TEXTBOOK BY DOCTOR OF MILITARY

SCIENCES GORDIENKO D.V. EKONOMIKA I UPRAVLENIE: PROBLEMY, RESHENIYA.

Pozdnyakova, U. A., Golikov, V. V., Peters, I., & Morozova, I. (2018). Genesis of the Revolutionary Transition to Industry 4.0 in the 21st Century and Overview of Previous Industrial Revolutions. Industry 4.0.

Proroković, D. (2020). American Geopolitics in Contemporary Eurasia: What Must Be Done and Can Global Leadership Be Preserved? Russia and Serbia in the Contemporary World: Bilateral Relations, Challenges and Opportunities.(Javed & Chattu, 2020)

Putnam, R. D., & Bayne, N. (1987). Hanging together: Cooperation and conflict in the seven-power summits. Harvard University Press.

R., T., Naylor. (2001). Economic Warfare: Sanctions, Embargo Busting, and Their Human Cost.

Rathbone, M., & Jeydel, P. (2017). United Nations Security Council Resolutions 2321, 2371, & 2375. International Legal Materials, 56, 1176–1208.

Richard, Garfield. (2002). Economic Sanctions, Humanitarianism, and Conflict After the Cold War. Social Justice.

Richard, Overy. (2022). The Economic Weapon: The Rise of Sanctions as a Tool of Modern War. Journal of International Economic Law, doi: 10.1093/jiel/jgac039

Rodrigue, T. T. (2018). Can Western Media Overshadow the China-Africa Storytelling? Case Study of the BBC Documentary "The Chinese Are Coming." New Media and Mass Communication, 75, 49–59.

Rodrik, D. (2018). "Straight Talk on Trade: Ideas for a Sane World Economy." Princeton University Press.

Rokem, J., & Boano, C. (2023). Towards a Global Urban Geopolitics: Inhabiting Violence. Geopolitics, 28, 1667–1680.

Rozman, G. (2011). The Nuclear Crisis in 2010. 237–261.

Rudnitski, R. (1996). Global Leadership Theory: Theoretical Roots, Principles and Possibilities for the Future. Gifted Education International, 11, 80–85.

Salih, A. (2024). Healthcare Statistical Highlights for First Quarter 2024. Healthcare Administration Leadership & Management Journal.

Salter, B. (2013). Governing Innovation Paths in Regenerative Medicine: The European and Global Struggle for Political Advantage. 194–216.

Salvage, J., & White, J. (2020). Our future is global: nursing leadership and global health*. Revista Latino-Americana de Enfermagem, 28.

Sassler, S. (2018). Families in the 21st Century. Contemporary Sociology: A Journal of Reviews, 47, 177–178.

Schneider, G., & Weber, P. (2018). Punishing Putin: EU Sanctions Are More than Paper Tigers.

Schropp, S., Latipov, O., Lau, C., & Mahlstein, K. (2023). Quantifying the Impact of the Latest US Tariff Sanctions on Russia: A Sectoral Analysis. Journal of World Trade.

Sedghi, H. (2017). Trumpism: The Geopolitics of the United States, the Middle East and Iran. Socialism and Democracy, 31, 82–93.

Serafini, F. (2012). Reading Multimodal Texts in the 21st Century. Research in the Schools, 19, 26–32.

Shang, J. (2023). Transformational Leadership Influences Employee Performance: A Review and Directions for Future Research. Highlights in Business, Economics and Management.

Sharma, R. (2012). Broken BRICs: Why the Rest Stopped Rising. Foreign Affairs, 91(6), 2-7.

Sharma, R. (2019). "The Rise and Fall of Nations: Forces of Change in the Post-Crisis World." W. W. Norton & Company.

Shaw, T., & Jobbins, D. (2009). Commonwealth Scholarships: Advancing Cosmopolitanism for 50 Years. The Round Table, 98, 777–787.

Sheriff, G. I., Thomas, A., & Ahmet, A. (2021). Impact of the Belt and Road Initiative on World Politics and Economy. African Journal of Economic and Sustainable Development.

Sigal, L. (2015). Sanctions Easing as a Sign of Non-Hostility. North Korean Review, 11, 103.

Simachev, Y., Fedyunina, A., & Kuzyk, M. (2020). Industrial Revolution 4.0 in the BRICS countries: What are the challenges for industrial policy? BRICS Journal of Economics, 1, 4-22.

Skripnuk, D., Davydenko, V., Romashkina, G., & Khuziakhmetov, R. (2021). Consumer Trust in Quality and Safety of Food Products in Western Siberia. Agronomy.

Slaughter, A. M. (2017). The Chessboard and the Web: Strategies of Connection in a Networked World. Yale University Press.

Sokolova, E. N., & Yakushev, I. (2023). Global Analysis of Modern Economic Sanctions. Federalism.

Sparks, C. "Communication & Global Power Shifts| Deconstructing the BRICS." International Journal of Communication, vol. 8, 2014, p. 27.(Binder & Payton, 2021)

Srivastava, U. K. (2024). A Study of Global Trade War and Its Impact on Indian Economy. International Journal For Multidisciplinary Research.

Stabinsky, D. (2015). Teaching and Practicing Climate Politics at College of the Atlantic: Student-inspired, Student-driven. Radical Teacher, 102, 24–29.

Stiglitz, J. E., & Greenwald, B. C. (2014). "Creating a Learning Society: A New Approach to Growth, Development, and Social Progress." Columbia University Press.

Stuenkel, O. (2015). The BRICS and the Future of Global Order. Lexington Books.

Stuenkel, O. (2020). The BRICS and the Future of Global Order (2nd ed.). Lexington Books.

Stuenkel, Oliver. "The Financial Crisis, Contested Legitimacy, and the Genesis of Intra-BRICS Cooperation." Global Governance, vol. 19, 2013, pp. 611-630.(Sudorgin et al., 2021)

Stulberg, A. (2013). Russia and the Geopolitics of Natural Gas: Leveraging or Succumbing to Revolution? PonarsEuarasia - Policy Memos.

Subramanian, A. (2011). "Eclipse: Living in the Shadow of China's Economic Dominance." Peterson Institute for International Economics.

Sung-Jo. (2018). The United Nations' Response Strategy for North KOREA's DENUCLEARIZATION. J-Institute.

Šupšáková, B. (2016). VISUAL LITERACY FOR THE 21ST CENTURY. IJAEDU- International E-Journal of Advances in Education, 2, 202–208.

Supyan, V. (2021). Long-term Factors of Economic Development of the USA during the Third Decade of 2the 1st Century. Russia and America in the 21st Century.

Takishita, K. M. (2005). [14PacRimLPolyJ515] U.S. Economic Sanctions Against North Korea: An Unsuccessful and Sanctimonious Policy Ripe for Modification.

Taskinsoy, J. (2020). The Great Pandemic of the 21st Century: The Stolen Lives. Health Economics Evaluation Methods eJournal.

Telarico, F. A. (2023). ARE SANCTIONS FOR LOSERS? A NETWORK STUDY OF TRADE SANCTIONS. НОВИ ЕКОНОМИСТ.

Teshaev, O.R. Ismailov, M.U. Khayitov, I.B., Babazhanov, A.B.. (2023). Understanding Twenty-First Century Power Shifts. doi: 10.1007/978-981-99-0714-4_4

Thakur, R. (2014). How Representative Are BRICS? Third World Quarterly, 35(10), 1791-1808.

Tomja, A. (2024). Internationalism of the Post-Cold War World: Clinton's Foreign Policy for the Global Age. Interdisciplinary Journal of Research and Development.

Toufik, Mansour., Reza, Rastegar., Alexander, Roitershtein., Mark, Shattuck. (2020). Shifting powers in Spivey's Bell number formula. Quaestiones Mathematicae, doi: 10.2989/16073606.2020.1848936

Trachy, E. (2011). State & Local Economic Sanctions: The Constitutionality of New York's Divestment Actions and the Sudan Accountability & Divestment Act of 2007.

Tran, D. (2018). The Law of Attribution: Rules for Attributing the Source of a Cyber-Attack. Yale Journal of Law and Technology, 20, 376.

Uğur, Ö. (2016). The Eu's Influence on Eastern European Stability in the Context of Ukrainian Crisis.

.Ulker, N., Gemalmaz, Ö., & Yüksek, Y. (2022). Towards 21st century citizenship through sustainable development goals in foreign language education. Towards a New Future in Engineering Education, New Scenarios That European Alliances of Tech Universities Open Up.

Ullrich, H. (2008). The Group of Eight and the European Union: The evolving partnership. G8 Research Group.

Velazco, J. J. H. G., Hernandez, A. C. C., & Pesantez, L. B. T. (2021). Knowledge management and key factors for organizational success in the perspective of the 21st Century. Revista Venezolana de Gerencia.

Vitale, A. (2020). THE REBIRTH OF ECONOMIC NATIONALISM- FROM NEO-PROTECTIONISM TO THE NEW WORLD GEO-ECONOMY.

Vlaskamp, M. C. (2018). The European Union and natural resources that fund armed conflicts: Explaining the EU's policy choice for supply chain due-diligence requirements. Cooperation and Conflict, 54, 407–425.

Vlaskamp, M. C. (2019). THE EUROPEAN UNION AND NATURAL RESOURCES THAT FUND ARMED CONFLICTS: EXPLAINING THE EU'S POLICY CHOICE FOR SUPPLY CHAIN DUE.

Vogelgesang, G., Clapp-Smith, R., & Osland, J. (2014). The Relationship Between Positive Psychological Capital and Global Mindset in the Context of Global Leadership. Journal of Leadership & Organizational Studies, 21, 165–178.

Walton, C. (2007). Geopolitics and the Great Powers in the 21st Century: Multipolarity and the Revolution in Strategic Perspective.

Watson, G. (1973). American economic sanctions against Great Britain, 1806-1812.

Wekke, I. S., Nusran, M., Henny, A., & Azis, St. N. (2024). Indonesia's Halal Future: Charting a Path to Global Leadership. Social Science Research Network.

Werthner, H. (2021). Geopolitics, Digital Sovereignty...What's in a Word? Perspectives on Digital Humanism, 241–248.

Whitty, M. D., Kim, S., & Crick, T. (2006). The Effectiveness of Economic Sanctions: The Case of North Korea. North Korean Review, 2, 50–65.

Woodley, D. (2015). Globalization and Capitalist Geopolitics: Sovereignty and state power in a multipolar world.

World Trade Organization. (2023). "World Trade Report: The Changing Landscape of Global Trade." WTO Publications.

Wright, J., & Conca, J. (2009). The GeoPolitics of Energy: Engaging the Public and Policymakers - 9557.

Yu, H. (2017). Motivation behind China's 'One Belt, One Road' Initiatives and Establishment of the Asian Infrastructure Investment Bank. Journal of Contemporary China, 26, 353–368.

Yu, S. (2019). THE BELT AND ROAD INITIATIVE: MODERNITY, GEOPOLITICS AND THE DEVELOPING GLOBAL ORDER. Great Potential, Many Pitfalls, 50, 187–201.

Zabella, A. A., Fiveyskaya, M., & Penkova, E. (2021). "One Belt, One Road" vs. "Free and Open Indo-Pacific": rivalry for regional integration (views from India and Japan). South East Asia: Actual Problems of Development.

Zhang, C. (2020). Regional Transformation of the Horn of Africa. China Quarterly of International Strategic Studies.

Zhao, Y. (2015). A World at Risk: An Imperative for a Paradigm Shift to Cultivate 21st Century Learners. Society, 52, 129–135.

Zhironkin, S., Cehlár, M., & Zhironkin, V. (2019). The Convergent Structural Base of Sustainable Development in the 21st Century. E3S Web of Conferences.

Дробот, Г. А. (2018). LEADERSHIP POTENTIAL OF RUSSIA IN WORLD POLITICS. Bulletin of Moscow University. Series 27: "Global Studies and Geopolitics."

www.ingramcontent.com/pod-product-compliance
Lightning Source LLC
Chambersburg PA
CBHW070803040426
42333CB00061B/1815